Sacred Discourse and
American Nationality

Sacred Discourse and American Nationality

Eldon J. Eisenach

ROWMAN & LITTLEFIELD PUBLISHERS, INC.
Lanham • Boulder • New York • Toronto • Plymouth, UK

Published by Rowman & Littlefield Publishers, Inc.
A wholly owned subsidiary of The Rowman & Littlefield Publishing Group, Inc.
4501 Forbes Boulevard, Suite 200, Lanham, Maryland 20706
www.rowman.com

10 Thornbury Road, Plymouth PL6 7PP, United Kingdom

British Library Cataloguing in Publication Information Available

Library of Congress Cataloging-in-Publication Data

Eisenach, Eldon J.
Sacred discourse and American nationality / Eldon Eisenach.
p. cm.
Includes bibliographical references and index.
ISBN 978-1-4422-1771-3 (cloth : alk. paper) — ISBN 978-1-4422-1773-7 (electronic)
1. Political science—United States—History. 2. Religion and politics—United States. 3. Progressivism (United States politics) I. Title.
JA84.U5E52 2012
320.50973—dc23

2012012465

♾™   The paper used in this publication meets the minimum requirements of American
National Standard for Information Sciences Permanence of Paper for Printed Library
Materials, ANSI/NISO Z39.48-1992.

Printed in the United States of America

Contents

Acknowledgments

Thanking everyone who had a direct or indirect hand in the many parts that comprise this book would be to replicate much of my intellectual biography. Instead, I would like to acknowledge the founding editors of two academic periodicals. These journals not only expressed and shaped my own ways of thinking about the relationship of political ideas to governing, they provided places for new generations of scholars to exchange ideas and further their shared intellectual projects. Thirty-three years ago, Janet Coleman and Iain Hampsher-Monk, both in the politics department at the University of Exeter, founded *History of Political Thought*. As a contributor, book reviewer, and articles referee, I was a constant witness to the scholarly fruits of Janet and Iain's initial labors and vision, which came to include a worldwide body of humanities scholars. Twenty-six years ago, Karen Orren and Stephen Skowronek, both in the political science department at UCLA, founded a semi-annual periodical, *Studies in American Political Development*. Simply put, this publication transformed the way political scientists study American politics, quickly attracting scholars from history and the other social sciences as well. Here, too, as a contributor and articles referee, I was able to enrich my own work with this emerging body of scholarship. And, as a member of editorial boards for both publications, I tracked the success of these founders and marveled at their ability to combine the extraordinary diligence and energy as founding editors with their equally extraordinary individual scholarly achievements. Institutions count, and these two journals have counted for me in more ways than I can number.

PERMISSIONS

Chapter 1, "Jumping Out of Ordinary Time: Sacred Rhetoric in American Political Discourse," was originally given as a paper for a Center for Research and Study in Contemporary American Society (Recherches et Etudes sur la Societe Americaine Comtemporaine—RESSAC) conference, Religion and Politics in the US, in Paris, December 2002, and published in *Tocqueville Review* (2004): 57–80. It is published here in a slightly abridged version with the permission of the publisher.

Chapter 2 is a revision of the paper "The Fateful Alliance of Liberal Religion and Liberal Politics," presented at the American Political Science Association meetings in Boston, 2008. The appendix to chapter 2 is one story (174–76) from "Bookends: Seven Stories Excised from *The Lost Promise of Progressivism*" by Eldon J. Eisenach, *Studies in American Political Development* 10, no. 1 (1996): 168–83. Copyright 1996 Cambridge University Press. Reprinted with permission.

Chapter 3, "Emerging Patterns in America's Political and Religious Self-Understanding," was originally given as a paper presented at the American Political Science Association meetings in Philadelphia, 2003. "Emerging Patterns in America's Political and Religious Self-Understanding" by Eldon J. Eisenach, *Studies in American Political Development* 18, no. 1 (2004): 44–59. Copyright 2004 Cambridge University Press. Reprinted in a slightly abridged version with permission.

Chapter 4, "Progressivism as a National Narrative," was given at a conference, Liberalism: Old and New, sponsored by the Social Philosophy and Policy Center, Bowling Green University, 2005. It was published as "Progressivism as a National Narrative in Biblical-Hegelian Time" in *Social Philosophy and Policy* 24 (2007): 55–83, also published as a book, *Liberalism: Old and New*, edited by Ellen Frankel Paul, Fred D. Miller, Jr., and Jeffrey Paul (New York: Cambridge University Press, 2007), 55–83. It is published here in a slightly expanded version with the permission of the publisher. The two appendixes to chapter 4 are two stories (168–71 and 176–78) from "Bookends: Seven Stories Excised from *The Lost Promise of Progressivism*" by Eldon J. Eisenach, *Studies in American Political Development* 10, no. 1 (1996): 168–83. Copyright 1996 Cambridge University Press. Reprinted with permission.

Chapter 5, "Progressive Internationalism," was originally given at a conference, Progressivism Then and Now, at Brandeis University, 1996, and appeared as a chapter in *Progressivism and the New Democracy*, edited by Sidney Milkis and Jerome Mileur (University of Massachusetts Press, 1999), 226–58. It is published here in a slightly expanded form with the permission of the publisher.

Introduction

Orientations and Arguments

The origin of this project stretches back more than twenty years, to the mid-1980s, when a colleague and I began collecting a bibliography for creating a course in American political development. We gathered together a very broad swath of research and writings in American political history and political science. What particularly interested me was the relationship of these materials on transformative political change to the history of American political thought and, more generally, to American intellectual and cultural history. As I explored this dimension of American political development I began to focus on the "producers" of political theory in America, whether political intellectuals, philosophers, social scientists, or activists, and especially some figures, such as John Dewey and other Progressive intellectuals, who combined all of these roles at once. In a sense, then, I began to think in terms of a "biographical" history of political ideas and how these biographies were part of our political history, especially in those moments that signal a marked shift in the ends and modes of governance.

As I explored more closely the contours of American political thought from this perspective, it became clearer to me that the boundaries between "political theory" and "political ideology," especially as, together, they empowered political change, were permeable. At critical moments in American political life, the combination of theory and ideology created coherent bodies of rhetoric motivating transformative political change, first by discrediting prevailing political ideas and then by explaining and justifying the new political order that was coming into being. This combination of destruction, explanation, and justification always included a deeper historical dimension, locating the new regime within the larger story of American political life. Whether more in the mode of continuity or of radical disjunction, every change in regime required a larger story to enframe it. And when the change was perceived as radically discontinuous—even apocalyptic—the enframing story was often anchored in a sacred discourse addressing religion and national identity.

The period that most strongly interested me, and the subject of my first book that took up these themes, was the Progressive Era.[1] From that era, I not only heard strong echoes from our distant political/cultural past, I saw ideas, ideals, and ways of thinking that persist into the present day. The chapters that follow, then, might best be understood as attempts to explore, in a variety of contexts, the interrelationship of political theory, political ideology, and political change in the story of American political life.

Before exploring some of these relationships, a unique feature of American political history should first be noted, one that is probably the main source of the attention paid to political change conceived as distinct "regimes."[2] Unlike all other modern and developed states, since the end of the eighteenth century America has had only one formal, written national constitution. Despite this seemingly fixed and durable foundation, the modes of governance, the shifts in power and policies, and the effective "governing ideas" appear disjunctive and even revolutionary when placed side by side and compared. From the standpoint of the authoritative institutions marking the separation of powers and federalism, one sees persistence and continuity. From the standpoint of authoritative ideas and values in the exercise of governance, one sees instability and discontinuity.

One way to sort out this conundrum is to reflect on the distinction between the formal institutions of government—their respective constitutional powers, resources, and policies—and the authority of the American "state" conceived as the combination of *all effectively governing institutions*—even local and "private" ones—that pursue common sets of ends and purposes.[3] In this view, one can then see that at some periods of American history we have had ostensibly small and weak "governments" but an authoritative and powerful "state." And, at other times, we have had periods when our national government has been big and intrusive but unable to generate enough authority to elicit support from the states and from other governing institutions to address commonly recognized problems and concerns. To take one obvious example of the former: the Northwest Ordinance of 1787, passed under the Articles of Confederation, forbade slavery in the federally administered territories. In the 1850s, under the aegis of the much more robust United States Constitution, the power to forbid slavery in the territories was so seriously contested that secession and civil war followed. Under one of the weakest forms of central government one could imagine, a whole sector of the continent was declared free of slavery. Under a much stronger set of national governing institutions, this elementary power of territorial governance was denied.

Thus, combinations of "big government/weak state" and "small (or invisible) government/strong state" require modes of explanation that lie quite outside political theory expressed as constitutional law and powers, bills of rights, and the whole universe of language embedded in individual rights and formal governing powers. Cryptically put, "not all political institutions are governmental" and yet they exercise governing power.[4] All students of American political history know that a new language and a new vocabulary of politics was created and institutionalized with the rise of mass, election-based political parties; that its vocabulary was often far removed from constitutional and other "theory" discourse; and that its "governing ideas" crossed not only political jurisdictions decreed by federalism, but the divide between public institutions and private associations and institutions. Just as clearly, we can discern this same kind of discourse before parties were organized "out of doors" and were confined to groupings of governing officials. In short, parties were part of the effective, authoritative "state" without which no formal political institutions could have governed at all. What I further suggest in the chapters here is that this discourse and its institutionalization continued and even gained in power in the twentieth century, when political parties were severely weakened. Indeed, this migration of rhetoric and power was already begun in the nineteenth century, when "antiparty" parties and movements were formed to raise pressing national issues that the party system effectively screened out. These movement parties were the seedbeds of a reform culture and its institutional structure which came to dominate the production, organization, and dissemination of the rhetoric that powered the authoritative "state" no matter whether "government" was big or small, visible or out of sight.[5]

I came to the serious study of American political thought only after receiving my primary training in political philosophy, with its history of canonical authors and texts speaking to each other across the ages in the universal language of epistemology and logic. Knowing instinctively that this approach was never very useful in the study of American political thought led me to the suspicion that it wasn't all that useful in the study of political philosophy more generally. Thus, my attraction to the "Cambridge School" of political theory and to the study of ways in which religion intersects with political theory in the writings of canonical political philosophers.[6] Less obvious, to me at least, was my later attraction to some of the leading ideas of what came to be known as phenomenology and antifoundationalism. Perhaps because of their genealogical methods and their distrust of universals, I found an affinity between their interpretive methods and my own. And, insofar as these perspectives became incorporated into feminist theory, I borrowed freely from that body of literature as well. While many of these strands and influences are evident in the materials that follow, my primary focus has always been on recovering and articulating "governing ideas" in America.

ORIENTING FRAMEWORKS

In the chapters that follow, there are four sets of ideas and distinctions that orient the analysis and arguments. Together, these frameworks provide an interconnected structure that seeks to align American political history and American political thought.

1. Regime Ideas. Political power, especially in liberal democracies, requires a high level of willing support by large numbers of people and passive acceptance by many others. This support and obedience require, at the minimum, ideas that both explain the institutional nature of that power and the manner of its exercise. These explanatory ideas must be supplemented by ideas that justify this power and those who wield it. And, at junctions of critical political change, the ideas explaining and justifying new modes of political power must be part of a larger set of ideas that discredit and delegitimate the authority they seek to displace. Indeed, many of the formative ideas for a new regime are embedded in the critique of the old one. In this process of creative destruction, especially when it requires the mobilization and assent of large sectors of the population, formal political ideas from higher intellectual culture and ideas permeating popular culture necessarily intersect.[7]

2. Ideology, Religion, and Political Identity. A recurring relationship in the chapters that follow is that between religious discourse, mobilizing political ideologies, and political change. In the Protestant, Bible-centered tradition, religious language is structured as a narrative that connects the political theology of the Hebrew Bible to the individual and collective story of salvation in the final Kingdom of God in the New Testament. From the Puritan founding in New England, through the American Revolution, to the vision of America as "redeemer nation" during the Civil War and thereafter, this discourse was particularly effective in using words as power in hard-fought political (and military) battles. First in ethnocultural partisan divides, then through the large complex of reform associations, this rhetoric, even as it became increasingly disconnected from its particular theological and denominational roots, has served to discredit, explain, and justify the exercise of political authority. This narrative connected person to political movement and personal biography to national history. Its ideology was a source of personal and collective identity, serving more the ends of meaning and agency than those of abstract truth and laws. And insofar as this narrative source of identity and meanings was independent of formal constitutional and legal distinctions—and indeed of formal citizenship itself—it contained a democratic imperative far more encompassing than the formal-legal categories of citizenship and public office, restricted as they initially were to adult white

males. One might conclude, then, that in America, political ideology can be distinguished from political theory because of its close alliance with personal identity, religious faith, and national patriotism.

3. Political Theory, Law, Constitutionalism. In contrast to the highly charged and extremely various ideological discourse sketched above, the language of political theory in America is highly formal and remarkably stable, if only because it is so strongly attached to the Constitution and the Bill of Rights and, therefore, to laws, separation of powers, and federalism. The political theory issuing from this source and its philosophical antecedents (e.g., John Locke) privileges the fixities of liberalism and individual rights over the fluidities of more democratic forms of discourse. As I suggest in the chapters below, however, theory discourse tends to be hostage to each successive political regime, needing to be reworked and restated even as it seeks to mask profound changes in modes of governance. Put cryptically, but considered more fully in chapter 3, in America the liberal truths of political theory always accommodate and sometimes must give way to the democratic and civic republican meanings of political ideology.

In a similar fashion, but more haltingly, constitutional jurisprudence follows a parallel trajectory. It is not always true that the Supreme Court follows the election returns (especially when it helps decide election results, as in 2000) but, during particular periods of judicial activism, Supreme Court decisions reflect decisive shifts in elite political and intellectual culture. And, as elite law schools have increasingly become centers of research and writing within the universities and higher intellectual culture, this process has become deeply institutionalized across much of the legal profession. One might go so far as to say that law school faculty and law journals have become major sources of sophisticated political theory, even at the cost of their doctrinal contributions and the training of working lawyers.[8]

4. Ideas and Institutions. Within the field of American political development (APD) there is a strongly felt methodological division between "historical institutionalism" and "ideational" approaches.[9] The former stresses the ways in which public policies are ordered by institutional structures and how, in interaction with other institutions, these policies are constrained and directed. The stress is on the interests of the actors and how those interests fare in the matrix of governing institutions. Ideational approaches point to the ways in which normative ideas and political rhetoric empower political movements, frame political debates, and structure institutional changes. The gap between the history of particular public policies and the larger political and intellectual culture is often very wide. Those who stress ideas think their job is done when those ideas are specified and begin to do their work. Those who stress institutions are satisfied with thick descriptions of the success or failure of particular policy initiatives in light of larger institutional settings. The chapters below, although they are clearly within the ideational camp,

differ from most such studies because the political theories and ideologies examined *are themselves placed in associational and institutional settings.* These settings are not institutions administering public policies, but institutions and associations either advocating political change or supporting the prevailing order, either seeking to alter the prevailing political culture or buttressing current political values and interests. The assumption is not that "ideas" somehow create political agency but that these institutionalized ideas create and express shared political identities and organize political will. And it is the interaction of these ideational institutions and associations with the institutions of public policy that powers political conflict and political change.

ARGUMENTS

Given the orientations sketched above, there are four theses allied to that framework.

1. Religion is embedded in American political thought. This assertion does not mean that Christian or Protestant *theology* plays a major role in our political ideas, but that liberal evangelical Protestant ways of thinking—regarding American nationality and destiny, regarding the relationship of religion to moral progress, and regarding the penetration of religious/moral values into all aspects of life—are foundational ways in which we shape our political ideas. Given this centrality, one argument that runs through these chapters is that America has always had some form of informal and voluntary religious "establishment" that sets the boundaries within which our political thought and political life are conducted. Put differently, at any given time and for every durable political regime some values and purposes are held to be sacred—or at least so vital to our national identity that to question or repudiate them *in public discourse* is to renounce political relevance and efficacy. Even the partly ironic use of the term *political correctness* is a gesture toward this impulse. In any case, informal establishments can be and have been discredited, attacked, and overthrown—but only to be replaced by new ones.

2. Conceptions of political time and history structure American political ideas. Take the simple distinction between the idea of America as a "new" nation and of America as a "young" nation, discussed later in chapter 3. The former suggests, in the words of Thomas Paine, that we can "begin the world over again" by breaking from England and the Old World. America as "young" suggests that the path to maturity is already set, that any future "rebirth" of freedom would be a dangerous deviation from that path. The former conception suggests that political time is often synchronic, periodical-

ly transformed by events that echo the distant past and presage a prophetic future. The latter conception suggests that political time, like all ordinary or secular time, is diachronic, consisting of endless chains of cause and effect that we can largely control through ordinary means and common sense. Synchronic time and ideals of rebirth have a religious origin, built into the Biblical understanding of prophecy and fulfillment, making America's moments of rebirth part of a sacred fulfillment story, the hidden but periodically revealed history of the "city of God." Diachronic time is anchored in the logic and values of the "city of man."

Embedded in the notion of America as a new nation is the assumption of American exceptionalism, first in contrast to Europe, then as vanguard and exemplar for the whole world. This self-concept was at first distinctly religious and articulated by New England Puritans ("city on the hill"), but soon became the sacred story of American national identity. And, as part of this migration, the city of God changed from existing at the end of time, and outside of history, to being the fulfillment of human destiny in historical time. A clever historian of ideas might say that the movement was from Augustine/Calvin to Hegel.

These distinctly American notions of time and history are periodically challenged by those seeking to discredit the "myth" of American exceptionalism. These attempts, I suggest, are in vain. Every political regime that seeks legitimacy must lay claim to this myth in some form (even, as jeremiad, of America as exceptionally bad) because it constitutes the very marrow of our nationality, what makes us one people. And no matter how hard political philosophers (and some Supreme Court justices) try to absorb our national creed into timeless categories of rights and reason, categories stripped of history and country, the assumption of American exceptionalism, overtly or covertly, permeates our political discourse and shapes our public policies.

3. American political change consists of distinct regimes. In common use for only the last thirty years in political science, the academic subfield of American political development posits that each durable regime comes to power by repudiating the leading ideas and policies of its opponents and with a set of alternatives that both propel its adherents into power and provide them with legitimacy and policy direction. Major regime changes are also changes in how we conceive ourselves as a people—a nation—because, for good or ill, how we govern ourselves reveals not only what we do but who we are. No other aspect of our common life and culture does this so clearly— hence the periodic outbreak of political "culture wars." Political development is important for understanding American political thought because it is in periods of the rise and fall of governing orders that *articulate political ideas are required to do battle*. In between, previously contested ideas attain the

status of largely unexamined "common sense," usually with a political science and a constitutional jurisprudence to prove it: this is the very meaning of hegemonic power and sets the conditions for its overthrow.

4. National political authority periodically changes its location. When Jefferson said that our "republicanism" is "not in our Constitution certainly, but merely in the spirit of our people," he meant that all governmental forms of political authority are subject to popular sovereignty—the authority of the people. But how and where is "government of, by, and for the people" represented and expressed? The first answer was interconnected coteries of local and national political elites, a "natural aristocracy" of virtuous leaders united by a shared commitment to republican principles and deferred to by a then narrow electorate. Following the breakup of these networks into contending factions, the formation of the Jacksonian Democratic Party quickly shifted authority to party organizations and leaders. Without political parties organized from the precinct level upwards, an effective political democracy could not have been achieved. With the institution of universal white male suffrage and the rapid rise of voter turnout, party-electoral victory was the font of both legitimacy and policy. And, as coalitions of local and state organizations, parties reinforced an extremely narrow reading of federal constitutional power and a very capacious understanding of local and states' rights.

The dominance of party organization as the location of political authority was both copied (the Whig Party) and contested by opponents who organized anti-Jacksonian "movement" parties (e.g., Anti-Masonic League, Liberty Party), reform movements (e.g., antislavery and temperance societies), and various Protestant ecumenical reform associations and their array of national publications. Party to them meant the dominance of self-interest and the protection of backward and even vicious ways of life. Moreover, political authority lodged in party organization not only subordinated the larger national interest, it slighted a larger public good represented by women and children, Indians, and, of course, slaves. The sudden rise of the Republican Party not only included women, children, and freedmen in its many auxiliary party organizations, it fused together the organizational matrix of Protestant church, mission, and reform bodies, along with their colleges and universities and their national publications. In combination with the Republican Party, during the Civil War and after this matrix of associations and institutions functioned as a powerful centralized "state," standing astride and directing the various governments they dominated.

By the turn of the last century, parties were progressively weakened as sources of authority. What replaced parties as institutional expressions of popular sovereignty? What people, values, and purposes did these institutions represent? Answers to these questions are suggested in the chapters that follow. A large part of the answer lies in the ways in which new institutions and organizations allied themselves with new governmental bodies. The rise of compulsory public schools, the establishment of research universities and their social science and social work departments, the founding of trade and professional organizations, and the formation of settlement houses and a "nonpartisan" press all contributed to the displacement of party as the source and locus of authoritative political ideas. In alliance with enhanced executive and bureaucratic power in the states and in the federal government, along with specialized regulatory bodies and the growth of professional networks connecting government, business, education, and charities (i.e., social services), the modern American "state" was formed. Paradoxically, then, the rise to dominance of the Republican Party, infused with antiparty values from the start, laid the ideological and policy groundwork for this replacement. These nationalist Republicans and, later, their breakaway offshoot, the Progressive Party, attacked the dominance of party on every conceivable front, and they were largely successful. This legacy remains with us today.

Needless to add, all of these changes in the location of political authority changed the production, dissemination, and content of our political ideas as well. We have inherited from these many changes a contemporary political universe that is a complex and perplexing layering of traditional governmental institutions (i.e., constitutional power), partisan election machinery, and a civil society, intellectual culture, and informational media of bewildering variety. My hope is that the themes and arguments in this book will help us to understand the changing contours of our political thought and thus to think and negotiate our way today into a fuller and more responsible citizenship.

I also hope that the chapters that follow convey some of the pleasure and excitement I had in researching and writing them. Attempting to place political ideas broadly conceived within the story of American political development was, for me, a series of revelations. The first was that so much of what I was taught as a student of the history of American political theory contained conundrums, paradoxes, and elisions that were only clearly revealed when placed against our political life conceived as the history of distinct regimes. The second revelation was that lying beneath the seemingly placid "common sense" of every successful regime are highly charged ideological components born of contention, sacrifice, and struggle. Thirdly, this ideological substratum of passion and commitment is also present in the moral psychology of individuals, especially in the officials and intellectuals who represent the values of the prevailing regime. No political actor is above the battle. Lastly, studying political ideas through distinct political orders in America revealed to me the centrality of narrative to political ideas, because the truth claims of political theory must be wedded to the agency power of ideology in order to constitute durable political regimes.

NOTES

1. Eisenach, 1994 and see Eisenach 2006b.

2. Orren and Skowronek, 2004, define political development in these terms: "a durable shift in governing authority" (123), and see 125 for the further distinction between "power" and "authority."

3. Orren and Skowronek, 2004, 22–24, use the term "plenary authority" to argue that all sites of political change already possess such generalized authority, whatever its source. This is to counter the common misperception that the growth of government is the same as an increase in authority. Thus, "America in the nineteenth century was no less fully governed than America in the twentieth; more of some forms of authority indicates less of others" (23).

4. Orren and Skowronek, 2004, 84.

5. Balogh, 2009. Although state governments commanded a vast proportion of fiscal resources and personnel (Novak, 1996) the national government was surprisingly effective in setting the larger policy goals (except for slavery) within which the individual states functioned. This conundrum was first articulated by Franz Neumann, a German intellectual, who contrasted England and America to continental European states, wondering how the former two formally "weak states" could generate so much power and so many resources in comparison with the "strong states" with powerful executives and centralized bureaucracies. Neumann, 1957.

6. Eisenach, 1981 and 2002.

7. Michael Freeden, 1996, 2003, 2004, has done a remarkable job sorting out the relationships between political theory and political ideology both philosophically and in terms of specific bodies of political ideas such as the "new liberalism." See also Marc Stears, 2004 and 2010. It might be said more broadly that the larger intellectual project of the Cambridge School of political theory over the past forty years, represented by Quentin Skinner, John Pocock, and John Dunn, has transformed the study of political philosophy into the study of texts from within larger linguistic, political, historical, and ideological contexts.

8. Posner, 1995, 81–108.

9. Glenn, 2004; Lieberman, 2002.

Part One: Sacred Stories and American Political Ideas

Chapter One

Jumping Out of Ordinary Time

Sacred Rhetoric in American Political Discourse

After the attack on the World Trade Center in September of 2001, a struggle immediately began over how to characterize that event. Was it an act of war or a crime? Those who wanted to contain the event within the framework of ordinary politics, to be handled by properly designated officials within preexisting procedures and language, said the act was a crime, the perpetrators were criminals, and those who aided the criminals should be apprehended and tried in a court of justice. The resulting punishment would complete the event and everything would proceed within ordinary, diachronic time. [1]

The lyrics of "God Bless America" that spontaneously sounded throughout the country drowned out the discourse of crime. War became the defining word. The country began to speak in a different voice and entered a different mode of time—a synchronic time in which past, present, and future become mixed up, reversed, and conflated. That song was in fact a late and generic coda to a host of patriotic hymns written by Unionists in the massively disruptive period of the American Civil War. The most famous is "Battle Hymn of the Republic" (technically, "Mine Eyes Have Seen the Glory"), whose verses track the path of the nation through the apocalyptic book of Revelation in the Bible: "He has sounded forth the trumpet that shall never call retreat; / He is sifting out the hearts of men before his judgment seat." Equally famous is another hymn of that era, "My Country, 'Tis of Thee." It begins with the Puritan nation founders and ends: "Our father's God, to thee, / Author of liberty, / To thee we sing; / Long may our land be bright / With freedom's holy light; / Protect us by thy might, / Great God, our King." [2]

3

The word "homeland" entered the public vocabulary, carrying with it what Sacvan Bercovitch calls America's "Christianography," a merging of providential nature and biblical prophecy.[3] A whole host of policies, symbols, and rituals arose as witness to the call. American flags appeared everywhere and on everything; blood banks were besieged with donors; hundreds of millions of dollars flowed into aid and charitable organizations. This massive response was as disproportionate to the need as it was to any realistic assessment of immediate further physical threats to our safety—as if to say that Americans entered so fully and spontaneously into these activities with a sense of relief, a release from their entrapment in the ordinary time, ordinary laws, and ordinary lives that divide and separate them. And this transformative release from ordinary time and ordinary priorities sets the stage for a new configuration of ordinary time constructed from the repertoire of possibilities contained within synchronic time.

A LITERARY RECORD

All students of American history and literature are familiar with John Winthrop's 1630 lay sermon in which New England becomes the biblical "antitype" of Jerusalem, marked out to be the site of mankind's final redemption in the Kingdom of God. This theme runs throughout our language and literature. In Herman Melville's novel *White-jacket* (1850), a character says:

> We Americans are the peculiar, chosen people—the Israel of our time; we bear the ark of the liberties of the world . . . We are the pioneers . . . ; the advanced guard, sent on through the wilderness of untried things to break a new path to the New World that is ours . . . Long enough have we been skeptics with regard to ourselves and doubted, whether, indeed, the political Messiah has come. But he has come in *us*, if we would but give utterance to his promptings.

This typology, however, is two-edged and has always been read in two distinct registers. The first register I call a "providential" reading—the working out in ordinary time and through ordinary actions and understandings the larger plan of an omniscient and moral God—a sort of tame, almost secular Enlightenment reading of time. Here is one example of this reading from the turn of the last century:

> The United States of America,—bounded on the north by the North Pole; on the South by the Antarctic Region; on the east by the first chapter of the Book of Genesis and on the west by the Day of Judgment . . . The Supreme Ruler of the Universe . . . has marked out the line this nation must follow and our duty must be done. America is destined to become the Light of the World. (Arthur Bird, *Looking Forward*, 1899)[4]

The rhetoric of this providential reading seeks to empower us as a people by adherence to the teachings of science, morality, and liberal-democratic constitutionalism. Extraordinary acts, such as the American Revolution, are seen as necessary, but entirely unsought, responses to the policies and actions of others that would reverse, stall, or impede "progress"—and progress itself is seen as the extension of what has transpired before. America is "young" and its path to maturity and fulfillment is well marked. Once these "external" barriers are removed (England, slavery), life will go on as before but on a higher level. We all participate in this providential and diachronic time by being ordinary rational, moral, and law-abiding citizens.

The other, more apocalyptic, edge of this typology is not only full of dialectic and paradox, it is also full of darkness and danger, replete with images of sin, failure, suffering, and death. This second register I will call "prophetic"—a way of being grounded in a covenantal relationship to a God who intervenes in history in ways that are outside both ordinary time and ordinary understandings of how the world works. America is "new" and will continue to be reborn in ways beyond our current reckoning.[5] Ordinary rational, moral, and law-abiding citizens are not only not the solution, they are often the problem. I offer three examples.

Winthrop began this prophetic strand by contrasting the law of nature—that of "mere justice" applicable to all men in all conditions and all times—to the "lawe of grace, or the . . . lawe of the gospel." This law rules only particular communities of men at particular moments in time and is part of the sacred history of salvation.[6] Walt Whitman's poem "Song of the Banner at Daybreak" symbolizes the two different imperatives that flow from nature and from grace. A banner and pennant, high up in the sky, beckon to a small child and the child wants to heed their call. The father warns the child: "Cease, cease, my foolish babe . . . / Behold with the rest again I say, behold not banners and pennants aloft, / But the well-prepared pavements behold, and mark the solid-wall'd houses." The child responds: "O my father I like not the houses, / They will never to me be anything, nor do I like money, / But to mount up there I would like, O father dear." To this the father responds with a final warning:

> Child of mine you fill me with anguish,
> To be that pennant would be too fearful,
> Little you know what it is this day, and after this day, forever,
> It is to gain nothing, but risk and defy everything,
> Forward to stand in front of wars—and O, such wars!—what have you to do with them?
> With passions of demons, slaughter, premature death?[7]

Finally, consider Abraham Lincoln's second inaugural address of 1865. After his reelection, everyone expected Lincoln to address the nation in an optimistic, triumphalist, and providential mode. It was clear that the Union armies were finally prevailing and that plans for the peace following victory soon would be undertaken. Lincoln defied these expectations. Not only did he explicitly refuse to predict a Union victory, he placed the entire nation, North and South, under divine judgment.

> One eighth of the whole population were colored slaves . . . all knew that this interest was, somehow, the cause of the war . . . Neither anticipated that the *cause* of the conflict might cease with, or even before, the conflict itself should cease. Each looked for an easier triumph, and a result less fundamental and astounding. The prayers of both could not be answered . . . The Almighty has his own purposes. "Woe unto the world because of offences! for it must needs be that offences come; but woe to that man by whom offences cometh!"

American (not southern) slavery was an offence to God which "He now wills to remove" by giving to both "North and South this terrible war, as the woe due to those by whom the offence came." And this woe, this suffering and death on all sides, must be accepted in faith as just. Even as we hope and pray

> that this mighty scourge of war may speedily pass away . . . if God wills that it continue, until all the wealth piled by the bondman's two hundred and fifty years of unrequited toil shall be sunk, and until every drop of blood drawn with the lash, shall be paid by another drawn with the sword . . . "the judgments of the Lord, are true and righteous altogether."[8]

Lincoln's major addresses and proclamations could be said to mark America's third refounding as a nation, following Winthrop's proclamation of America as the covenantal "city upon a hill" and Thomas Paine's call "to begin the world over again" by declaring independence from England.[9] Lincoln could proclaim "a new birth of freedom" at Gettysburg only after America had renounced its deceitfulness and pride and acknowledged again "the necessity of redeeming and preserving grace." National sin, suffering, and repentance are necessary elements in this rhetorical reenactment of national identity.[10] These elements are quite outside of and independent of the US Constitution and its underlying state constitutions and laws. As Lincoln said in his inaugural address of 1861, "the Union is much older than the Constitution."[11] American national identity is not only older in time, it exists, in its biblical and typological articulation, outside of ordinary notions of time altogether. This "Hebraicism" at the roots of our national identity embeds in our political discourse disruptive elements that can and do suddenly appear to transform our self-understandings and our political, constitutional, and legal systems. In this sense, the presence of sacred rhetoric in our political discourse constitutes an always available—and often dangerous—repertoire from which to critique and transform existing political procedures, practices, and understandings. Without this sacred rhetoric—with only "timeless" philosophical-constitutional-legal principles—our frozen institutions and practices would have shattered long ago.

SACRED RHETORIC, POLITICAL PARTIES, AND POLITICAL TRANSFORMATION

Students of American political history like to say that other countries (they are actually thinking of France) have had many revolutions and many different constitutions, while America has had many realigning or "critical" elections but only one constitution. Nevertheless, like French revolutions, realigning elections produce distinct regimes that last over many decades.

Without entering into the intricacies of argument about realigning elections and regime change,[12] I want to discuss the differences in rhetoric or "voice" between our two political parties. Beginning with the Federalist vs. Jeffersonian-Republican conflict in the 1790s and continuing through today, our major parties speak in decidedly different voices, none of which can be construed as simply "conservative" or "liberal." I want to discuss four of these ways.

The first is David Greenstone's distinction in mid-nineteenth-century party politics between the "reform liberalism" of National Republicans/Whigs versus the "humanist liberalism" of the Democratic Party.[13] Let me illustrate:

National Republicans (Whig):

> We wish, fully and entirely, to nationalize the institutions of our land and to identify ourselves with our country; to become a single great people, separate and distinct in national character, political interest, social and civil affinities from any and all other nations, kindred and people on the earth . . . We have all the elements of becoming a greater people, a mightier nation, and more endurable government than has ever held a place in the annals of time. (*American Republican* [Whig], November 7, 1844)

Democrats:

> 1. That the Federal Government is one of limited powers, derived solely from the Constitution, and . . . ought to be strictly construed. 2. That the Constitution does not confer upon the General Government the power to commence or carry on a general system of internal improvements. 3. That the Constitution does not confer authority. . . . 4. That justice and sound policy forbid . . . 5. That it is the duty of every branch . . . to enforce and practice the most rigid economy . . . 6. That Congress has no power to charter a United States

Bank . . . 7. That Congress has no power . . . to interfere with or control the
domestic institutions of the several states . . . 8. That the separation of the
money of the government from banking institutions is indispensable for the . . .
rights of the people. 9. That the liberal principles embodied by Jefferson in the
Declaration of Independence, and sanctioned in the Constitution . . . makes
ours the land of liberty. (Democratic Party platform, 1840, repeated verbatim
in 1844, 1848, 1852, and 1856)[14]

The National Republican voice is project- and future-oriented, pointing to a
program of personal and national development within a world-historical setting. The Democratic Party voice is principled and static, as if our political
order rested, once and for all, on a contractual agreement among clearly
delineated jurisdictions and groups who, for their own separate reasons,
agree to authorize the national government to undertake strictly defined and
limited ends.[15]

This suggests a second way of putting this difference: that between a
stress on a shared, consensual national purpose that should shape and dominate constitutional-legal understandings and a stress on neutral proceduralism itself—"constitutionalism"—as the primary unifying bond. Here I offer
the example of Woodrow Wilson, first as a good Democratic Party constitutional theorist in 1908.

Woodrow Wilson as Democrat:

> There is no such thing as corporate liberty. Liberty belongs to the individual,
> or it does not exist . . . [and] liberty is the object of constitutional govern-
> ment . . . Constitutional government can exist only where there is actual
> community of interest and of purpose, and cannot, if it be also self-govern-
> ment, express the life of any body of people that does not constitute a veritable
> community. Are the United States a community? In some things, yes; in most
> things, no. (*Constitutional Government in the United States*, 1908)

Now I give you President Woodrow Wilson, accidentally elected as a Democrat in a Republican era, leading the nation into a war that his own party
strongly opposed but his Republican-Progressive opponents enthusiastically
supported.

Woodrow Wilson as National Republican:

> Our participation in the war established our position among the nations . . . the
> whole world saw at last . . . a Nation they had deemed material and now found
> to be compact of the spiritual forces that must free men of every nation of
> every unworthy bondage . . . The stage is set, the destiny is disclosed. It has
> come about by no plan of our conceiving, but by the hand of God who led us
> into this way. We cannot turn back. We can only go forward . . . to follow the
> vision. It was of this that we dreamed at our birth. America shall in truth show
> the way. (speech to the Senate, July 10, 1919)

A third way of putting this difference is ethnic and religious. The electoral base of the Republican Party, starting with the Federalists, has been evangelical-Protestant, a sort of covenantal core constituency that sees itself as representing and articulating the permanent and higher interests of the American nation in history. In contrast, the Democratic Party has never had a homogeneous base, but has consisted of a coalition of marginals united by a common distrust and even hatred of the "core" and held together by fair procedures, log rolling, and trade-offs. Each coalition member seeks group advantage and protection from outside interference.[16] As David Greenstone has argued, decisions and policies of this heterogeneous constituency can be predicted by game theory models of interest-group struggles, where each group strives to maximize its advantages within the party through bargaining and trade-offs. In contrast, at any given period the Republican Party is more united by shared conceptions of the national good, and thus by commitments to shared substantive principles. The Republican Party, heir of both the Federalists and Whigs, has always been a "national" party and, therefore, uses a narrative language and employs sacred rhetoric as the means to address the nation as one body. The Democratic Party, heir to Jefferson and Jackson, not only distrusts a central authoritative state (but not big government), it distrusts the "aristocracy" or "elitism" implicit in narratives of national purpose and destiny. For them, it goes without saying that every national project is also a hegemonic one, privileging certain ways of life over others.[17]

Even in the twentieth century, when the Democratic Party captured the national government in the period 1932–1980, Democratic presidents have had to govern with the help of traditionally Republican-Progressive institutions and elites (Wall Street, national research universities, professional associations) while using the expanded powers of the national government to incorporate new groups and interests (while devaluing some older ones) into its ruling party coalition. Put differently, the long-lived New Deal coalition that governed America for half a century and literally defined what came to be known as democratic pluralism thrived under a national-consensual canopy that was not of its own making. This canopy was not the US Constitution but the "liberal establishment" of institutional elites first constructed by Republican Progressives at the turn of the twentieth century.[18] The ideological materials constituting this canopy were first antifascism and then anticommunism, the American commitment to save the "free" (and Christian) world from totalitarian godlessness and materialism. Under this canopy and this set of nonnegotiable priorities (i.e., a "bipartisan" foreign policy), interest-group liberalism combined with constitutional proceduralism could operate quite freely. Once this canopy was shredded—roughly at the time of the Vietnam War—the resulting complex of power called interest-group pluralism was robbed of its national legitimacy.[19]

This suggests a fourth and last difference in the rhetorical voices of the two parties. The Republican Party voice speaks under the assumption that a moral-spiritual consensus exists or must be brought into being for effective governance to take place. Every Republican regime (but not Republican presidents elected in Democratic Party regime periods) that comes into power incorporates into its rhetoric the assumption of a national spiritual consensus—an informal and voluntary national "religious establishment"—that gives purpose and direction to formal and coercive governments. The Democratic Party voice tends to speak under the assumption that law, the national constitution, and the various state constitutions clearly delimit the purpose and reach of government, and that these boundaries between public and private and between politics and religion must be clearly defined and maintained. Their language is "rights talk."[20] But here arises an obvious flaw and an often fatal weakness: at any given period of history, the particular construction of these boundaries and the particular way in which rights are understood are held hostage to a *previous* national consensus. In short, the constitutional and rights talk that is the dominant voice of the Democratic Party is not and can never be intentionally "transformative" because it has no repertoire of resources and no morally and culturally coherent constituency through which to set priorities and make hard choices.[21] Constitutional and rights talk can only encode prevailing powers, entrenched interests, and extant values, themselves the product of previous transformations; this is what gives the contemporary Democratic Party such a backward-looking cast.

These four sets of differences in voice and rhetoric can be combined and restated. The differences can be seen as two different responses to what European observers from Tocqueville through Max Weber have termed our "statelessness." The Democratic response is that statelessness is a good in itself. The pluralism that flourishes under the interrelated systems of law and is mediated through bargaining and compromise maximizes individual liberty and group power. This response assumes that the interests and groups that comprise this pluralism are clearly defined and that our primary identities are constituted by these various groups and interests. Like an economic market, policy decisions should be an aggregate result, not an intended purpose. Democrats, of course, can never govern the nation on this theory, so they become dependent upon a rather unfettered system of presidential-executive power. The Republican response is that the only cure for statelessness is an enhanced national consensus. In the words of Mary Follett, a Progressive intellectual at the turn of the last century, "the state must be no external authority which restrains and regulates me, but it must be myself acting as the state in every smallest detail of life."[22]

SACRED NARRATIVES AND CONSTITUTIONAL PRINCIPLES

In my book *The Next Religious Establishment*, I boldly (some would say recklessly) asserted a number of propositions.[23] Among them were these:

1. National politics always requires help from beyond the constitution and electoral victory, and this help is in the form of national religious establishments—i.e., consensus on national purposes and values within which disagreement and governance take place. I call this help shared moral orientations. Politically, these orientations provide one party with the energy and power to dominate national politics and discourse, winning not just votes but commitments and purposes, while the party in opposition is either ineffective and irrelevant or plays a me-too role, waiting for the dominant party to stumble.

2. This establishment is voluntary, somewhat informal, and articulated by national elites through national institutions—economic, professional, educational, cultural, religious, and intellectual. It is also "sacred," embodying a political theology in which the American people/nation (not individual church bodies) is the object of God's intentions and will.

3. Our cultural-political history has consisted of a series of voluntary religious-political establishments divided by a series of disestablishments. Each new voluntary establishment is constructed on the ruins of the old. Because we are a nation as well as a constitution, there has never been and will never be a durable, stable, and effective disestablishment—some timeless, fair, universal, principled, neutral, value-free set of governing ideas—*even though each victorious establishment justifies its victory in these terms.*[24] These timeless principles always conceal the power, values, and purposes of the particular groups that dominate our thinking and governing. To oppose capital punishment today on biblical/religious grounds—polls show this is the dominant reason given by opponents—is perfectly acceptable in today's liberal intellectual culture, as acceptable as it was to meet in churches to pray and organize for civil rights in the South. To oppose abortion on religious grounds today, however, is to seek to impose one's "private" religious values on other people through political coercion. Why? Because opposition to abortion is not rational, just, or progressive. And why is that? Because we say so. And who is we? Enlightened, disinterested, rational, responsible, professional, expert people. Needless to add, this argument no longer wins elections and no longer intimidates foes of abortion into shamed silence: we are in an era of disestablishment.

4. It is only in periods of disestablishments, periods when national will and purpose are up for grabs and deeply contested, that boundaries defining group identities become fixed and rigid. Disputes within those groups are ruthlessly put down, while conflict between groups gains in intensity because mutually contradictory moral standards and national identities are up for grabs. Supreme Court Justice Clarence Thomas is not authentically black; Reverend Jesse Jackson is. To many on the outside, Jackson is a sinning charlatan—a sort of Al Sharpton with a divinity degree—and Thomas a brave Catholic Christian persecuted by his own people. When effective national political/ religious establishments are in place, boundaries between groups are more permeable and shifting and plurality within each group is more accepted. Individual identities become more open and free as well, because everyone in each group assumes it is under a shared national canopy within which they civilly negotiate identity and purpose.

These four propositions are meant to complement current scholarship that stresses the ways in which America has periodically transformed itself even while seeming to maintain its commitment to eighteenth-century constitutionalism. Here I am thinking of the work of Bruce Ackerman on constitutional transformations, Morton Horwitz on the transformation of American law, and Stephen Skowronek on the transformative rhythms of presidential succession.[25] I point to the ways in which sacred narrative and sacred rhetoric are the means by which constitutional and philosophical principles can become reinterpreted and relegitimated, first by discrediting their attachment to extant powers and interests and then by inviting new values, new powers, and new interests to interpret their purposes in light of new national ones. This process often takes early form among intellectual and moral countercultures whose voices and purposes are not honored in the prevailing national regime. Here, I think, the Progressive intellectuals and moral reformers of the 1880s and 1890s are an exemplary case[26] —not unlike the neoconservative intellectuals in journalism, think tanks, and (some few) law schools beginning in the 1970s.

To the question of whether or not we are entering or have already entered a period of reestablishment—spiritual, cultural, and political—I think the answer thus far is no, and it is to this issue that I now turn for my conclusion.

OUR CURRENT POLITICAL AND CULTURAL CONDITION

In an earlier period, 1876–1896, neither the Republican Party nor the Democratic Party could consolidate its electoral victories. Over this twenty-year period, no president succeeded himself, and none of these presidents had both House and Senate majorities during their entire four-year term of office. In this same twenty-year period, party control of the House changed hands five times and that of the Senate four times. In three consecutive presidential elections (1880–1888) the winner's margin was less than 1 percent of the total vote.[27] Between the election of President Carter in 1976 and the reelection of George Bush in 2004, we have had divided government (president of one party and at least one house of Congress of another) during twenty of those twenty-eight years. Between 1980 and 2000, only in Clinton's first two years has a president had party majorities in both the Senate and the House. The brevity of Clinton's triumph was repeated by President Obama in 2008–2010.

One appropriate response to this comparison is to say that now, but not then, our national governing institutions can hardly be limited to the three formal branches of the national government. One should also ask about the nature and values of the elites running the national bureaucracy, regulatory agencies, and military within the government and, outside the formal government, elites in national corporations and financial institutions, the national media, national book publishing, national churches, national law schools, and national research universities. If you are going to speak of collective moral orientations and informal religious establishments, surely these elites and institutions must be taken into account. That is to say, even as the Republican Party consolidated its electoral and even constitutional power before the election of 2008, it showed no clear signs of winning over many of the institutions that constitute our national political culture and our national identity. In short, the culture war continues.

I think that this reading is essentially correct, but I also think that there are movements within our larger intellectual culture—especially in our universities—that suggest that this culture war, this long period of religious disestablishment, is coming to an end. Moreover, unless the Democratic Party is able to rethink itself (or, as the 2008 election seems to bear out, find itself a charismatic leader who can transcend the party's incoherence and even appeal to Republican Party symbols such as Reagan), this ending of the culture wars will still benefit the voice and discursive style, if not necessarily the particular policies, of the Republican Party.

We are now deeply divided into two camps. One I call "democratic universalism," the ideology of the liberal intellectual and professional elite whose ideas can no longer win elections. The other I call the "restoration-

ists," comprised of the Protestant Christian right and neoconservatives, usually Jewish and Catholic, who together have effectively discredited the older
liberalism electorally and provided the source of most new ideas and directions for national policy, but who have no real weight in many other national
institutions, ranging from Wall Street, the American Bar Association, the
American Medical Association, and corporate America to Hollywood, the
national news media, and, most significantly, the universities. Most national
elites, especially in law schools, the foundations, the professions, and the
media, continue to act as if they are still the leaders of a successful national
intellectual and moral establishment and as if their rights-based discourse and
their understanding of equality, justice, and rationality are the only legitimate
and embracive national discourse. [28] And, in order to enforce this illusion—
because democratic elections and local political majorities certainly have
not—they must become ever more strident in keeping out other voices. That
is, every failure to persuade requires the diminution of democratic politics—
even at times, the discrediting of democratic politics—in the name of a creed
they insist necessarily and in principle includes everyone. [29] They are in a
political battle, but claim to be above it. This has become an increasingly
futile battle, both politically and intellectually. Stanley Fish calls this strategy
the attempt to characterize their opponents as belonging to "an epistemological criminal class" and to parade one's own political preferences and ethnic
and class biases as universal principles. [30] In short, neither side is hegemonic,
capable of winning both elections and the hearts and minds of the losers.

It goes without saying that the universities have been the intellectual and
moral center of the rights-based language of democratic universalism an-
nexed to a "principled" multiculturalism—the idea that all ethnic, racial, and
religious groups (at least as they choose to define them) should be accorded
equal rights, standing, and respect. Presumably, this should help the Democratic Party. I think, however, that this abstract and universal language of
rights, one that seems so easily to meld into a philosophically dogmatic
reading of the US Constitution, has come apart at the seams. As I view higher
intellectual culture in the universities over the past two decades, I see both
the ideas and the outlines of a reconstituted sacred-national consensus that is
neither restorationist nor democratic-universalist, but nationalist and pragmatic.

If our current condition, as a nation and as a university, flows from the
turmoil beginning in the late 1960s, we must examine this period with some
care before deciding whether the American university as American church
will—or even can—reclaim its originating purpose. The most recent disestablishment of the American university is heavy with irony. The first irony is
that in the 1960s, the establishment *defense* of the university against New
Left disestablishmentarians was *that the American university had no soul* of
its own. The modern research university was explicitly defended as a soulless

"multiversity" whose neutral creed was service to all of the various values and interests of a "pluralist democracy." Berkeley's Clark Kerr, lecturing at Harvard, proclaimed that the university was "value free" and morally neutral *because* it embodied and served *all* of American society in all of its diversity.[31] Here enters the second irony: the university, without a soul of its own, defended its authority because it was the veritable dynamo of America's moral, economic, political, and spiritual virtue/power in the world, shaping and channeling the energies of America into the defense of democracy and freedom at home and abroad. The university did not need a distinct soul because *America* was the soul; the university as the seminary authorizing American political theology existed only to nourish, articulate, and preserve that soul. The virtue and power of the national government and its leaders was defended on exactly the same value-free terms as the national university: social scientists declared the end of ideology and proclaimed the birth of a new value-free "pluralist" democracy in which all values become interests, all interests get a hearing, and no single interest is permitted to dominate. The "constitution" of freedom is procedural neutrality. The substance of freedom and equality is defined by the value-free social sciences.[32]

In retrospect these twin defenses appear almost as parodies of intellectual-spiritual complacency and moral-political hypocrisy. And worse, they do not begin to do justice to the operative religious values and the moral and political accomplishments of the liberal-internationalist (i.e., anticommunist) establishment being defended.[33] What these defenses do indicate is an intellectual, political, and cultural establishment on the brink of dissolution because the rhetorical and spiritual power of synchronic time had become frozen into the diachronic time of science and common sense.

The ironies of establishment denial are mirrored in the ironies of disestablishment desire. The first irony is that the New Left desperately wanted the university *to regain its soul*, to become reborn as a democratic and confessional church in order to witness against an imperialist American state and a racist and corrupt society. Their jeremiad was a call to conversion and higher service, a call that requires opposition and sacrifice and suffering. Regarding the Vietnam War and racial segregation, they were singularly successful in this call. Within the university, however, there began a period of intense struggle on all fronts, administrative, disciplinary, and curricular.

A third of a century of intellectual and bureaucratic power struggles in the university, however, have *not* ended in mutual exhaustion. I would point first to critiques starting in the 1960s in the social sciences and humanities that have now transformed the moral and political orientations of these disciplines. Not only have many areas of the social sciences jettisoned behaviorism and other superficial claims of value neutrality, they have come together under the rubric of the "human sciences" that draw upon the moral sources and resources of philosophy, cultural history, religion, and ethics. This shift has typically resulted in practically ignoring older departmental boundaries and creating new communities of scholarship based on the "experiential foundations" of shared moral orientations.[34] And the orientations driving these fields are precisely those that take seriously the role of values and commitment in human agency and in human history. Even academic philosophy—at least the academic philosophy that other intellectuals and academics now read—has rediscovered phenomenology and pragmatism. This, too, is a source of religious depth, for phenomenology and pragmatism place spirit, experience, and purpose *inside* thought and therefore inside the history of thought. Social history generally and women's studies in particular—despite their beginnings in ressentiment—have rediscovered spirit as a guide to understanding, infusing history, the humanities, and the social sciences with issues of identity and directing reflection on and research into the moral and religious sources of the self.

My own field of moral and political philosophy has attained an energy, reach, and attractive power far outside of political science departments even as it has drawn on resources and ideas quite outside its earlier boundaries. With these resources, political theorists have launched a many-sided reconsideration of the foundations of liberalism, individualism, and rights. Entailed in this reconsideration is a rediscovery of "civic republicanism" either as an alternative to or as a deeper understanding of liberalism. In seeking to recover more civically oriented ideas of individuality and citizenship, this enterprise has necessarily drawn upon narratives and ideas excluded from the dominant story of liberalism and modernity that ended in the ahistorical and procedural ideal of the "unencumbered self."[35] Moral and political philosophy has rediscovered the history of religion and power that has enabled it to write the history of and chart a future for liberalism that includes religious spirit and moral purpose. Here, the writings of Charles Taylor are both exemplary and causal.[36]

As more scholars envision common projects of scholarship and study, so they construct common pasts to shape that future. These narratives, moreover, are primarily *national* constructs addressed both to American universities and to *national* audiences of political intellectuals and other opinion leaders. Alisdair MacIntyre has reminded us to pay attention to stories, because it is through personal, professional, institutional, and political narratives that one tracks and interprets the growth and decay of spirit.[37] From the 1960s onward, every deep critique of an academic discipline and every creation of new scholarly communities required at some point a story, both to unmask and to show new directions. Is there any doubt that these critiques are political-theological? At bottom, these narratives proclaim what *national* covenants have been broken, what *national* commitments have not been kept, and what *national* errands have gone unfulfilled in our scholarship and our teaching. These same proclamations are invitations to reform and to reclaim the national covenant on a higher level.

In the academy, as in the larger society, one might say that spiritually dead establishmentarians are routinely hoisted on their own petards because those petards were constructed from real spiritual experiences, moral choices, and political commitments now most vividly remembered by their critics. This was as true at the time of the First Great Awakening in the 1740s as it was in the 1960s.[38] At these moments it is the critics who seek to reclaim history—and reintroduce a rhetoric of synchronic time—because they claim the duty to call America back to its obligations.

It remains a very open question whether all of the resulting spiritual and intellectual agon in the university will ultimately produce a reconstituted political theology for the nation. It is, I think, rapidly producing one in microcosm and for itself that effectively includes participants who, in the larger political and cultural world, are neither speaking to nor understanding each other. Whether these emerging "master narratives" uniting previously distinct moral orientations and scholarly communities in the humanities and the human sciences will achieve spiritual mastery of—and reconstitute the soul of—the university is the first question. Whether this newly inspired university can or will reclaim its spiritual role in the larger society is the next one. The best we can do for now is to look for the signs and help call them forth.

What has all this intellectual ferment and change done for our politics? Well, it has certainly not converted die-hard rights- and race-obsessed Democrats into moralistic and conservative Republicans! What it has done is unsettle and disorient the strident recourse to abstract democratic principle on the left, and thus undercut a kind of antinational, cosmopolitan, and principled "multiculturalism" in favor of more nuanced, open-ended, ironic, and experiential views of groups, of "otherness," and of the many meanings of inclusion. Affirmative action as a fixed principle is dead; experiments by both conservatives and liberals to diversify entry into the university (and into a common American culture) are thriving. Prominent figures on the left like Richard Rorty and Michael Lind[39] have been very influential in this regard. Harold Bloom's *The American Religion* is only the most notable of scores of books coming from university religious studies and history departments that look at the many-sided appearances of religion in our common culture rather than its formal-institutional expressions in the churches.[40] These writings represent rediscoveries of America and the sources of American national patriotism that are also implicit critiques of the idea that we are constituted by and through universalistic constitutional ideals.

CONCLUSION

G. K. Chesterton is famous for saying that America is "a nation with the soul of a church." He is less remembered for saying "There is nothing the matter with Americans except for their ideals." What I have been arguing is that underlying every particular statement of our constitutional, political, and moral ideals—and oh, how we love to parade our ideals!—is a deeper and sacred narrative, one that has the capacity to mock our prevailing ideals and prepare us for their reinterpretation and transformation.

The American reception of Abraham Lincoln's second inaugural address was both mixed and bewildered. All the newspapers noted its odd biblical-theological content, but few knew what to make of it. Some thought the recourse to sacred rhetoric was an intellectual embarrassment; others thought it was an attempt to take refuge in piety; still others saw it as a simple evasion of the responsibility to spell out a political and constitutional program for the next four years. In marked contrast, reports on responses from London and Paris suggest that thoughtful journalists from these countries saw more clearly what Lincoln was doing. Both Englishmen and Frenchmen, I suggest, knew the power and symbolism of "divine sovereignty,"[41] first from their monarchical traditions and then from their own revolutionary moments. An English journal favorably compared Lincoln to Cromwell. American officials and journalists in Paris first noted that the address was both accurately translated and widely diffused—evidently a rare occurrence for an American state paper—and then noted that the French particularly remarked on its absence of boasting regarding the American past and future—what I have termed providential-diachronic time. Instead, they praised the address for its simplicity and Christian dignity and, therefore, as expressing a fundamental truth about ourselves and about the nature of political life.

NOTES

1. Even after the crime description was overwhelmed by that of war, and even after the invasion and occupation of Iraq, some leaders of the Democratic Party and some of its candidates for presidential nomination still vainly insisted that the first priority continue to be the apprehension of Osama bin Laden. Even with the capture and killing of bin Laden under the direction of a Democratic president, however, the "war on terror" continues both institutionally and rhetorically.

2. Julia Ward Howe, 1819–1910; Samuel F. Smith, 1808–1895. And see James Russell Lowell, 1819–1891, "Once to Every Man and Nation." For an analysis of the lyrics in "Battle Hymn of the Republic," see Tuveson, 1968. For a discussion of various models of time, see Zerubavel, 2003.

3. Bercovitch, 1975, 98–108.

4. Quoted in Bercovitch, 1975, 148.

5. The distinction between young and new is discussed in chapter 3, below.

6. Quoted in Michael Levy, 1982, 7–8.
7. Whitman, 1955, 240–42.
8. Quoted in White, 2002, 18–19.
9. Paine, 1976, 120. On the American Revolution and constitution as events in sacred history and prophecy, see Bercovitch, 1976; Clark, 1994; and Hatch, 1977.
10. MacPherson, 1991; Murphy, 2008; Ross, 2009.
11. "First Inaugural Address" (1861), quoted in Michael Levy, 1982, 227; and see McPherson, 1991.
12. Burnham, 1970; Jensen, 1971; Kelley, 1979; McCormick, 1986; Kleppner, 1987 and 1970; Plotke, 1996; Shefter, 1978; and Skowronek, 1993 and 1982.
13. Greenstone, 1993.
14. Johnson and Porter, 1975, 1–2.
15. Wilson, 1974, distinguishes between national republicans seeing America existing in time and democrats seeing America as existing in (ever-expanding) space. The most ambitious attempt to catalogue the differences in partisan voices and purposes is Gerring, 1998.
16. Handy, 1991; Howe, 1979; Kohl, 1989; Jaenicke, 1986; and Jensen, 1971.
17. Kohl, 1989, and Gerring, 1998.
18. This is the meaning of the term "liberal establishment" that gained currency in the 1950s and 1960s. This establishment was not the Democratic Party, but the national institutional elites clustered around a greatly expanded and strengthened presidency. See Plotke, 1996; Silk, 1988; Galvin, 2009; Hodgson, 1976; William McGuire King, 1989; and Zunz, 1998 and 1990.
19. Lowi, 1969, and Hodgson, 1976.
20. Glendon, 1991.
21. Lowi, 1969.
22. Follett, 1918, 138.
23. Eisenach, 2000.
24. Hutchison, 2003, makes this argument.
25. Ackerman, 1993 and 2000; Horwitz, 1992; Skowronek, 1993; and see Morone, 2003.
26. See chapters 4 and 5, below, and Eisenach, 1994; Crunden, 1984. For contemporary conservative mobilization, Teles, 2007 and 2009.
27. Keller, 1977.
28. Teles, 2007; Spragens, 2009, chapter 2.
29. The best recent example is Gutmann, 2003.
30. Fish, 1999, 191.
31. Kerr, 1963.
32. Dahl, 1967 and 1956; Truman, 1951; Neustadt, 1976; and Hodgson, 1976.
33. Dudziak, 2002; Silk, 1988; and King, 1989.
34. A good discussion of this dynamic is Green, 1996, 24–28.
35. Sandel, 1996; Neal, 1997.
36. Charles Taylor, 2007, 2001, 1991, 1989, and 1985; and see Hunter, 2001. Kloppenberg, 2011, places President Obama—but not the Democratic Party nor its supporting body of progressive intellectuals—squarely within these new bodies of thought.
37. MacIntyre, 1984, and see the excellent collection of writings on this theme in Hinchman and Hinchman, 1997.
38. Contrast, for example, the tone and spirit of Kerr, 1963, to the rejoinder by Wolff, 1969.
39. Rorty, 1998; Lind, 1996. For a more theoretically nuanced discussion of these same themes, see Smith, 2003.
40. Bloom, 1992; Stout and Hart, 1997; Moore, 1994; Butler and Stout, 1998; Fox and Westbrook, 1998; Marsden and Longfield, 1992. I develop this idea more fully in chapter 3, below.
41. Engster, 2001.

Chapter Two

Liberal Religion and Liberal Politics

Shortly before John Dewey left the University of Michigan for the University of Chicago in 1894, he gave an address to the Students' Christian Association entitled "Christianity and Democracy." Dewey begins by rejecting the idea that religion consists of cult and doctrine, that is, "a collection of specific acts to be performed, and of special ideas to be cherished in consciousness" that separate it from other acts, "secular, profane, commercial, or merely moral—that are not communion with God." On the contrary, recent research shows that "religion is an expression of the social relations of the community . . . its dogmas and mysteries are recognitions, in symbolic form, of the poetic, social and intellectual value of the surroundings." Unfortunately, these dogmas and mysteries often become condensed into symbols and rites that separate religion from its life-giving sources, forcing vital religion to seek "revelation and expression in more adequate relations and truths." Jesus is the expression of this authentic understanding of religion: he "had no cult or rite to impose . . . there were no special religious truths which He came to teach . . . his doctrine was that Truth . . . is one as God is one." Drawing on a recent book by Elisha Mulford,[1] Dewey concludes that "the very universality of Christianity precludes its being a religion" of cult and doctrine. Christianity is not a creedal religion but a continuous revelation of truth that "must continue as long as life has new meanings to unfold, new action to propose." Any attempt by any body of men or any set of institutions to assume guardianship and administration of this revelation betrays the essence of Christianity. God "is essentially and only the self-revealing, and the revelation is complete only as men come to realize Him."[2]

At this point, the relationship between Christianity and democracy is drawn. Man must live and act in free societies, for his social relationship "is the only organ he has for receiving and appropriating" God's continuously revealed truths. Democracy, then, "appears as the means by which the revelation of truth is carried on" and, through democratic life, this truth "is made a common truth enacted in all departments of action, not in one isolated sphere called religious." "Democracy is a spiritual fact and not a mere piece of governmental machinery" precisely because "freedom means giving this truth a chance to show itself . . . with more conscious and more compelling force." And, as it does so, humanity will become ever more spiritually unified, a "community of truth" progressively realizing "the brotherhood of man" that "Christ called the Kingdom of God."[3] As Dewey states in a contemporaneous address: "The next religious prophet who will have a permanent and real influence on men's lives will be the man who succeeds in pointing out the religious meaning of democracy, the ultimate religious value to be found in the flow of life itself. It is the question of doing what Jesus did for his time."[4] When one adds two later essays, "My Pedagogic Creed" (1897) and "Religion and Our Schools" (1908), Dewey's ambitious project for the democratization of American politics and society through shared religious belief becomes clear. Education is "a regulation of the process of coming to share in the social consciousness" by continuously helping the student to reconstruct and, therefore, to understand, internalize, and share "in the inherited resources of the race, and to use his own powers for social ends." In bringing together in common schools "those of different nationalities, languages, traditions, and creeds, in assimilating them together on the basis of what is common and public in endeavor and achievement, [teachers] are performing an infinitely significant religious work. They are promoting the social unity out of which in the end genuine religious unity must grow." Common education, therefore, is the "paramount moral duty" of the community, and the teacher "the prophet of the true God and the usherer in of the true kingdom of God."[5]

The editor of Dewey's *Early Works*, writing in 1970, dismisses these early essays as "quaint remnants" to serve as a "reminder of opinion and interests within which Dewey was working."[6] Today we must be more subtle in our understanding. Read in the light of American Protestant theology from Theodore Parker, William Ellery Channing, Nathaniel Taylor, and Horace Bushnell prior to the Civil War, and from Henry Ward Beecher, Lyman Abbott, John Bascom, Washington Gladden, Josiah Strong, and Theodore Munger after, Dewey's early essays can more clearly be viewed not as quaint religious remainders but as attempts to appropriate and transport this liberal theology into philosophy and psychology in the universities and thence into the public schools. This project would not only displace denominational creeds and control,[7] it would tap into the power and energy of new ideas in philosophy and the natural and human sciences. And read against the English philosophers and churchmen Samuel Taylor Coleridge, Frederick Denison Maurice, John Stuart Mill, and T. H. Green, and the German philosophers and theologians Fredrich Schleiermacher, G. W. F. Hegel, Christian Baur, Albrecht Ritschl, and Adolf Harnack, one sees affinities and relationships among liberal Protestant intellectuals all across the transatlantic world.[8]

This understanding of Dewey, and of his forebearers and contemporaries, is made more convincing given recent scholarship on the relationship of religion and politics over the course of American history.[9] Much ground has been cleared—and more ground needs to be cleared—in order to grasp both the inner and the outer relationships in the alliance between liberal religion and liberal/reformist politics in America. The problem I set myself was to ask what must be learned—and what must one unlearn—in order to give a coherent account of the relationship between liberal religion and liberal politics in America. Who were its thinkers and leaders? What were the primary sites in which, and the media through which, they did their work? Did these sites and these media change over time? How and when did the liberalization of Protestant theology become appropriated by liberal social and political reformers—or was the causal chain reversed, where social and political reform ideas stimulated revisions in Protestant theology and social teachings?[10]

These questions are asked against a background that assumes very high levels of success by this alliance in the period beginning in the 1840s, reaching its highest moment in the Civil War period, and then powerfully reconstituted as the Progressive movement at the turn of the last century. The success of Progressivism continued, but with major alterations, both in parts of the New Deal program and through what became known as the postwar "liberal establishment" that dominated both political parties and all upper reaches of national institutions through the 1960s. This series of successful political/cultural regimes itself suggests further questions. To what extent was the post–New Deal liberal establishment also a liberal Protestant establishment? And how had liberal Protestantism and political liberalism themselves been altered—institutionally, demographically, and in self-understandings—between their mutual collapse in the 1920s and their reconstitution during World War II and the Cold War? Finally, when did this alliance finally prove fatal to both parties? When did liberal religion and liberal politics go on the defensive, serving more as a refuge of condescending bitterness and arrogant anger than as a dynamic and creative force in American life?

This chapter can only give rough indications of how these questions might best be addressed. And because so much has been written and is already known about the history of liberal-reform politics in America, most attention will be paid to liberal religious ideas and social teachings. Even this attention will often be condensed in short biographies of writers and leaders who exemplify the connections between liberal religion and liberal politics. Even this modest beginning, however, requires some preliminary deconstructive work, if only to open ourselves to understandings that pass over and around a series of intellectual roadblocks that stand in the way. Two of these roadblocks must be confronted at the start.

The first barrier is erected by starting with the question—much mooted today—of whether America is or ever has been a "Christian" nation. This question is both silly and wrongheaded, however ingeniously or disingenuously one attempts to answer it. The second barrier to understanding is to frame the general relationship between religion and politics as a "constitutional" question of the proper relationship between church and state. Both of these barriers are hopelessly abstract and do violence to American thought and experience.

To address the first roadblock: the primary fact is that America was from the earliest colonial beginnings a profoundly Protestant nation—and in some respects it remains a Protestant nation. It remained anti-Catholic in its national identity so long as the Catholic Church stood apart from and criticized the reigning voluntary and informal religious establishment. In weird ways, this remains true even today. The interesting issue is whether this Protestant identity was and is also a "Christian" one. To what extent can a noncreedal, transchurch, and liberal-ecumenical Protestantism be identified as "religious" in a Christian understanding of religion? This is not a recent issue. Dewey is a good example, but one could add Jane Addams and many leading academic social scientists and philosophers at the turn of the last century. One could arguably say that Dewey and these others had scant regard for Protestant theological creeds and church doctrines and often did not identify with or attend any particular Protestant denominational church. The same could be said of many of the leading lights of the ecumenical Protestant divinity schools and of the leadership of some of the colleges and universities founded by the leading Protestant churches.

It is no accident, however, that almost all of the intellectual leaders in the academy, the foundations, and higher journalism in the late nineteenth and early twentieth centuries came from seventeenth-century New England stock and were raised in mid-Atlantic or Midwestern states by Republican parents who attended either Congregational or Presbyterian churches.[11] Did church-going Protestants and their clergy successfully reject them as heretics or as repudiators of Christianity?[12] To the contrary, the liberal Protestantism they represented became increasingly dominant as it became ever-less dogmatically Christian and ever-less centered in churches. The energies and power of liberal Protestantism had migrated (often using what appears to be "secular" language) out of denominational bodies and into both ecumenical and secular settings. This migration explains its unending string of moral, social, and political victories and, for liberal theologians and churchmen, serves as proof of a sign of religious success. Here is Dewey's vision restated in a recent article: "A key paradox of liberal Protestantism—one that must be a cornerstone of any history of liberal Protestantism—is that its goal has always been, in part, to sanctify the secular, to bring forth out of the natural and human worlds the divine potential contained within them. Secularization can be seen, in some of its forms, as a sign of success for liberal Protestantism, not a marker of defeat."[13] It is only at one's intellectual peril that one underestimates the theological, historical, and philosophical energy and sophistication that went into the achievement of this paradox—not only in America, but in Germany and England as well.[14]

In a sense, the second roadblock to understanding has already been approached. While church and state became legally separated in the early nineteenth century (Massachusetts Unitarians and Connecticut Congregationalists were the last holdouts), religion and politics have continuously been intermixed. The rise of competitive mass-based political parties in the 1840s immediately created religious divisions along partisan lines—divisions that were already anticipated in the factional struggles in the revolutionary and constitutional periods.[15] This intermixture of religion and democratic politics was not only present at the creation, it has continued into the present era with greater or lesser strength and with different mixes of religious, ethnic, and racial divisions. To ask that religion and politics be separated is to ask that culture and politics, or intellectual life and politics, or nationalism and politics, or morality and politics be separated. Each and every vital sphere in American life confronts democratic politics and must respond. All of these spheres, directly or indirectly, intersect with religious issues and questions.[16] Put in stark terms, calls for the separation of church/religion and state/politics have frequently been part of a political strategy *by some religious interests against other religious interests*—whether the issue was keeping "religion" out of the schools in the nineteenth and early twentieth centuries[17] or current opposition to voucher systems. An even more obvious example is the divide over "faith-based" welfare systems.[18]

LIBERAL PROTESTANT THEOLOGY

An exponent of liberal Protestant theology in America, Daniel Day Williams, characterized it this way: "By 'liberal theology' I mean the movement in modern Protestantism which during the nineteenth century tried to bring Christian thought into organic unity with the evolutionary world view, the movements for social reconstruction, and the expectations of 'a better world' which dominated the general mind. It is that form of Christian faith in which the prophetic-progressive philosophy of history culminates in the expectation of the coming of the Kingdom of God on earth."[19]

This definition seems ideally suited to show the relationship of liberal religion and liberal politics: liberal Protestantism seemed specifically designed to serve the ends of American reform politics. Indeed, written in 1949, it better reflects than explores the power of this alliance in the early twentieth century. This definition, however, overlooks key elements put in place earlier, first in Germany and England and then in America. These earlier elements were not primarily directed outward toward the reform of society, politics, and culture, but directed inward toward dominant Protestant creeds and theological teachings. [20] Religious thinkers in each of these countries confronted specific problems. In Germany it was the falling intellectual and moral prestige of the state churches in the Protestant lands—especially in the universities and state administration—and, in some states, the rift between Lutheran and Reformed churches. In England it was the long-standing conflict between low and high church parties in the national church as well as the energetic and growing body of dissent outside the church. In America, the main issue was the fall in prestige of the New England clergy in the face of state disestablishment and the proliferation of new churches resulting both from schism and the religious entrepreneurship occasioned by revivalist movements. This resulted in an intense struggle over educational, moral, and religious leadership in the new western settlements. Despite these domestic differences, however, churchmen in all three countries confronted some of the same intellectual and theological conundrums flowing from the Enlightenment and scientific rationalism—and the new possibilities raised by Romanticism. [21]

If one were asked to identify the most prominent early liberal Protestant thinkers in America, any short list must include William Ellery Channing, Theodore Parker, Nathaniel Taylor, and Horace Bushnell. All four were influenced directly by Samuel Taylor Coleridge (1772–1834) in England and indirectly by Friedrich Schleiermacher (1768–1834) in Germany. Both Coleridge and Schleiermacher grounded theology as an intellectual discipline not on external authority—whether that of God, the Bible, or the church—but in imagination and feeling. Schleiermacher's series of addresses, first published in 1799 and then, with revisions, translated into English in 1821, *On Religion: Speeches to Its Cultured Despisers*, sparked a revolution in Protestant theology. [22] At the conclusion of his second speech, for example, Schleiermacher addresses the issue of immortality:

> The true essence of piety . . . is our immediate consciousness of the deity as we find him in ourselves and in the world alike. And this is precisely why the aim and character of a religious life is not immortality, as so many wish and believe . . . It is not that immortality which is outside and beyond time—or rather after this time but still in time—but only that immortality which we can

already possess in this temporal life of ours . . . In the midst of finitude to become one with the infinite, and to be eternal in every instant—this is the immortality of religion.[23]

Coleridge, in his *Aids to Reflection* (1825), echoed this same idea: "That which we find within ourselves, which is more than ourselves, and yet the ground of whatever is good and permanent therein, is the substance and life of all other knowledge."[24]

Both theologians situated religion in acknowledgement of our incompleteness and dependence, our realization that we do not exist from ourselves. Like Coleridge, with his distinction between reason and understanding, Schleiermacher places religion on a footing that not only incorporates all the human and natural sciences but makes it immune to attack from those quarters. As Schleiermacher wrote to a colleague, "every dogma truly representing an element of our Christian awareness can also be formulated in such a way that it leaves us uninvolved with science."[25] If, as they both maintained, God is immanent in human consciousness and experience and, therefore, in history, access to God can be gained from many different starting points and from many different ways of knowing. But it must be acknowledged that the canopy they created clearly *subordinated* all historical expressions of "church" Christianity to this new universal grounding. And this subordination was clearly a *Protestant* one, premised on the inner recognition in each believer of God's continuous revelation/grace through all the various resources and expressions of man's spirit.

This "essence of Christianity"[26]—what Dewey claimed made it not a conventionally understood religion at all[27]—holds open the possibility of a national/universal church with no authoritative creeds and rituals, standing astride all of the various church bodies, each with their particular members, doctrines, and practices. Like Coleridge, Schleiermacher did not intend to do away with standing modes of worship and confessions of faith—let alone destroy the nationally established church—but to ground religion on a basis from which everyone, from the most sophisticated philosopher to the most ordinary of people, could partake in a higher life of the spirit. Coleridge explicitly held that the Church of England need not be Christian in any creedal sense. Under Coleridge's influence, John Stuart Mill thought that a reformed national church should be maintained by the state, serving as a public repository and recognition of the primacy of man's spirit over man's nature and as a counterweight to commercial and materialist values driven by lower human desires and interests.[28]

Viewed in this light, the philosophical/theological canopy could be quite radical when measured against conventional Christian beliefs. Theodore Parker, a close reader of *Aids to Reflection*, not only grounded religion in the sense of transcendence flowing from our intuitions and feelings, he relegated to the realm of the transient all church authority and teachings that do not flow from an immediate sense of this transcendence. Even the personal authority of Jesus cannot stand against these feelings. The truths of Christianity, Parker said, would prevail even if it were proved historically that Jesus never lived and that the Gospels were fabrications. Parker—like Schleiermacher and Coleridge—saw himself as completing the work of the Reformation. [29] Truths grounded in reason and spiritual intuition carry their own authority. In this sense, according to Parker, "each man must be his own Christ, or he is no Christian." [30] Parker and Channing had dreams of transforming the Unitarian church in Massachusetts—itself a denominational fragment of New England Congregationalism—into just such a national church, driven by the power of its moral ideals and its rationalist footing. Their dreams were quickly dashed in the face of the Second Great Awakening and in the superior intellectual, moral, and financial power of liberal evangelical Protestantism to "Christianize" the ever-expanding American west. [31]

An Ethical Turn to Moral Governance

The failure of these dreams, however, hid a huge paradox: the leading ideas of Schleiermacher, Coleridge, and those they influenced in America generated a resurgence of Protestant liberal theology that, by the late nineteenth century, became intellectually and culturally hegemonic in all three countries, albeit in different institutional ways and with differing political results. [32] This resurgence was not the result of their skepticism regarding historical forms of Christianity, but of the ways this critique freed Protestant theology to embrace the primacy of individual morality and social ethics as the central feature of a Christian life and to stress the power of individual and collective spirit to fulfill Christ's promise on earth.

In America, the first battles to be fought before this "ethical turn" in Protestantism could be completed were over the intertwined doctrinal issues of predestination, human depravity, free will, and the meaning of Christ's sacrifice and atonement. Without delving into the complexities of the arguments made and the intense controversies they generated, [33] the result was the transformation of liberal Protestantism almost wholly into morality: "It is absolute, pure Morality; absolute, pure Religion; the love of man; the love of God acting without let or hindrance." [34] The connection between man and God is a shared desire for the moral governance of the world. Horace Bushnell characterized this intuition of right and wrong as "a kind of revelation."

"Here then," he says, "will I begin. If there is a God, as I rather hope there is, and very dimly believe, he is a right God. If I have lost him in wrong, perhaps I shall find him in right. Will he not help me, or, perchance, even be discovered to me . . . ? And the dimly groping cry for help, what is that but a feeling after God, if, haply, it may find him, and actually finding him not far off? And what is the help obtained but exactly the true Christ-help? And the result, what, also, is that but the kingdom of God within, righteousness and peace and joy in the Holy Ghost?[35]

This early statement soon became a liberal Protestant mantra, endlessly echoed in the writings of famous Protestant spokesmen after the Civil War. Henry Ward Beecher (1813–1887), the most influential Congregational clergyman of his day and an early exponent of what later became known as the social gospel, put it most vividly: "Morality is the indispensable ground of spiritual fervor . . . An elevated morality blossoms into spirituality. And eminent spirituality sends down the elaborated sap into every leaf, fiber and root that helped create it." Religious creeds of the future will begin where the old ones ended, "upon the nature of man, his condition on earth, his social duties and civil obligations, the development of his reason, his spiritual nature." Man's religious spirit "will ascend from the known to the unknown."[36] John Bascom, another Congregational clergyman who later became president of the University of Wisconsin, put this relationship even more succinctly: religion "is not so much the foundation of morals, as morals is the foundation of religion."[37]

Now that America had finally forged itself into a coherent nation through the northern victory in the Civil War and become consecrated through the life and death of Abraham Lincoln, this nation must become equipped to serve as the vanguard in the achievement of what Nathaniel Taylor had earlier termed "moral government of God."[38]

A further influence on and carrier of liberal Protestant theology was revivalism and related religious and moral reform movements. These provided a crucial link between the Progressive alliance of liberal religion and liberal politics in the twentieth century. The earliest expression of politico-religious revival is, of course, found in the abolitionist, temperance, and women's movements prior to the Civil War. All had their origins and main centers of strength in areas swept by religious revivals in the 1820s and 1830s.[39] After the Civil War, "social Christianity" shared these same revivalist and social movement characteristics.

A representative early figure uniting revival, liberal Christianity, and social Christianity is Charles Grandison Finney (1792–1875). Beginning as a revivalist preacher in upstate New York, he became the minister of one of the largest Protestant churches in New York City, concluding his career as a professor of theology and then president of Oberlin College. As he articulated and refined his "new measures" for religious revival,[40] he succeeded in winning over leading liberal Protestant intellectuals and seminarians. These new measures, theologically premised on the promise of general atonement, not only democratized religious worship and preaching styles, they confirmed the relationship between man's initiative in conversion and his ability to translate religious conversion into personal and social reform. By attacking as pharisaical the more condescending forms of Christian philanthropy tied to a religion of respectability, Finney helped forge a more democratically inspired social engagement with poverty, the new immigrants, and other problems occasioned by rapid industrialization. And by opening up religious participation and religious education to women (Oberlin was the first coeducational college in America), the later social gospel movement recruited a vast new constituency for social reform and political action.[41]

NARRATIVES OF THE LIBERAL PROTESTANT IDEOLOGY OF SOCIAL REFORM

A leading element connecting liberal Protestant theology to the social gospel and thence to what became the Progressive movement was the stress on inward conviction and the power of collective opinion to transform both self and society. From the theological side, the stress on experience and feeling and on the relationship of ethics to religion not only denigrated legalistic and hierarchical forms of authority, but lodged authority in the renewed power of individual belief and collective opinion.[42]

Dewey's stress on shared consciousness as the source of all religious and social progress was one of the central themes in the new Progressive social sciences.[43] In one of his earliest essays, he sought to identify the specifically ethical dimensions of democracy. Any ethical conception, he begins, must reject from the start an abstract and mathematical conception of democracy, reducing men "into merely numerical individuals, into ballot-projecting units."[44]

> Society and the individual are really organic to each other . . . He is not merely its image or mirror. He is the localized manifestation of its life. And if, as actually happens, society be not yet possessed of one will, but partially is one and partially has a number of fragmentary and warring wills, it yet follows that *so far* as society has a common purpose and spirit, *so far* each individual is not representative of a certain proportionate share of the sum total of will but is its vital embodiment. And this is the theory, often crudely expressed, but none the less true in substance, that every citizen is a sovereign, the American theory, a doctrine which in grandeur has but one equal in history, and that its fellow, namely, that every man is a priest of God.[45]

Moral Religion and Democratic Opinion

In a socialized and ethical democracy, personal development and social progress are interdependent because both require "a unified and articulate will."[46] Without this will, every association for the achievement of common ends would remain temporary and artificial. In his widely used college text-book, *Ethics*, Dewey stated that "a common end which is not made such by common, free voluntary cooperation in process of achievement is common in name only . . . It has to be continually buttressed by appeal to external, not voluntary, considerations; bribes of pleasure, threats of harm, use of force. It has to be undone and done over."[47]

The effective embodiment of a common will requires a coherent and consensual "public opinion." For the social psychologist Charles Horton Cooley, one of Dewey's early colleagues at the University of Michigan, "public opinion is no mere aggregate of separate individual judgments, but an organization, a cooperative product of communication and reciprocal in-fluence. It may be as different from the sum of what the individuals could have thought out in separation as a ship built by a hundred men is from a hundred boats each built by one man."[48] To the sociologist Franklin Gid-dings, a sociologist and later colleague of Dewey's at Columbia, "society is democratic only when all people without distinction of rank or class partici-pate in the making of public opinion and of moral authority."[49]

Famous for the establishment of Hull House in Chicago, Jane Addams was also a prolific and influential writer. In an early essay, "The Subjective Necessity of Social Settlements," she spoke of why educated young people experience "a fatal want of harmony between their theory and their lives, a lack of co-ordination between thought and action." They know that "it will be impossible to establish a higher political life than the people themselves crave; that it is difficult to see how the notion of a higher civic life can be fostered save through common intercourse;. . . that the good we secure for ourselves is precarious and uncertain, is floating in mid-air, until it is secured for all of us and incorporated into our common life."[50] These hopes are an ascending hierarchy: "The first contains the desire to make the entire social organism democratic, to extend democracy beyond its political expression; the second is the impulse to share the race life, and to bring as much as possible of social energy and the accumulation of civilization to those por-tions of the race which have little; the third springs from a certain *renais-sance* of Christianity, a movement toward its early humanitarian aspects."[51]

Progressives not only acknowledged the importance of moral and relig-ious vanguards, they made identification with this vanguard a large part of their appeal. This, I think, is most evident in those who explicitly combined Protestant evangelicalism and Progressive social reform.[52]

"Evangelizing" America by establishing new churches and colleges in the west had long been a project of New England and, later, Midwestern Protes-tants. Additionally, antebellum "evangelical united fronts" created many ecu-menical national reform movements, most notably, temperance and antislav-ery. New England "theocrats" like Horace Bushnell and Henry Ward Beecher advocated projects to "Christianize America" not only through "home missions" but through the reformation of the family, creating common schools and asylums, and starting crusades against drink and prostitution. Post–Civil War "social Christianity"—which came to be called the "social gospel"—was unique, however, in its alliance with the new social sciences, and in its equanimity at the prospect of having much of the church's traditional educational and social missions being taken over by governmental or other nonsectarian institutions.

The Master Narrative

These two features were welcomed and, indeed, more or less implicit in liberal evangelical theology grounded in revelation driving an evolutionary theory of history.[53] Lyman Abbott wrote three books on the evolution of Christianity. The first traces the history of Christianity as a spiritual force, the second, the history of Christianity as a social development, and the third, Christianity as it has evolved into a new ethical system.[54] When the three books are set alongside two other books of Abbott's, on the history and evolution of human freedom and on the making of America,[55] the result is a comprehensive narrative underpinning for the Progressive reform project. Abbott's narrative was seconded by many others.[56]

In this perspective, experience of the spirit takes place in time and history; for each age of man, authentic religion "is always new" and must find new forms of articulate expression. Christianity is evolutionary because God "manifests himself [to man] in growth."[57] History "is but the record of the process of this evolution of the divinity out of humanity. It is a continuous progressive change, from lower to higher, and from simpler to more complex. It is according to certain definite laws of the moral and spiritual life."[58] Progressive revelation turns religious life toward ethics and the life of the church from inward maintenance to outward action. Because God is disclosed ever more fully through man in his larger moral and social life, God "is training children to be free like himself, and by their own free choice to become partakers of his nature." Evidence of this disclosure is in man's increasing capacity for "righteousness."[59]

Abbott's political-religious narrative is also a history of ideas that encompasses Europe's leading theologians, scientists, philosophers, and political thinkers. As this history moves toward the present time, American reformers take center stage, as if all earlier history of man's spirit reaches fulfillment. In this spiritual history, the "New Theology" is seen to migrate out from the constraints of creed, church, and state in order to permeate the entire society, with America as the vanguard.[60]

Abbott's narrative was a transatlantic one, with a decided emphasis on the Anglophone world. This emphasis is understandable when one examines, for example, how intellectual leaders of the "Broad Church" movement in mid-nineteenth-century England constructed their ideological narrative.[61] In 1860, a book of essays on Christianity appeared, written in 1858–1859 by seven broad churchmen, all with Oxford connections. The presentation and format of *Essays and Reviews* is modest to the point of diffidence. There is no acknowledged editor or introduction. The preface consists of ten lines holding each author responsible for his contribution only and avowing that the articles were written "in entire independence of each other." Initial appearances to the contrary, *Essays and Reviews* soon created a sensation, quite eclipsing Darwin's *Origin of the Species*, published the year previously.[62]

The primary distinction running throughout the essays was the same one that grounded John Stuart Mill's "moral sciences," the distinction between "internal/spiritual" and "external/material" ways of perceiving and knowing man, his culture, and his history. In the *Essays*, this common historicist perspective placed both biblical history and church history inside a larger story of man's spirit, a story that embodied both "lawlike" truths and the highest source of personal and social meaning.

Summaries of two of the essays capture this shared orientation. In the lead essay, "The Education of Man," Frederick Temple begins by distinguishing the material (external) and spiritual (internal) worlds, placing man within the lawlike characteristics of each, and then traces the workings of the "laws of the spiritual . . . world" in sacred history. Following Gotthold Lessing, from whom Temple borrowed his title, the essay becomes an extended analogy of the individual and society as they are "educated" from childhood to adulthood. The child is educated by positive rules and punishments, the youth by the force of example, and the adult by his own free choices. So too is the progress of the education of mankind: "First comes the Law, then the Son of Man, then the Gift of the Spirit."[63] It is only in the adulthood of man that freedom becomes central to his further development. Having been prepared and disciplined in these earlier ways, the education of modern man now rests with "the office of the spirit," not as the immediate source of external truths but as the "guide . . . into truth." Modern man "looks inwards . . . He is free." The remainder of the essay is a plea for the fullest intellectual freedom as the only means of incorporating new forms of knowledge into theology. The Bible is the central site of Christian faith, so freedom to interpret the Bible from the standpoint of man's evolved inner life—his conscience—becomes the contemporary imperative for the church. Protestantism, the only tenable modern standpoint, has both created this new condition and been slow to recognize its implications. Toleration is now inseparable from a commitment to "spiritual truth and religiousness of life."[64]

Henry Bristow Wilson's article on the idea of the national church is an extension of the distinction between external and internal. As in Dewey's early essays, Wilson held that formal creeds and dogmas are only contingent and external statements of the condition of man's spirit at any given time and therefore should never become fixed or finally authoritative. As he put it in the 1851 Bampton Lectures at Oxford (anticipating Mill's famous phrase in *On Liberty*), such reliance "is inconsistent with man's condition as a progressive being."[65] Turning to the national church, he concludes that it must primarily be concerned "with the ethical development of its members" and not with external creedal forms and verbal formulas expressing speculative doctrine. The intellectual method appropriate for this new-modeled national church is termed by Wilson "the application of ideology," that is, religious knowledge understood within a larger history of the human spirit. This is so because only "the ideologian [literally, scientist or historian of ideas] is evidently in possession of a principle which will enable him to stand in charitable relations to persons of very different opinions from his own, and of very different opinions mutually." The ideologian is uniquely equipped to further the progress of revelation at its highest intellectual and spiritual level.[66]

Although charges of heresy were filed (but failed), the essayists went on to successful careers at Oxford and in the church: Benjamin Jowett as master of Balliol College, Mark Pattison as rector of Lincoln College, and Temple as archbishop of Canterbury. They and many of the other essayists lead successful campaigns to reform the universities and to ally themselves with many other reform movements championed by Mill and his followers.[67]

The power of this Anglo-American liberal Protestant narrative of personal, religious, social, and political reform was evident in the many books in political and social economy that charted the progress made in human welfare as markers of the progress of the kingdom of God. Given the parallel developments in liberal theology and social teachings, reformers saw themselves as part of a "Progressive Internationale." Most remarkable in this regard was the publication, in 1908, of *The New Encyclopedia of Social Reform*, compiled by William Dwight Porter Bliss (1856–1926). The son of Congregational missionaries in Turkey, he founded the Christian Socialist Society and edited *Dawn*, served as national lecturer for the Christian Social Union, became editor of *American Fabian*, and served a president of the National Reform Union. After a few years with the US Bureau of Labor, he worked with Josiah Strong's American Institute of Social Service. A summary statement of his ideas and vision, however, are encapsulated in the *New Encyclopedia*. Successor to a less ambitious version published earlier, the new edition promises to be a compendium of "all social-reform movements and activities, and the economic, industrial, and sociological facts and statistics of all countries and all social subjects." Contributors, mostly American, consisted of an all-star cast of intellectuals and reformers.[68] Billed as "contributing" only because their writings are so extensively quoted are Jane Addams, Richard Ely, Sidney Webb, and Theodore Roosevelt.

While these materials are discussed more fully in a later chapter, it should be noted that as the power of social Christianity grew ever stronger, its leading American articulators increasingly portrayed this movement in world-historical and geopolitical terms. Lyman Beecher's call for planting churches and schools in his 1835 *A Plea for the West* became Josiah Strong's more ambitious call for saving America in *Our Country* (1885). By 1915, Strong's *New World Religion* outlined a program of world redemption. In organizations such as the newly formed Federal Council of Churches of Christ in America and the Anglo-American Salvation Army and YMCA, Strong saw the seeds of world transformation.[69] These and other social service organizations were, in the words of Frances Willard of the Women's Christian Temperance Union, "living monuments to a dead church."[70] Unless churches emulate these organizations, Strong argued, they will remain mired in "individualist Christianity" and serve as a barrier to the achievement of the Kingdom.[71]

This larger social-evolutionary and historical framework incorporated the academic disciplines of sociology and social psychology and was the dominant framework in the study of political economy. And, through this narrative, the emerging industrial and financial economy was both legitimated and regulated with an end to recruiting its resources and abundance into the larger moral and political missions of the reformers. Within this narrative, the alliance of liberal religion and liberal politics could claim that it was inviting and enlisting the talents and energies of *all* good Americans and, by doing so, creating bonds of national loyalty and purpose that would overcome the forces and traditions that divide us. Finally, the authority of this liberal "political theology" depended not on destroying or even discrediting more traditional understandings of both religion and politics, but only in *subordinating* and then incorporating them as particulars into the national universal.

THE LONG MARCH THROUGH THE INSTITUTIONS

Antonio Gramsci (1891–1937), the leading theorist of "hegemonic domination," coined the phrase "the long march through the institutions" to highlight his point that political regimes rule through the institutional ligaments of the entire national culture. To overthrow an existing regime and found another requires the conquest not only of the national bureaucratic state, but of all of the dominant institutions of civil society.

While a case can certainly be made that, in America, the allied forces of liberal Protestantism and liberal/Progressive politics did, indeed, "conquer" many powerful institutions (dominant Protestant churches and seminaries, national journalism, universities, professional associations), Gramsci's model presumes not only the preexistence of a powerful state but also the preexistence and hierarchical durability of the dominant institutions in civil society. America not only lacked a centralized administrative "state" to conquer, its matrix of national institutions was both thin and constantly undergoing changes in its constituent elements. The most striking features in the rise to hegemonic power of liberal religion and liberal politics, then, were not only the *conquest* of existing and powerful national institutions but also the *creation* and *building* of national institutions combined with the *transformation* and *displacement* of existing ones.

Universities and Colleges

I had suggested earlier a kind of paradox: as liberal theological and social teachings were going from victory to victory from the 1880s onward, the institutional churches that originated and spread those teachings, dominantly Congregational and Presbyterian, became an ever-smaller part of denominational Protestantism. And, during this same period, specifically religious talents and energies were shifting to Methodist, Disciples of Christ, and American Baptist churches. The talents and energies that had earlier graced Unitarian, Congregational, and Presbyterian pulpits and seminary lecterns increasingly moved into university departments in the emerging academic disciplines of sociology, social and political economy, and social psychology, while their ecumenical seminaries shaped their curriculum from these new academic sources.[72] And reform ideas that informed "institutional [i.e., social service] churches"[73] increasingly found more congenial residence in settlement houses and the emerging profession of scientific social work, both of which had stronger ties to the new research universities than to liberal Protestant churches.

Contrast the institutional continuity, national power, and protean reproductive energies from the late nineteenth century onward of Harvard, Yale, and Princeton universities with those of their respective denominational founders, sponsors, or successors, namely, the Unitarian, Congregational, and Presbyterian churches.[74] Next, contrast the contributions to American intellectual and cultural life of clergymen in and of those church bodies to those of the faculty in these universities. And note the power of these universities and the newly established research universities—Cornell (1867), Johns Hopkins (1876), and Chicago (1891)—to extend and enforce their standards, values, and curriculum on other colleges and universities.[75] Exemplary in this regard were the Protestant-led research universities and the Carnegie Foundation that established and funded the national retirement system for private college and university professors in 1906. Participation required that boards of trustees replace majority clergy control with majority lay control.

The effect was not to de-Christianize private higher education but to shift power from diverse denominational Protestant churches to a more uniform and nondenominational liberal Protestantism. Needless to add, no Catholic and no fundamentalist Protestant institution took up the offer.[76]

Without going into detail concerning the major leadership roles played by liberal Protestant clergymen in both state and private universities in this period,[77] it might be recalled that twenty-three of the fifty founders of the American Economics Association in 1885 were liberal-evangelical Protestant clergymen. They, along with this first generation of professionally trained economists, almost all studied in Germany or were taught by those who had. Even the fact that four of the five major intellectual journals— *Princeton Review*, *Unitarian Review* (Harvard), *New Englander* (Yale), *and Andover Review* (Andover Seminary)—folded in the period 1888–1894 exemplifies this larger paradox of migration.[78] In the decade that followed, academic professional journals in sociology, economics, and political and social science were founded, but the contributors to both old and new journals were many of the same people. And almost all of the editors of the old religious journals, like the new disciplinary journals, had received their advanced academic training at the same universities in Germany.[79]

Two prominent institution builders in the research universities illustrate the migration of liberal Protestantism into the universities and thence into national political life. Albion Small (1854–1926) was professor of sociology at the University of Chicago at its founding in 1892 until his death. He was a founding member of the American Sociological Society, serving as president, 1912–1914, and the founder and editor of *The American Journal of Sociology* (1895–1926), a leading venue for Progressive scholarship and reform causes. After degrees from Colby College and Newton Theological Institute, Small studied in Germany and then returned to receive his PhD from Johns Hopkins University. Small used his journal as a clearinghouse for Progressive ideas, welcoming nonacademic reformers such as Jane Addams, Florence Kelley, and Charlotte Perkins Gilman to its pages.[80]

Simon Patten (1852–1922) was born in Illinois, the descendent of eighteenth-century Scotch-Irish settlers in New York. Educated at Northwestern and at Halle, where he received his PhD, Patten was one of the many German-trained founders and early presidents of the American Economic Association. Along with Albion Small and six of Patten's doctoral students, he was also one of the founders of the American Sociological Society, serving as its president as well. Patten followed Edmund J. James, another son of Illinois and a Halle PhD (and later president of the University of Illinois), to the University of Pennsylvania, where they were professors in the Wharton School, the newly founded professional business school that combined the study of economics, public finance, and business management. Together, Patten and James founded and lead the American Academy of Social and

Political Science and edited its publication, the *Annals*. This journal became a high-level meeting place not only for German-trained academics in America, but also for leaders in business, finance, and government. Patten's many graduate students (called Patten Men) included Walter Weyl of *The New Republic*, Edward Devine, general secretary of the New York Charity Organization Society, and two who later made major contributions to the New Deal: Rexford Tugwell and Frances Perkins. Patten is credited with inventing and popularizing the term "social work."

Two features animate the thought of Small and Patten. The first is the primacy of an ideological narrative that fused together liberal Protestantism and Progressivism, providing the moral, intellectual, and institutional basis for political mobilization. The second feature of their thought is its confidence that historical modes of social and political inquiry would produce "laws" of progress that would guide social organization and practices and provide a set of values that would integrate self and society on a democratic foundation.[81] Informed by the theoretical writings of Simon Patten and the sociology department and divinity school at the University of Chicago, Christian charity became "scientific charity" and "social work." *Survey*, the journal of charity and social work organizations,[82] and the many books written by Edward Devine legitimated this transformation.

On the eve of the last century, William Rainey Harper, president of the University of Chicago, speaking at Berkeley, summed up the sacred tasks of the new research university. He equated its animating spirit with a "religion of democracy"; the university is at once the "prophet," "priest," "philosopher," and "Messiah" of the mission to democratize America and the world. If free from interference by church and state, the American university can discover, reveal, and inculcate man's highest possibilities, becoming a liberal-evangelical national church by serving as the primary agent of God's progressive revelation.[83]

Social Service Organizations

Another set of new institutions that had a deep influence were Protestant ecumenical bodies dedicated to social service. A biographical sketch of one such founder-leader, John R. Mott (1865–1955), illustrates the trajectory from liberal-evangelical religion to liberal culture and politics. While an undergraduate at Cornell, Mott was caught up in the revivalism of Dwight L. Moody. After serving as a successful president of Cornell's YMCA, Mott was appointed traveling agent and then senior secretary of the North America section; under his leadership, membership in the American YMCA doubled.[84] In college, Mott also founded the Student Volunteer Movement for Foreign Missions (SVM) for the "evangelization of the world in this generation." Through summer conventions bringing members of both groups together, over the next thirty years SVM recruited, trained, and placed more than twenty thousand American student-missionaries abroad. In cooperation with British student leaders, in 1895 Mott also organized and, for the next thirty years, headed the World Student Christian Federation, an American-led holding company of liberal-evangelical Protestant student organizations. He also continued to help the YMCA expand in Asia. With no theological or graduate school degrees, he was offered, but turned down, the positions of dean of the Yale Divinity School and president of Oberlin College. President Wilson made him a member of the Root Commission to Russia in 1917. During World War I he organized twenty-six thousand YMCA volunteers to work with prisoners and refugees. Following World War II, he instigated the formation of the World Council of Churches and, in 1946, received the Nobel Peace Prize.[85]

Courts

While today we think of the US federal courts as one of the remaining governmental bastions of political liberalism, legal education was one of the last citadels to be conquered by the alliance of liberal Protestantism and liberal politics. The path of this late conquest involved two factors, the closer institutional integration of law schools with their affiliated universities and the importation of the social sciences into legal education.[86]

Reform of legal education first entailed intellectual emancipation from "traditional illusions." Chief among them, according to Herbert Croly, was the "tendency to regard the existing constitution with superstitious awe, and to shrink with horror from modifying it even in the smallest detail." If this emancipation is not achieved, "the American ideal will have to be fitted to the rigid and narrow lines of a few legal formulas; and the ruler of the American spirit, like the ruler of the Jewish spirit of old, will become the lawyer."[87] In *Progressive Democracy*, Croly extends this criticism to the constitution itself when viewed as standing above and outside of democratic political life: "The Constitution was really king. Once the kingdom of the Word had been ordained, it was almost as seditious to question the Word as it was to plot against the kingdom. A monarch exists to be obeyed. In the United States, as in other monarchies, unquestioning obedience was erected into the highest of political virtues."[88] This age has now passed. Democracy and the monarchy of the constitution are now in conflict, and monarchy must give way. "The ideal of individual justice is being supplemented by the ideal of social justice . . . Now the tendency is to conceive the social welfare, not as an end which can be left to the happy harmonizing of individual interests, but as an end which must be consciously willed by society and efficiently realized."[89]

Roscoe Pound, who began his twenty-year tenure as dean of Harvard Law School in 1916, had the most influence in shaping legal education to the contours of the new social sciences.[90] By the 1920s—well after the electoral energies of Progressivism had been spent—the key assumptions and values of Progressivism were starting to become institutionalized in the curricula of elite law schools, in the federal regulatory bureaucracy, and eventually in the judiciary.[91] By the time of the realigning election of 1932, the New Deal not only found a well-developed administrative branch to serve its ends,[92] it found a court system that increasingly deferred to the will of legislative majorities and expert administrators.

Political Parties

The most powerful set of institutions that stood in the path of alliance success was the locally based, election-oriented, and patronage-driven political party. While the Whig and Republican parties always contained strong "antiparty" elements, the infusion of liberal-religious enthusiasms at the turn of the last century provided the energies for waves of antiparty regulatory legislation.[93] John Dewey's animus against parties was intimated in the materials presented above.[94] His animus was mild compared to that of hundreds of magazine articles, pamphlets, and books written against party machines and political corruption. Samuel Batten, a social gospel minister and professor in Iowa, wrote a conclusion to these critiques. The party system "stands between the people and the government and makes a fully democratic government impossible." The "subtle and silent . . . tyranny" of party mirrors the despotism of the selfish appetites of the unredeemed American individualist. At its best, party government "means stagnation . . . commonplace ideas and past issues," at its worst, it "spells compromise and not principles . . . it means mediocrity and inferiority where it does not mean cowardice and corruption. A good partisan cannot be a good citizen."[95] So long as party politics is played as a game for the most votes, party government will be open to corruptions of all kinds and remain incapable of serving the larger public interest.

The formation of "antiparty parties" was a recurrent feature in the Whig-Republican tradition because their party base was overwhelmingly evangelical Protestant. The most successful "antiparty," the Progressive Party, was a product of three decades of incessant antiparty writings and the celebration of an informed "public opinion" that stood above mere party allegiance. The Progressive Party nominating convention, held in Chicago in August 1912, was a curious affair. In the style of Protestant conversion narratives, every delegate was given five minutes for political testimony. Theodore Roosevelt's address was titled "Confession of Faith." Periodically, the delegates would break out singing "Battle Hymn of the Republic."[96] The party's platform planks on social and industrial justice were drafted largely by Florence Kelley and Jane Addams. Addams seconded Roosevelt's nomination.[97]

This high point was no accident: the major institutions of Progressive ideas, along with the new industrial economy, were thriving. Mass journalism, the new universities, citizen-oriented book series, women's clubs, and the infrastructure of reform organizations, churches, social workers, teachers, and professional and academic associations, each with their magazines and journals, were at the peak of their energies and morale. The combined effect was to infuse all three contesting parties with the language of reform.[98] Despite the defeat of Theodore Roosevelt, President Wilson was compelled to govern largely on the basis of Progressive ideas; once America entered the war, Wilson became dependent on Progressive intellectuals, journalists, administrators, and academics to manage the mobilization of popular support— and in the process, a few of them even became Democrats!

THE TWISTED PATH FROM PROGRESSIVISM TO THE LIBERAL ESTABLISHMENT

Most date the death of Progressivism as a political movement to the 1920s. Almost everywhere one looks, evidence for this judgment abounds. The Republican Party candidate for president in 1924 was Warren Harding; his Democratic Party opponent was John W. Davis, who later achieved fame as the lead attorney for the defenders of segregated schools in the *Brown* case. More importantly, the transition from Progressivism to liberalism—in part caused by the creation and defeat of the Progressive Party itself—weakened the power of liberalism in the Republican Party without liberalism becoming clearly centered in the Democratic Party.

This incomplete transition and its effects require further analysis. Until the realigning elections of 1932–1936, liberal reformers did not have a clear party home, even as the preponderance of their influence remained in the Republican Party because that was where liberalism's electoral base resided. Many liberal-democratic academics and intellectuals, however, were becoming estranged from the Republican Party, both because of the increasing power of national financial and business institutions in the party (amply confirmed in the organization of the economy during World War I) and because they found themselves at odds with the religious values and practices that continued to prevail in Protestant churches, despite the advanced theological and social teachings in the seminaries and ecumenical organizations of these churches.[99]

But where to go? The Democratic Party had no *nationally coherent* electoral base. From its Jacksonian beginnings it was coherent only because its constituent elements were bound together negatively, in common opposition to nationally oriented political and economic elites and to all reform movements that sought to impose consensual moral and cultural values. And when it did begin to use the national government in positive ways, its primary motive was not to achieve common national projects but to reward its various electoral constituents and to attract new ones. [100] And, finally, the Democratic Party and its major constituents remained attached to the *values* of partisanship and local party loyalty, evidenced by its urban political machines and the political culture of the south. Additionally, for many of its members, strong partisanship was necessitated by the fact that the Democratic Party was the *only powerful national organization* that could protect their local ethnic, religious, and economic values and interests. All other national organizations and institutions—universities, the media, the professions, finance, and corporate business—were firmly in the hands of the liberal religious and political elites, who were Republicans. [101]

When the Democratic Party won national election victories in the 1930s and later became entrenched as the majority party, they were not coherent enough or powerful enough *as a party* to pursue a liberal-reform agenda on their own. For a long time this weakness could be disguised. Voluntarist national military and economic mobilization for World War I necessarily meant that liberal-Republican–dominated institutions in society played dominant roles. This model was immediately repaired to in the first term of FDR's presidency and became institutionalized during and after World War II. By the mid-1950s, this previously "voluntarist" model became a permanent part of the effective national government, best characterized as liberal corporatism. [102]

From the 1940s through the 1960s, as domestic economic planning was subordinated to the priorities of war and national defense, the Democratic Party became even less capable, *as a party*, of creating and sustaining a national reform agenda. Foreign policy and therefore defense planning and therefore national economic planning and priorities were sustained through bipartisan coalitions. This congressional coalition of northern Democrats and liberal Republicans was sustained by a bipartisan electoral "coalition" that could not become institutionalized in Congress. The result was to concede to the executive branch almost all major national policy initiatives. In turn, the executive branch could neither create nor sustain its national policies without the active participation of the defense establishment (now including the major research universities), national financial institutions, national business corporations, and national labor unions. Dreams of turning the Democratic Party into a self-consciously liberal party with shared national goals were not only very unlikely to succeed, they were always deferred, because the achievement of many of those same goals could be partially and more readily achieved under the aegis of national defense and the imperatives of the Cold War.[103] There was, of course, a heavy price to pay. As Dewey put it in his ethics text fifty years earlier: "It has no support and guarantee in the activities which it is supposed to benefit, because it is not the fruit of those activities. Hence, it does not stay put. It has to be continually buttressed by appeal to external, not voluntary, considerations; bribes of pleasure, threats of harm, use of force. It has to be undone and done over."[104]

Liberal politics became increasingly sustained by a regime that came to be described, variously, as "corporate liberalism," "polyarchy," "pluralist democracy," or "interest-group politics." Whatever the name, however, it was not a liberal *party* regime sustained by a self-conscious national electorate. While the elites at the top of almost all national institutions remained nominally liberal Protestant, if not by direct affiliation, then in style and values,[105] this type of liberal Protestantism was more a sign of superior education and high status than a living faith. It was a marker that its holder was committed to some sense of a larger national good.

Institutionalizing Liberal Protestantism

Before turning to how vulnerable this alliance of liberal religion and liberal politics had become under these conditions—and how easily it became discredited and demoralized—attention should be given to the fortunes of liberal Protestantism itself, both in its main church bodies and in its attempts to institutionalize itself in larger religious bodies. An early sign of weakness was the failure, immediately after World War I, of the most ambitious attempt to institutionalize liberal Protestantism. This initiative was called Interchurch. Following rapid military and governmental demobilization at the conclusion of World War I, Progressive intellectual, religious, and political leaders became disabused of their hope that the spirit and unity of preparedness and war mobilization would continue to animate the national government. This was especially true of wartime leaders who came from Protestant ecumenical organizations that had enjoyed unprecedented prestige and support during the war.[106]

The plan was to create and fund a gargantuan umbrella organization called the Interchurch World Movement. This organization, American liberal Protestant in its initial funding and leadership, would not only embrace *all* the churches in America representing all faiths in America, but also call on the support of non–church affiliated leaders in government, labor, finance, and industry to help underwrite this national "church of America," a superstate/superchurch to organize and spearhead the drive for democracy and justice at home and abroad. In 1920, Interchurch, with a paid staff of 2,600 in New York City and expenditures exceeding a million dollars a month, began its drive to raise more than a third of a billion dollars over a five-year period. With the support of prominent leaders in Washington[107] and help from major New York advertising agencies, the funding campaign to fulfill the kingdom covenant at home and abroad was finally launched. While the campaign within most of the thirty founding churches for their own use was quite successful, support for the organization itself was a colossal failure. Not even 10 percent of the funding goal was met. The initial denominational under-writers of the venture (Methodist, American Baptist, Presbyterian, Congrega-tional, and Disciples of Christ) quickly bailed out, and Interchurch simply faded away. This failure paralleled a precipitous decline in Protestant ecu-menical social service, missionary, and student organizations as well.

The failure of the Interchurch initiative should not be seen as a failure of the alliance of liberal religion and liberal politics. Here the same paradox raised earlier enters. The constituent denominations continued to thrive as churches and seminaries. More importantly, members of these church bodies continued to grow in power in proportion to the growth in power of the national institutions they led. But a different logic obtains regarding church federation. Given the rich institutional pluralism of *churches* in America, any federated church of churches would demand *some* creedal grounding. But any formal expression of such grounding having normative weight and sub-stance would either divide the constituents from within or be perceived from without as so thin and insubstantial as to be the object of derision *as the authoritative moral source and moral orientation for the nation.* Moreover, since no formal federation could embrace all institutional embodiments of American Protestantism—not to speak of American Catholicism and American Judaism—the very institutional presence of a unified and powerful federation would also appear either as aggrandizing and oppressive or (and this would be worse) as weak and ineffectual.

The National Council of Churches, formed in 1950, is proof of this logic. To be sure, its organizing constituent churches were high in cultural status but were soon to become ever lower in relative numbers, evangelical energy, and will to power. And worse, its formation gave rise to a counter-group of more traditional Protestant churches. In short, while the National Council of Churches (and its international counterpart, the World Council of Churches, founded two years earlier) represented itself to America as the enlightened voice of social conscience and internationalism, it could no longer presume to interpret God's word to the American people. Speaking more as a trans-religious ethical voice in shaping public policy, it was relegated to another public-spirited interest group similar to Common Cause, not so much active-ly opposed as ignored by other faith traditions. Moreover, because it was so closely identified with *much more powerful institutions* in the liberal estab-lishment, its power did not come from its constituent churches but through its ties to the institutional matrix of the larger liberal establishment.[108] And, when this claim of symbolic religious hegemony was attacked in the name of a much deeper religious pluralism in America, its spokesmen were forced to mount an illiberal defense.[109]

Throughout the 1950s and 1960s, however, liberal religion and its churches and seminaries were quite complacent because, as they looked outward, their members, values, and traditions seemed to prevail. Signs of this complacency were not confined to the liberal churches. Political and social policies that were previously defended as substantive moral values to be achieved by political and religious mobilization were increasingly represented as nonideological social requisites of advanced industrial societies. Berkeley's Clark Kerr, lecturing at Harvard, proclaimed that the American national research university—he termed it the "multiversity"—was value free and morally neutral because it embodied and served all of American society in all its diverse interests and values. The constitution of freedom is procedural fairness and neutrality.[110] To be sure, dangerous ideological impulses existed in American society on both the right and the left, but so long as social science and common sense held, so would "the vital center."[111] And the center would hold because the elites heading most powerful national institutions were liberal-democratic elites in this nonideological sense: tolerant, committed to procedural fairness, and, because of their interactions and bargaining with other institutional elites, committed to a larger public good.[112]

When the New Left began its attack on the liberal establishment in the late 1960s, the first place it turned to was the national research university and its social sciences. The New Left desperately wanted the university *to regain its soul*, to become reborn, in President Harper's sense, as a prophetic voice for the democratic community in order to witness against an imperialist American state and a racist (and, later, sexist) and materialist society. And, they reasoned, once the university was conquered, all of the national institutions that require social knowledge and articulate moral values would follow in its train.

In retrospect, it is remarkable how quickly the liberal establishment folded and how tepidly it defended its institutions, especially universities, churches, foundations, and national media. This explains the rapidity with which leadership in the universities, and research and teaching in the social sciences, humanities, and law, became infused with the values and spirits of the New Left. And it explains the ease with which New Left critics came to occupy positions of power—almost overnight becoming part of the institutions they had condemned. These conquests, however, did not extend to electoral success—in part because the Democratic Party would lose more of its older electoral constituency than it gained in attracting new and spiritually charged ones.[113]

RETHINKING AMERICAN POLITICAL THOUGHT

John Dewey and Herbert Croly are totemic figures in the pantheon of American liberalism; both were critical links in the passage from Progressivism to liberalism. Except for very early in Dewey's career, neither was associated with formal religion or the social gospel. And yet, after World War I and the collapse of Progressivism, both men wrote on the need for "a common faith." This need was both personal and political for, without a common faith, there can be no "people," no coherent nation, and no coherent electorate. Unlike Walter Lippmann, Croly's colleague at *The New Republic*, Croly grounded political democracy in public opinion. But personal opinions could only become common political will if they bound individuals together in a shared desire to achieve higher human goods. Both Lippmann and Croly recognized that Progressivism had what current liberalism seemed to lack. The older alliance of liberal religion and liberal politics had been torn asunder and needed to be reconstituted on a new basis. [114] Without a shared faith, the only time this common will shows itself is in cases of war or other national emergencies and, under these extreme conditions, this will is easily corrupted and manipulated.

Only a few of the many recent writings on the rebirth of liberal-progressivism recognize this same need, put largely in terms of a call for a national patriotism that replicates, in some fashion, the early national Progressivism of Dewey and Croly. Because the only conceivable vehicle for this resurgence is the Democratic Party, however, this new nationalism must eschew any hint of "church religion"—not to speak of the style and rhetoric of evangelical Protestantism! [115] I want to conclude, therefore, by suggesting how the foregoing analysis of the alliance of liberal religion and liberal politics might alter how we view the contours of American political thought. These suggestions are admittedly sketchy and will be disappointing to those who think that rethinking the intellectual dimensions of the problem will reinstall a hegemonic liberalism in American political life. That is not possible, because, as Dewey might put it, political life is also a matter of spirits and worldviews that are not altered through the process of truth seeking so much as reinterpreted and transformed in a common search for purpose and meaning. [116]

Progressivism as Strong State; Liberalism as Big Government

Four years before becoming president, Woodrow Wilson gave a series of lectures on constitutional government in the United States. As a southerner, a Democrat, and a trained lawyer, he believed that "liberty is the object of constitutional government" because "representatives of government have no authority except such as they derive from the law." But authoritative constitutional government can only exist if it is constituted by a people, an "actual community of interest and purpose." The crucial question is then posed: "Are the United States a community? In some things, yes; in most things, no." Needless to add, Wilson as a war president immediately called on "one nation, under God" to buttress his extraordinary authority.[117] Once the war ended, demobilization rapidly reduced the government to its constitutional limits. Unlike the Republican Party, which had constructed the ligaments of a strong state in the 1920s and had always supported state "authority" in its pronouncements, the Democratic Party has never, in principle, defended a strong national state, even as it has presided over the massive expansion of government.[118] These are not the same thing.

In his book *The End of Liberalism* (1969), Theodore Lowi seized on this distinction to argue that big government generated by interest-group liberalism served to weaken the state because it could not prioritize choices and policies within a shared conception of public good. I would extend that argument to suggest that, without a shared conception of common good (war, depressions, and other emergencies excepted), liberalism necessarily subverts itself: public good becomes an empty rhetoric to justify every particular interest. Without a national-ideological narrative to underwrite shared conceptions of public good, principled rights claims soon become just another interest, an interest whose organizations and leadership might not even require the participation of the claimants or those most closely tied to those claimants.[119] Attacks on big government as an inevitable result of patronage-driven political parties were routinely made by Progressives reformers more than a century ago. They insisted that all beneficiaries of public policies provide a "strong state" justification with clear connections to public and shared ends that should be given priority over competing claims. And, they added, state and local governments and many private organizations often serve these national ends better than the federal government. Their conception of the state included all authoritative institutions in America, public as well as private.

In refusing to make this distinction, contemporary defenders of liberalism too often end up defending entrenched and older interests and values and preventing the articulation of new ones. That was the brunt of the New Left argument against pluralist theories of democracy and the "liberal establishment"—an argument that was soon forgotten as the critics soon took their places in that establishment. But this argument was quickly appropriated by intellectuals on the right and became a major part of its political appeal to evangelicals seeking to understand their civic responsibilities.

Progressivism as National Union; Liberalism as National Constitution

A recent letter to the *New Yorker*, responding to an article on the decline of newspapers and the rise of the "blogosphere," asserts the following: "The United States is in the unusual position of never having been a nation in the sense of sharing a common culture or language. Our monumental faults notwithstanding, this country exists as an idea—an attempt to better organize society. The Constitution came first, not 'the people.'" The writer concludes by voicing the cosmopolitan hope that America will become "the first nation forged through the community of the World Wide Web."[120]

Curiously, this understanding obversely reflects that of a southern senator, James Beck, writing in 1875: "There is that contemptible word *Nation*—a word no good Democrat uses, when he can find any other, and when forced to use it, utters in disgust. This is no nation. We are free and independent states" under the constitution.[121] This tradition lives on in other strains of contemporary liberalism: justifications for affirmative action that echo Calhoun's defense of states' rights and concurrent majorities[122] and the defense of multiculturalism on quasi-constitutionalist grounds of equal group rights. Those who define the ligaments of American nationality as a panoply of constitutional/universal rights forget that abstract rights discourse and constitutionalist logic can justify many very different public policies. And this same argument necessarily means that all who went before us misread the constitution or were inferior rights philosophers. Our national history, with a few shining exceptions, then becomes one of hypocrisy, greed, injustice, and error.[123] Worse, defenders of contemporary liberalism have ceded national patriotism to the religious right, often perceiving in American nationalism itself an unwholesome mixing of religion and politics. This perception contains some truth. National identity discourse necessarily contains strains of "sacred rhetoric" and this rhetoric, in turn, is often infused with Protestant-biblical-Hegelian elements.[124] One only need read the speeches of Abraham Lincoln, or earlier Whig Party documents, or Paine's *Common Sense* to recognize this connection. There is also some truth in the fact that using national patriotic speech necessarily downplays and even devalues the importance of universalistic "principles" that have become so prominent today in turning fluid democratic political argument into rigid court briefs. The rhetoric of national union used so powerfully by Lincoln and the Progressives was, to use contemporary language, addressed to a whole people and not to a federal appellate court or graduate seminar in political philosophy.

Absent a national ideological narrative to provide guidance for interpreting abstract principles and rights, contemporary liberalism is often compelled to shape its political ends in terms of bare "rights talk." The earlier alliance of liberal Protestantism and liberal politics, in contrast, was hostile to such claims, seeing them as specious covers for both antisocial individualism and the protection of private interests adverse to the public good. This alliance was informed by an inherent pragmatism because it sought moral and political direction from *within* the processes and shared experiences of the material world. John Dewey remained such a powerful influence in this culture because of his insistence on this very possibility of revelatory transcendence within experience itself.[125] Shared experiences require high levels of social interaction and communication. Rights should be distributed only *after* the issues of common goods are publicly aired and after all participants have laid their commitment cards on the table. Pragmatic critics of liberalism today—usually from the left—reflect this earlier background.[126]

Toward a New Liberal Narrative

Although a rethinking of contemporary liberal political thought is no guarantee of its political and moral rebirth, thoughtful liberal intellectuals are quite aware that the intellectual weaknesses sketched above are tied to ideological, political, and moral weakness in the larger culture. Concluding on a note of hope, I point to a recent book that both critiques contemporary liberal thought and suggests that the path to reconstruction is a narrative one that often intimates elements of the sacred.

Michael Lind's *Next American Nation* also faults contemporary liberalism for its abstract and legalistic ways of thinking. Starting from the premise that "a constitution is not a country; an idea is not a nation," he not only constructs a narrative of distinct political regimes in American history, he suggests that the ideal of a "multicultural republic" denies America its nationhood and has proved incapable of sustaining an authoritative political order. He calls for an ideological narrative that incorporates a form of civic religion that parallels, but does not replicate, Protestant and Judeo-Christian ones that came before.[127]

Lind's argument and two similar ones discussed in chapter 4, below,[128] require a more articulate moral psychology that is entailed by this turn to national/sacred narrative. Such a psychology, I suggest, must include a theory of human agency quite different from that of, say, John Rawls, and much closer to that of Charles Taylor.[129] Rawls presumes the psychological possibility (and liberal necessity) of isolating comprehensive moral/religious doctrines from politics; Taylor asserts that such isolation would make political life alien and incomprehensible. Through and with the company of others we must interrogate our experiences and intuitions to discover both the moral sources and the moral power to sustain human agency and democratic citizenship.[130] Taylor's notions of agency and freedom are experiential and, thus, grounded in the relationship of personal to collective narratives. And, he would add, such narratives, even in our secular age, always touch on the sacred.[131]

APPENDIX: GEORGE HERRON AND EDWARD STEINER

The story below captures the way in which liberal Protestantism at the turn of the last century could extend its reach to embrace, but not replace, both secular socialism and secular Judaism.

***

Iowa College, later called Grinnell, was founded by the famous "Iowa Band" of twelve New England Congregational clergymen pledged to Christianize America. The economist Henry Carter Adams was the son of its leading founder and an early graduate. Albert Shaw, the municipal reformer and founder of *Review of Reviews*, also attended Grinnell. The institution became famous in the 1890s under the leadership of President George Gates, who pledged that "Iowa College . . . will always teach the actual applicability of the principles of Jesus Christ to every department of human life."[132] With the appointment in 1893 of one the most famous reformers of his day, the Reverend George Herron, and the funding of a rich and widowed ex-parishioner and very close friend of Herron's, Mrs. E. D. Rand, Gates's pledge was institutionalized in the Department of Applied Christianity. This project was buttressed with the founding of *The Kingdom*, a weekly edited by Gates, and the creation of an outreach program of campus conferences, called the School of the Kingdom, a national center of social gospel activism. Herron joined and inspired many reform organizations, working with Richard Ely and John Commons, Henry Demarest Lloyd, Jane Addams, John P. Altgeld, and Eugene Debs. A divorce and "companionate" remarriage following a long-standing relationship with Carrie Rand, the daughter of his benefactress, led to his early retirement and President Gates's resignation from Grinnell in 1899. Despite his notoriety, Herron gave the commencement address at the University of Nebraska in 1902 and, with the help of many clergymen, continued to give public lectures all over the country, especially in colleges and universities.[133] Herron campaigned for Debs in 1900 and gave one of his nominating speeches at the Socialist Party Convention of 1904. The best summary of the evangelical theology represented by Grinnell was supplied by President Gates in 1894: "The Kingdom of heaven and the Kingdom of God does not refer to a life beyond the grave; the Kingdom of God does not mean the Church or any other institution; such an identification of the King-dom with the Church either concrete or invisible being 'one of the most dangerous of heresies;' the Kingdom of God [means] a society upon this earth in which all human affairs exhibit the nature and spirit of God."[134]

In 1903, another professor came to Grinnell and stayed until his retire-ment in 1941. He also brought some fame to the institution and of a more long lasting and less controversial kind. Foreign-born, he had a PhD from Heidelberg and became expert on US immigration patterns and policies, eventually writing fifteen books for a popular audience, most of them on problems of immigrants and immigration and on the meaning of his own immigrant experience. An ardent champion of the immigrant, he was also acutely sensitive to problems of adjustment and assimilation. The brunt of his message was a call for sympathy for and understanding of the various nation-alities streaming into America. For example, of the Jews and their relation-ship to an America that was overwhelmingly Christian, he wrote "the task of historic Christianity . . . is not an easy one." For all Jews, from the most Orthodox and culturally narrow to the most sophisticated Zionists or Social-ists, "becoming a Christian means separation from the race . . . he must not become a Christian, even if to him Christianity is the only escape from the narrow tribal idea and from his own outgrown race consciousness, into the broader realm where he can say that he is a member of the human race, and as such is under the obligations of brotherhood to all men." The ceremonies, the ecclesiastical practices, and the theology of historical Christianity are "repellent to all these Jews, from the extreme radical to the extremist Ortho-dox." Typical methods used to attempt to convert Jews are equally repellent and have always been ineffective.[135]

> I have the conviction that when Christ comes fully to His own in the church, He will also come to His own in the synagogue; certainly no sooner, and perhaps not much later. When He emerges from the tangle of Greek philoso-phy, Roman legalism and Byzantine traditionalism—when "in deed and in truth" He becomes the Gentile's Messiah, He will also become the Messiah of the Jew. As a working basis for the right relation between Jew and Gentile, I wish to quote Rabbi Sonnenschein, formerly of Des Moines, Iowa . . . "I want to live so, that when you see me, you will say: 'There goes Rabbi Sonnensche-in, who is a Jew; yet he is a better Christian than I am.' And I want you to live so, that when I see you, I will say: 'That man is a Christian; but he is a better Jew than I am.'"[136]

The person writing this was the successor to George Herron's position as professor of applied Christianity. After Heidelberg, he studied at Oberlin for a divinity degree and became an ordained Congregational minister, serving various pastorates in the Midwest before taking the position at Grinnell. His wife, Sara Williams, was the daughter of a Congregational minister in Ohio named Mark Levy. George Herron's successor was a Jew, Edward Alfred Steiner, born in Slovakia and raised in Vienna. Without renouncing his Jewish identity, he could also be a social gospel Christian and (therefore?) an American. His books include *Introducing the American Spirit, Nationalizing America,* and *The Making of a Great Race,* as well as an earlier autobiography, *From Alien to Citizen.*[137] They all show clearly that his Judaism-Congregationalism (he also became a Quaker in 1947) was indistinguishable from a "religion of America" of the sort proclaimed and celebrated by Will Herberg in *Protestant, Catholic, Jew* (1955).[138]

NOTES

1. Mulford, 1882. Mulford, a student of the liberal theologian Theodore Munger at Yale, became an Episcopal priest and was the author of two books reflecting Munger's views. On Munger, see Welch, 1985, 230–31 and Dorrien, 2001, 262–304.

2. Dewey, 1894, 3–6, passim.

3. Dewey, 1894, 7–9, passim.

4. Dewey, 1893, "The Relation of Philosophy to Theology," *Early Works,* 4:367.

5. Dewey, 1897, 93 and 87; 1908, 175; 1897, 94–95.

6. *Early Works,* 1:xiii.

7. See Dewey's scathing characterization of the practice of periodic religious instruction by clergymen in the public schools in 1908, 172–74.

8. Welch, 1972 and 1985; Dorrien, 2001 and 2003; Kloppenberg, 1986.

9. Especially as denominational church history was replaced by religious and cultural history. See chapter 3, below, and Stout and Hart, 1997.

10. This argument is made in Oshatz, 2008, regarding the role of antislavery and liberal Protestant theology.

11. For biographies and analysis of nineteen such intellectual leaders, see Eisenach, 1994, 31–47.

12. Even though some attempts were made and heresy charges pursued. See for example, Dorrien, 2001, 335–70.

13. Richard W. Fox, 1977, 400, and see Richard W. Fox, 1993. To paraphrase a recent study of Hindutva, the ideology of Hindi national political movements, liberal Protestantism secularizes Christianity by sacralizing the nation (Ruthven, 2007).

14. The common trope of "spirit" vs. "matter" that pervaded and structured Victorian intellectual life in all three countries is a product of this same Protestant religious achievement. Here, Hegel and Mill stand as exemplars at either end of this period.

15. Jensen, 1971; Robert L. Kelley, 1979; Kleppner, 1970 and 1987; Phillips, 2000; Swierenga, 1990; Carwardine, 1993.

16. This is also true even when issues of race, gender, and sexual orientation become salient, if only because responses to these issues are interpreted through religious commitments.

17. Eisenach, 2000, 3 and 83–93; Hamburger, 2002.

18. Monsma, 1996.

19. Quoted from Dorien, 2001, xix.

20. See Dorien, 2001, xiii–xxi, and Welch, 1972, 57–127.

21. Welch, 1972, 22–56. Romanticism was integrated into liberal Protestant theology through evolutionary and historicist scholarship. See Abrams, 1973.

22. See, for example, Karl Barth, 1959: "The first place in a history of theology of the most recent times belongs and will always belong to Schleiermacher, and he has no rival . . . He is as a modern man and therefore as a thinker and therefore as a moral philosopher and therefore as a

philosopher of religion and therefore as an apologist and therefore finally as a dogmatist determined on no account to interpret Christianity in such a way that his interpreted statements can come into conflict with the methods and principles of the philosophical and the historical and scientific research of his time" (306 and 326). See also William Adams Brown, 1921, whose classified bibliography in his widely used *Christian Theology in Outline* has the headings "Protestant Theology from the Reformation to Schleiermacher" and "European Theology since Schleiermacher" (429 and 431). William Adams Brown (Union Seminary) was one of the major liberal Protestant theologians in America at the turn of the last century.

23. Schleiermacher, 1969, 156–57.

24. Quoted from Dorrien, 2001, 60.

25. Quoted from Barth, 1959, 326. Here Schleiermacher would include the historical and social sciences.

26. A good restatement of this position is William Adams Brown, 1906. The three thinkers he credits for shaping this modern position are Schleiermacher, Hegel, and Ritschl. See especially his conclusion at 309. Adolph von Harnack, a leading German theologian at the turn of the last century, also wrote *The Essence of Christianity* in 1900, but it was translated into English as *What Is Christianity?* It makes the same historical analysis as Brown's but stresses the centrality of the Gospels rather than Brown's stress on modern developments in theology represented by Schleiermacher, Hegel, and Ritschl.

27. Dewey never abandoned this distinction—he only ceased to call it Christianity. Dewey, 1934.

28. See Eisenach, 1998. This national church was understood to include Oxford and Cambridge universities as its primary component.

29. F. C. Baur and Albrecht Ritschl are the clearest exponents of this view; see Welch, 1985, 1–30 and 173–75, on the relationship between Protestantism and a historical-ethical imperative.

30. Quoted from Dorrien, 2001, 99. Parker wrote this in 1841. In 1911, the modernist theologian and leading church historian Frank Foster wrote: "Though Jesus should be proved never to have existed, the truth which has come down to us and which we have received because of its own self-evidencing value, and which we have found to work out such great results in the liberation of our spirits . . . it would still be true and its effects would remain unaltered. In this sense a historical Christ is unnecessary" (quoted in Bowden, 1971, 215).

31. In his early years, Coleridge had this same vision for the Church of England. In America, the victory of the evangelical churches, led by Congregationalists and liberal Presbyterians, was also a decisive victory of Yale over Harvard in the two decades after the Civil War. As Harvard drew its students increasingly from the urban elites along the East Coast, Yale attracted students from all over the nation. The founding presidents of the three newly established research universities, Cornell, Johns Hopkins, and Chicago, were all undergraduates at Yale. See Eisenach, 2000, 86.

32. For America, see Dorien, 2001, 261–334 and 393–411; for Great Britain, Howard Murphy, 1955; for Germany, America, and England, Welch, 1985, 212–65. Again, it was Schleiermacher's theology that first incorporated this ethical turn, in his lectures of 1817 and published from his notes in 1827–1828. See Schleiermacher, 1989.

33. These issues are exhaustively explored in Frank Hugh Foster, 1907, and Haroutunian, 1964, and see Dorien, 2001; William Brown, 1921, 235–373; and Elwyn Smith, 1971, 154–82.

34. Theodore Parker quoted in Dorien, 2001, 86.

35. Quoted in Dorien, 2001, 113–14, and see discussion of free agency and moral government by Nathanial Taylor in Haroutanian, 1964, 252–54.

36. Quoted in D. H. Meyer, 1976, 72–73.

37. Quoted in D. H. Meyer, 1976, 71, and see Henry Churchill King, 1902, 29–34 and 86–104.

38. Nathaniel Taylor, 1859, and see Elwyn Smith, 1971, 161–63.

39. Cross, 1950; Walters, 1977; Dorrien, 2001, 179–260.

40. Ted Smith, 2007.

41. Ted Smith, 2007, 140–81.

42. Curtis, 1991.

43. Eisenach, 1994, 74–103.

44. John Dewey, 1888, 8.

45. Dewey, 1888, 14.

46. Dewey, 1888, 22; *Early Works*, 1:239.

47. Dewey and Tufts, 1908, 304. This text was published continuously until 1942.

48. Cooley, 1909, 121.

49. Giddings, 1898, 315, and see Edward A. Ross, 1901, 93–105. Henry Churchill King, 1902, uses Giddings to ground his argument that Christian theology should always reflect an evolving social consciousness because that consciousness contains God's continuing revelation.

50. Addams, 1893, 2.

51. Addams, 1893, 7.

52. Dewey incorporated these same hopes in his ethics textbook when he stated that the increase in rights has been accompanied by an increase in personal responsibility as social norms become internalized and widespread in democratic societies and where "the external control of force has been replaced by the moral control of duty" (Dewey and Tufts, 1908, 153).

53. William McGuire King, 1983.

54. Abbott, *The Evolution of Christianity* (1892), *Christianity and Social Problems* (1896), and *The Theology of an Evolutionist* (1897).

55. Abbott, *The Rights of Man* (1901), *America in the Making* (1911). The latter was part of the Yale Lectures on the Responsibilities of Citizenship series; previous lecturers included James Bryce, Charles Evans Hughes, Arthur Twining Hadley, Elihu Root, and William H. Taft.

56. His contemporary and president of the University of Wisconsin, John Bascom (1827–1911), wrote four books that almost exactly parallel those by Abbott: *A New Theology* (1891), *An Historical Interpretation of Philosophy* (1893), *Evolution and Religion; or Faith as Part of a Complete Cosmic System* (1897), and *Growth of Nationality in the United States: a Social Study* (1899).

57. Abbott, 1892, iii and v.

58. Abbott, 1892, 254.

59. Abbott, 1892, 237 and 247. This analysis is also found later in the writings of Rauschenbusch, 1914, 201–10.

60. For more discussion of these themes, see chapter 4, below. The last chapter in Abbott, *Rights of Man* (1901), is subtitled, "To what extent and in what sense democracy and political Christianity are synonymous." The Hegelian element becomes clear when paired with the subtitle of the previous chapter: "The grounds for believing that democracy in some form is the ultimate and permanent form of government."

61. This movement is discussed in chapter 5 below and in Eisenach, 1998.

62. Three editions of 1,000 copies each were sold in the first year. In 1861, 13,000 more copies were sold, the sixth edition selling out in six hours. By early 1862, some 20,000 copies had been sold, and twelve months later, another 2,250. The bishop of Oxford, Samuel Wilberforce, wrote an early critique in the *Quarterly Review*, an issue that itself went through five editions. Altogether, by 1870, just short of 150 pamphlets, tracts, and books addressed against the essays were published (Altholz, 1977, 148; Ellis, 1980, 116–17 and 125).

63. *Essays and Reviews*, 2 and 5.

64. *Essays and Reviews*, 32–34 and 45.

65. Quoted in Ellis, 1980, 14.

66. *Essays and Reviews*, 202.

67. Eisenach, 1998. On the role of Pattison in university reform, Jones, 2007.

68. Among them were Edward Devine, Florence Kelley, John R. Commons, Franklin Giddings, Arthur Hadley, Samuel Gompers, Morris Hillquit, J. Cardinal Gibbons, Booker T. Washington, and William Lloyd Garrison.

69. Earlier, Strong wrote a report for the Department of Social Economy for the United States Commission to the Paris Exposition, *Religious Movements for Social Betterment* (1900).

70. In Strong, 1915, 458.

71. Strong, 1915, 275.

72. Cherry, 1995. Henry Churchill King, 1902, is an excellent example of this.

73. Strong, 1900, 42–90.

74. This despite the fact that the formal church presence in their respective universities was continuous and pervasive at least through the 1920s and, in some respects, through the 1950s.

75. Over 90 percent of the doctoral degrees granted in 1900 came from the fourteen universities that founded the AAU (American Association of Universities). The American Association of University Professors, founded in 1915, was a product of these same universities and the academic professional organizations that their faculties had created. Five universities (Harvard, Columbia, Hopkins, Chicago, and Berkeley) produced over half of all doctorates; these and the nine other charter institutions of the AAU, founded that same year, granted 90 percent of the total. In the 1920s, five private and three public universities from this same group still produced more than 60 percent of all doctorates. These percentages are even more impressive in view of the rapidly growing numbers of graduate students. From fewer than 900 in 1885, in five years they increased to 2,382, ten years later to 5,832, and reached almost 10,000 by 1910. Within roughly this same period the resources of these same universities increased dramatically: endowments at Johns Hopkins from $3 million to $24 million; Yale, $4 million to $58 million; Columbia, $9 million to $68 million; and Harvard, $10 million to $86 million. Eisenach, 1994, 12–13.

76. Reuben, 1996, 87. Barrow, 1990, 60–123, sees this as part of the conquest of higher education by business and capitalist interests.

77. See Eisenach, 2000, 83–93.

78. The lone survivor, *Bibliotheca Sacra*, moved from Andover Seminary to Oberlin and was renamed, *Bibliotheca Sacra: A Religious and Sociological Quarterly*. For the takeover of theology by liberals at Andover, see Williams, 1970.

79. Eisenach, 1994, 92n25, 100, and 140; Kuklick, 1985, 203–15.

80. Small's life and work and the careers of Kelley and Gilman are discussed more fully in chapter 4, below. The sociology department at Chicago welcomed its first female doctoral students in America in 1894 and, by the early 1900s, was producing one-third of all female social science PhDs in America (Fitzpatrick, 1990, 13, 29–30).

81. Symbolic of this connection are two formative texts in political economy, *Studies in the Evolution of Industrial Society* and *Outlines of Economics*, by Richard T. Ely. Both of these books were first published as part of a "home reading series" of the Chautauqua movement, a Methodist-inspired summer camp and later a national lectureship series dedicated to melding together nondoctrinal Christianity, family life, ethical values, and responsible citizenship. And see chapter 4, below.

82. Its earlier name, *Charities and the Commons*, came in turn from a merger of *Charities*, the magazine of Edward T. Devine's New York Charity Organization Society, and *The Commons*, a magazine of the Chicago settlement house movement edited by Reverend Graham Taylor of Chicago Theological Seminary. By the early twentieth century the gathering of social statistics through citywide and national surveys of social conditions became a rallying point for ecumenical religious groups such as the Men and Religion Forward movement. In 1911, this group planned the largest Protestant evangelization effort ever tried in the United States. Part of the plan was to conduct a social survey in each of the seventy-six largest cities in America undertaken by committees of one hundred men in each city prior to the revivals. What began as an ancillary effort became the primary focus of the entire revival campaign. Bateman, 2001.

83. Eisenach, 2000, 122–23.

84. The YMCA was founded in London in the 1840s, coming to North America in 1854. By 1910, three-quarters (2,339) of its paid staff, one-half (405,000) of its worldwide membership, and one-quarter of its associations were North American. Annual expenditures in this period were over $5 million, much of it used to support overseas programs. Eisenach, 1994, 235.

85. The biographies of Albert Shaw (1857–1947) and Robert Elliot Speer (1867–1947) show parallel trajectories through higher journalism (Shaw) and church federations (Speer). See Eisenach, 1994, 36, 228–39, and 241n.

86. Later, this included the destruction of most proprietary and freestanding law schools through the imposition of ever-higher accreditation criteria by the Association of American Law Schools (Stevens, 1983).

87. Croly, 1909, 278–79.

88. Croly, 1914, 25, 44–45, 131.
89. Croly, 1914, 148–49.
90. For more discussion of Pound's writings, see chapter 4, below. Pound wrote three very influential articles in the previous decade that made his reputation and became programmatic statements for legal reformers. See Pound, 1908, 1909, 1910. He was succeeded as dean by James M. Landis, drafter of legislation establishing the Securities and Exchange Commission and author of a book justifying the use of regulatory agencies rather than courts to regulate most economic relationships. Landis, 1938.
91. A recent cri de coeur lamenting this takeover is Epstein, 2006.
92. Skowronek, 1982.
93. The literature on antiparty legislation in this period is extensive. See, for example, McGerr, 1986, and McCormick, 1986.
94. His ethics textbook is even more forthright; see Dewey and Tufts, 1908, 474 and 478.
95. Batten, 1909, 239–40.
96. For more on this convention and the Progressive Party, see chapter 4, below.
97. Crunden, 1984, contains the best description of the convention. The social planks echoed some of the social platform of the Federal Council of Churches, founded four years earlier. Handy, 1991.
98. Four books, all published in this period, reflect this optimism: De Witt, 1915; Lippmann, 1914; Rauschenbusch, 1914; and Weyl, 1912.
99. Dewey, 1922.
100. Kohl, 1989; Greenstone, 1993; Gerring, 1998; Galvin, 2009.
101. Note that this is a reverse image of the position of the evangelical right and the Republican Party today.
102. Lustig, 1982.
103. In a series of three books, James MacGregor Burns provides an almost perfect ideological map both explaining and justifying this system and criticizing the barriers to its fuller achievement (Burns, 1949, 1965, 1967). And see Hodgson, 1976. In marked contrast, Brinkley, 1995, argues that the New Deal signaled the end of reform.
104. Dewey and Tufts, 1908, 304.
105. Cuddihy, 1978.
106. Ernst, 1974, 35–69; Eisenach, 1994, 253–57. In the words of one prominent religious publication, "War drives for world freedom [were] passing into Christian drives for world redemption . . . Christian churches mobilize when armies demobilize" (quoted in Ernst, 1974, 59).
107. Ernst, 1974, 73–74. Among those actively promoting Interchurch were the secretaries of state, treasury, and navy; Mrs. Woodrow Wilson; the vice-president; the Speaker of the House; and General Pershing.
108. Silk, 1988; Gaustad, 1989; Marty 1996. The one noteworthy exception was Reinhold Niebuhr. While most liberal Protestant thinkers were condescendingly noted by liberal academics and intellectuals, Niebuhr was lionized, his writings celebrated, and his opinions eagerly solicited. Perhaps it was because Niebuhr was both thoroughly within the high intellectual and philosophical traditions of liberal Protestant theology and a critic of American millennialist optimism. His theology, for example, centers on the Father and Son, but leaves out almost entirely the Holy Spirit. A subtle sociological explanation for Niebuhr's exalted position is in Cuddihy, 1978, and see Dorrien, 2001, 435–83.
109. *Christian Century*, June 13, 1951, 701–3.
110. Ciepley, 2007 and see discussion in Eisenach, 2006a, 56–61.
111. Schlesinger, 1949. *The Vital Center* was republished in 1962 and in 1999. Recently, a collection calling for the reconstitution of liberalism replicates many of Schlesinger's arguments: Jumonville and Mattson, eds., 2007.
112. This elitist defense of the liberal establishment was mirrored in writings critical of this establishment, both from the right and the left. From the right, these elites were socialists and fellow travelers, willing to sell our sovereignty to world government; from the left, they were a thinly disguised capitalist power elite whose leaders circulated freely between government, foundations, universities, finance, and business corporations.

113. These developments, along with the rise of the New Right, are discussed in chapter 1, above.

114. Dewey, writing in *The New Republic* in 1922 ("An American Intellectual Frontier," May 10), was quick to recognize this; his essay remains to this day a prescient analysis. *A Common Faith* (1934), the Terry Lectures at Yale, is Dewey's extended reflection and response to this analysis. Not surprisingly, it echoes many of the same ideas about religion articulated in Protestant liberal theology developed in the nineteenth and early twentieth centuries—and even his early essay "Christianity and Democracy." See, for example, 22–28. In the early 1920s Croly completed a book manuscript, "The Breach in Civilization," that located spiritual break-down with the Reformation and called for a new, more catholic, spiritual rebirth. Just as the book was about to be published, Felix Frankfurter dissuaded him, thinking such a book would embarrass Croly and hurt his reputation. David Levy, 1985, 290–99, and see Stettner, 1993, 152–53.

115. Rorty, 1998; Dionne, 1996; Lind, 1995; Tomasky, 1996; Jumonville and Mattson, 2007. Isaac, 2003, critiques some of these and similar writings.

116. This dimension of the problem is more fully explored in Eisenach, 2006a.

117. Woodrow Wilson, 1908, 18, 51. Note that Wilson used the plural "are," just like most pre–Civil War Americans referred to "these United States." In these same lectures he mounts a strong defense of both states' rights and patronage-driven, locally based political parties. See discussion in Eisenach, 1994, 122–29. In his 1919 speech to the Senate, President Wilson portrayed America as "a Nation . . . compact of the spiritual forces that must free men of every nation of every unworthy bondage . . . The stage is set, the destiny is disclosed. It has come about by no plan of our conceiving, but by the hand of God who led us into this way. We cannot turn back . . . It was of this that we dreamed at our birth. American shall in truth show the way" (July 10, 1919).

118. Gerring, 1998; Eisenach, 2000, 29–49.

119. See Skocpol, 2003. For discussion of the transition from interest-group liberalism to "rights talk," see Eisenach, 2006a, 56–61 and 64–67.

120. *New Yorker*, April 26, 2008, 5.

121. Quoted in Eisenach, 2000, 32.

122. Skowronek, 2006.

123. An almost perfect expression of this view is Higonnet, 2007.

124. See chapter 1 above and chapter 4 below.

125. Kestenbaum, 2002, and see Rogers, 2008.

126. Butler, 1996; Fish, 2001.

127. Lind, 1995, 244. Lind terms the Protestant period the "Anglo-American" regime (1789–1861) and the Judeo-Christian period the "Euro-American" regime (1875–1960s). The civil religion he suggests for our fourth republic, "Trans-America," is "civil familism."

128. Rorty, 1998; Rogers Smith, 2003.

129. Charles Taylor, 1989 and 1991.

130. Block, 2002, has written a history of American political thought constructed on the premise of human agency.

131. An ironic coda to this discussion is found in the recent discovery and publication of John Rawls's writings on religion as an undergraduate at Princeton. Thomas Nagel's introductory essay to these writings shows how Rawls both imported and transformed/suppressed a kind of social gospel Christianity when he began writing his political philosophy. Rawls, 2009.

132. Crunden, 1984, 43.

133. Crunden, 1984, 40–51; Dombrowski, 1936, 171–93.

134. Dombrowski, 1936, 112–13.

135. Steiner, 1909, 273–74.

136. Steiner, 1909, 275.

137. During this same period, popular Jewish writers such as Mary Antin (*From Plotzk to Boston, The Promised Land*) and Israel Zangwill (*The Melting Pot, Children of the Ghetto*) expressed these same ideas. Both of these writers were published in Lyman Abbott's *Outlook* and became associated with Theodore Roosevelt.

138. Herberg, (1955) 1983.

Chapter Three

Emerging Patterns in America's Political and Religious Self-Understanding

In his book *The Study of Politics* (1959), Charles Hyneman (president, American Political Science Association [APSA], 1961–1962) remarked that "religions appear to be virtually untouched" in mainstream political writing. "Certainly," he writes, "no American political scientist has provided a noteworthy analysis of the idea-system . . . that characterizes religion in general. Neither has an American political scientist carefully explored the significance for legal government of the belief-system, organization, and rituals we call Christianity."[1] By any measure, the study of religion in American politics, history, and culture, and in political philosophy today, is not only flourishing, it threatens to overwhelm us. This is true not only in the bureaucratic sense of the Religion and Politics Section of the APSA, but in the focus on religion across the discipline and in the use by these political scientists of the work of political, social, cultural, racial, and gender historians and literary critics.

I recently chaired a prize committee for the Religion and Politics Section that was to select the best recent dissertation on religion and politics. What struck me was the freedom and sophistication of these younger scholars, particularly in American and comparative politics, concerning the relationship of liberalism, modernity, and modernization to religious consciousness. These studies were not framed as if religion were a premodern and atavistic ghost at the banquet of neoliberalism or a merely external mobilization link of self to politics which, having done its job (sometimes violently), can quietly fade away.

These dissertations, like much recent work by American historians, suggest four emerging theses on the relationship of religion and politics:

(a) The secularization thesis/narrative is not only wrong, it distorts scholarship by leading us away from some of the constitutive elements of what is political by forcing our gaze to what is decidedly un- or antipolitical, whether it be bureaucratic and instrumental rationality, economic determinism, or therapy. To study politics seriously is to take religion seriously.

(b) Taking religion seriously means that religion is not seen simply as a vehicle for empowerment, moral agency, and mobilization for those previously excluded from politics (e.g., the civil rights movement in 1960s America). Accommodating new or newly emergent religious discourses is often constitutive and transformative of both persons and states, providing a way of discrediting frozen truths that have excluded newer values and interests and replacing them with more capacious ones.

(c) The boundaries separating secular and sacred in political philosophy, social and political theory, and political rhetoric and practices are permeable. And just as there is a variety of religions and of religious beliefs, so there is a variety of secularisms and secular beliefs, many of which have their origins and articulations in religion.

(d) Religious belief, religious/political ideas and rhetoric, and religious institutions are and will remain primary sources of both political conflict and political consensus, and will remain in but not of politics, both subversive and supportive of political orders.

America's political self-understanding is gradually being transformed by and through contemporary academic scholarship on religion and American culture and politics. In this chapter, I touch upon each of these theses in a variety of contexts. First I outline a paradigmatic and often unconscious divide in contemporary American self-understanding regarding religion and American politics. I then turn to historical studies representing the new ways in which religious history is being written and new ways in which cultural and gender studies and political history incorporate religion more fully into their analyses. A third articulation of this scholarship is at the level of political theory. I discuss this third topic in the context of critiques of liberalism, especially that represented by John Rawls, by his many critics, most notably Charles Taylor; by the "postmodernists"; and by the advocates of a new pragmatism in political theory. Generalizing from these historiographical and philosophical critiques, one result, which I take up as my fourth subject, is a set of arguments that posit multiple secularisms. To suggest that secularism comes in many forms and intersects with value and religious pluralism in many different ways is also to hold that there is no single or clear epistemological boundary between secular and sacred. I conclude, then, with some reflections on the ways in which "sacred" discourse and rhetoric can intervene in and interrupt more secular forms of political discourse and rhetoric, thereby resituating and redirecting political life itself.

TWO PORTRAITS OF AMERICA

One can distinguish between two perspectives on the relationship between religion and politics in America through two leading self-understandings. A liberal-enlightened understanding, best articulated in Louis Hartz, *The Liberal Tradition in America* (1955), can be contrasted to a democratic conception found in Alexis de Tocqueville, *Democracy in America.*[2]

One portrait is "liberal" in three senses: (1) it rests on highly abstract/legal distinctions between public/state and private/church; (2) it translates religion into "interests" that, like other private interests, seek recognition and advantage in political struggles; and (3) it distinguishes and isolates religion from other private interests when religion (illegitimately) seeks to shape constitutive features of the polity. This paradigm has tended to reign in law and political science.

The other portrait is "democratic" in three senses: (1) it focuses on national-consensual and moral-civic values lying underneath and inside external political forms and practices; (2) it stresses struggles and conflicts over the definition and import of these shared values; and (3) it concerns inclusion in, exclusion from, and assimilation into the larger society, culture, and polity.[3] This paradigm is increasingly powerful in the humanities and the human sciences, represented by culture and gender studies.

The Liberal Portrait (A)

America has become increasingly religiously pluralistic, just as it has become increasingly racially and ethnically pluralistic. Divisions within a still-dominant Protestantism have divided us even more. Any attempt to create a new religious or sacred-national consensus on the order of previously existing informal and voluntary establishments, successively WASP (Protestant), Euro-Christian, and Judeo-Christian,[4] is either quixotic or dangerous. American political unity must derive from constitutional values that are, in turn, grounded in universalistic ideals of human rights, equality, and representative government. While both the American past and the American present have been witness to many religiously motivated social and political movements (running the gamut from the good to the bad and the ugly), and while some of these movements have even resulted in major legal and constitutional changes, all of these political-religious movements can be understood and integrated into a larger "moral interest group" model of political action and conflict.

Like the individualism assumed in voting, religion is understood politically as religiously motivated individuals coming together in groups or social movements and seeking to translate those understandings into political influence. Professionally trained analysts of these phenomena are presumed to be able to stand outside and to convey the results of their studies in replicable, scientific form. Running parallel with this universalistic posture of the scientific analyst is the universal posture of liberal constitutional rules and principles that keep these claims and conflicts within the bounds of civility and good order. The patriotic aspect of this model has been termed "civic nationalism."[5]

The National-Democratic Portrait (B)

This more internal and historical portrait begins by asking us to set aside particular churches, religious interests, and "faith traditions" interacting with politics or taking sides in contemporary political battles. We are asked to look instead to the larger patterns and spirits in our national history and culture. America, proclaimed the English Catholic G. K. Chesterton in the 1920s, is "the nation with the soul of a church."[6] The patriotic aspect of this model has been termed "ethnic" nationalism because of its commitment to substantive principles and ethically (and often ethnically) constitutive stories that are presumed to constitute the national bond.[7] From the Puritan commonwealth to the American Revolution, understood as an Anglo-American religious civil war, Americans evidenced from the start a pervasive religiosity that was built into their political culture.[8] And in the nineteenth century, as attested by foreign or foreign-born analysts such as Tocqueville and Phillip Schaff, religious belief was a constitutive feature of republican citizenship, inseparable from our politics in the sense of creating the very preconditions for our political institutions and practices. Students of the "partisan period" in Jacksonian America as well as analysts of the origins of the Republican Party and the Civil War in the party-stalemate period that followed further attest to the religious structure of contending partisan and regime values.[9]

Given this interweaving of religion and politics, this portrait makes religion so pervasive, so deeply embedded in our culture and practices, that to be distinctly American is to be distinctly religious, even for those who proclaim to hold only "secular" values. These long-standing foreign observations and historical studies are increasingly being rediscovered and restated in new registers by contemporary American scholarship. The proper object of inquiry about the relationship of religion to politics in America is the American nation itself, not its particular churches and not its particular religiously inspired interests and social movements. [10]

Once one is open to the assumption that religious ideas and understandings are as constitutive of our political culture and political discourse as are formal constitutions, some interesting intersections and comparisons suggest themselves. Religiously inspired political and social movements and political and social interests must be seen as both external and internal to our politics. Religion is, from liberal portrait A, contestable from the outside in the name of constitutional and secular political values and institutions. Religion is, from portrait B, also contestable, but from the inside, when particular religions and religious practices are deemed outside a shared American faith. [11] Religion is, from portrait B, often incontestable, again from the inside, when it is atmospheric or hegemonic, when our secular political values and institutions are themselves so interwoven with religious assumptions and nationalist-religious discourse that there is no acceptable place to stand outside of religion's purview. Religion is, from portrait A, also incontestable, but from the outside, when it is seen as an individual and constitutionally protected right.

When Americans have attempted to keep religion permanently "outside" of politics in the name of liberal-constitutional order and individual rights, these attempts have not only been short-lived and in vain, they have often served to suppress the very resources and energies that power democratic politics and political change. [12] Conversely, when we have attempted to place religion permanently "inside" politics in the name of national consensus and patriotism, these attempts have also been short-lived and in vain, often suppressing new spirits and new revelations as a "civil" religion comes to buttress existing secular powers and interests.

Both portraits intersect in our histories and in our self-understandings, even as each understanding seems to confound itself as it seeks to become definitive—as if each paradigm harbors, within itself, subversive features. Portrait A is vulnerable to the argument that political liberalism as a historical and theoretical project was itself the secular product of a very specific kind of Protestant Christianity, that it remains a "comprehensive moral doctrine," and that it therefore seeks a philosophical-religious imperium over competing religious beliefs (and participatory democratic values) under cover of fairness and neutrality. Portrait B is also vulnerable to self-subversion. As the embodying churches of "Christian America" become an ever-smaller slice of the American faith salami, so, too, does the distinctly Protestant-Christian content of the religion of America. The more pluralistic the number and variety of churches and faiths, the more need for theological modernists (i.e., liberal Protestants) to set the conditions and norms for getting along. As these conditions and norms became stated in increasingly secular and liberal terms, they are transformed into a civic religion of tolerance and mutual respect standing above all particular creeds and churches. The ironic result (and happy coincidence) is an almost exact restatement of American liberal constitutional and moral values and a formidable barrier to distinctly religious voices in future democratic contestations and struggles. [13]

SOME HISTORIOGRAPHICAL MOVES

In outlining these two portraits and their potentials for self-subversion, it is apparent that historical understanding is deeply implicated, both as paradigmatic historiographical foundations and as ways to contest, amend, and transform these foundations. In this section, I consider both these implications in looking at religious history, women's history, and regime change theory.

Religious History

One area of scholarship that is important for understanding the relationship of religion to American politics, is—after the title of a recent book collection—new directions in American religious history. [14] This body of inquiry contends that, through most of the twentieth century, American religious history was in fact written as church history. Produced mainly by professors in liberal interdenominational divinity schools tied to major national research universities, this history treated dominant liberal or liberal evangelical Protestant churches as Protestant religion, Protestant religion as Christianity, and Christianity as the religion of America. The church history story that was told about the nineteenth century, however, tended to discount the role of particular (Protestant) church creeds and doctrines, stressing instead a sort of pan-Protestant evangelical "spirit" that left in its wake freedom-loving republican citizens. And while certain churches (i.e., Congregational, American Baptist, Presbyterian, Methodist, and Unitarian) more clearly embodied these values than did other Protestant bodies, this embodiment was usually confirmed sociologically by patterns of cultural, social, and intellectual deference and hierarchy. And, when Americans were true to their authentic national purposes, these hierarchies would be confirmed by national political dominance as well. [15]

One must note first that the teachings of this church history were two-sided. From the constitutional and liberal outside, state and church were clearly separated, but, from the national and democratic inside, this separation released the energies and spirits of evangelical Protestantism in its project to "Christianize" both America and the world. [16] The institutional meeting point was not the separate and separated churches but the many reform causes undertaken by the ecumenical institutions of an evangelical united front, institutions that successively included the Whig, Liberty, Republican, and Progressive parties. The major tension that emerged within church history as it addressed the twentieth century was between a rearguard and hagiographic defense of the older Protestant ascendancy (too much religious pluralism is a threat) and an attempt by this Protestant ascendancy to adapt to a more pluralistic environment by increasingly secularizing its doctrines and its methods of study. This latter solution, however, not only made the resulting "American religion" thin, it tended to submerge distinctly Christian and, arguably, distinctly religious content. [17]

So long as the implicit political theology of church history was safely tied to constitutionalism and moderate reform, it melded easily into prevailing academic political science and sociology. Indeed, the "political science" that church history embraced for twentieth-century America was a kind of political sociology in which denominational markers were demographic markers that could, in turn, be translated into partisan political commitments. In short, the older church history both supplemented and confirmed mid-twentieth-century pluralist political science, and both disciplines legitimated an increasingly secular liberal establishment. Translated into political theory and constitutional values, this mode of church history posited an elite consensus of secular liberals presiding over and providing an inclusive political consensus for increasingly diverse sets of believers and faith communities, often overlapping with racial and ethnic differences.

The entry of a new and different scholarly spirit in American religious self-understanding can be quite clearly marked. In 1990, the journal *Religion and American Culture* was founded to serve the growing constituency outside of divinity schools to address issues of religion in history, religion, and humanities departments. In 1998, the most distinguished academic journal in the field, *Church History*, not only moved from the University of Chicago to Duke but added a new subtitle: *Studies in Christianity and Culture*.

The "new religious history" is trying to tell us something beyond the negative message that the older church history has reached a series of unproductive dead ends that now are barriers to American self-understanding. As befits the journal name change, the issue is not (and perhaps never really was) the relationship of churches to each other and to the state, and is not the role and effects of organized religious movements, interests, and institutions on politics. The positive message is that we must study how religion and politics intertwine and interpenetrate each other in and through the larger culture. [18]

Women's History

Another area of scholarship that indicates this newer approach to religion and politics is women's history. How did women—who could not vote and were not church ministers—become active agents in American political life and religious culture in the nineteenth and early twentieth centuries? The very question moves the meaning of what we might mean by politics and political regime away from parties, elections, and constitutional-legal structures and toward civil society and patterns of authority and practices in the culture and society. This question simultaneously alters the meaning and location of religion, out of separate and separated churches as ministerial-led institutions for Sunday worship and into moral reform associations, evangelism, philanthropic institutions, and even popular fiction. [19] These parallel shifts suggest that agency and power in the larger culture set the terms of political discourse and action more than overt partisan-political struggle itself, and that participants at the overt level of political conflict operate within a set of tacit understandings over which they have little control.

While it could be said that women turned to religiously based political activity because they were excluded from formal political participation, so were they without formal authority in churches. In neither case would marginalization or prejudice explain why so many men participated alongside them and why the implicit antiparty ideas contained in these new forms of politics became such a large part of electoral-political argument both before and after the Civil War. [20] Moral-religious discourse and its organizational expression were not only constitutive of women's individual and collective agency, the innovations they and their male allies launched, and the cultural-political victories they won, carried this discourse and its organization into the larger civil and political society.

Regime Theory and Constitutional Transformations

A third body of scholarship that carries some of these same implications regarding the deeper relationships of religion and politics is the study of American national politics as a series of distinct "regime periods" that define the contours of our political life. While critical elections (e.g., Lincoln 1860, McKinley 1896, Roosevelt 1932) mark the demise of one regime and the start of a new one, the values, purposes, and discourse of each of these new regimes were not created de novo in and by the electoral campaign, but were embedded in the larger culture, now made articulate in the national government. [21] New regimes represent "new" agendas, authoritative warrants, and discourses, but their rhetorical and intellectual components must already be present for the discourse of the new regime to be comprehensible. New regimes may be occasioned by particular issues and disjunctive events, but these issues and events must themselves be interpreted in ways that discredit not just the policies of the standing regime, but the authoritative and prevailing understandings that sustained them. The "reconstructive discourse" of the new regime, then, makes visible and public what was before opaque or deemed nonpolitical or private.[22] The critical actors lying behind and before this transformative process might not be party-political activists at all, but reform leaders, social movement activists, intellectuals, journalists, and writers, where the lines separating public and private, secular and sacred, or church and state are much less salient.

In this sense, the new religious history, women's history, and regime-period political history are implicitly "interpretivist," addressing ideas of identity and meaning that combine sacred and secular, spiritual and material, private and public. This fusion is both at the psychological and the intellectual-ideological level. Religion is not only implicated in these cultural modes of understanding our politics, it is in many ways constitutive of the identities and meanings that go into the constructions of the meaning and purpose of politics and the meaning and purpose of civil society.

Two recent books[23] by political scientists indirectly confirm some of the spirit of this new scholarship. In *Hellfire Nation: The Politics of Sin in American History*, James Morone's reading of three epochs in American political life is premised on the religious and moral resources in the larger culture that make possible our capacity to mobilize nationally to undertake—for good or ill—the political projects we have undertaken. In *A Nation of Agents: The American Path to a Modern Self and Society*, James Block probes even more deeply behind this religious and moralistic culture to uncover the religious dimension in the very concept of the self that constitutes the actor or citizen in a free society. In America's early modern philosophical foundations in Hobbes and Locke, in the seventeenth-century Puritan revolution, and in the political ideas of the revolutionary and constitutional founding, citizenship and political agency are a complex amalgam of philosophy and theology, of hard-earned experience and visionary hope, of body and spirit. From Jonathan Edwards through John Dewey, in the words of a now classic book, the American churchman and the American philosopher combine.[24] Perhaps the most vivid recent example of combining political and religious ideas in American self-understanding, however, is *Lincoln's Greatest Speech*.[25]

SOME THEORETICAL CONTESTATIONS

Political theory both causes and reflects changes in our understandings of the relationship of religion to American politics. It is causal in two ways. Political theory articulates and helps to make consciously paradigmatic the different forms of understanding. In so doing, however, especially when refining and extending the logic of the dominant understanding, it reveals anomalies and other difficulties, helping to cause, as it were, its own critique and even its overthrow as hegemonic. Political theory reflects changing understandings when it seeks to articulate new or emerging ideological and cultural divides in the polity.

If any two contemporary political philosophers could be said to stand for different styles of contemporary liberal-democratic political theory, they would be John Rawls and Charles Taylor. Rawls asks to be judged on the truth and internal logic of his argument. In *Theory of Justice*, especially, the "God of reason" speaks, independently of the persona of the truth teller. In contrast, Taylor's *Sources of the Self* asks us to interrogate our own intuitions and reflect on our own individual and collective experiences, first to discover intimations of, and then to articulate philosophically, the moral orientations and moral sources that shape our overt principles and practices. Echoing Max Weber's distinction, Rawls comes to us as the "ethical prophet" with fixed principles and rules, while Taylor comes to us as the "exemplary prophet," calling us to destinies and destinations yet unknown. In more conventional terms, Rawls articulates the core ethic of contemporary liberalism and Taylor the many-sided moralities of democracy. Today Rawls represents the solid centerpiece of a well-wrought liberal theory of justice, while Taylor stands for a series of energetic and sometimes incongruent peripheries seeking more transformative forms of politics.

In a nutshell and for America, Rawls's theory has been taken to encode a narrative of secularization and cosmopolitanism. No matter what our historical past might have been and no matter what our own felt experiences of political agency might be, our political present and future should be guided by public principles that are neutral and fair. Public/democratic discourse and the standards regulating action and decision in the public realm must not be contaminated by privately held religious and other comprehensive moral doctrines. When major political choices are contested, holders of those doctrines are to constrain themselves (or be constrained by others) not to use those comprehensive arguments directly. Legitimate political discourse must be a translation of what is "privately" felt and believed true into secular, scientific, and pragmatic forms. The resulting discourse produces a "public reason" that is "political" and not metaphysical or religious: "it neither criticizes nor attacks any comprehensive doctrine, religious or nonreligious, except insofar as that doctrine is incompatible with the essentials of public reason and a democratic society." Shielding the public realm from these doctrines prevents that realm from claiming that its decisions regarding fundamental political questions are decided "according to [some] idea of the whole truth."[26]

Rawls's liberal theory can be set against two alternatives, one stressing more open-ended theories of political democracy and limited government (to stop an imperial secularization penetrating all the way down) and the other more historically and sociologically grounded arguments about the American polity and the origins of liberal democratic states. Both types of alternatives charge that a Rawlsian self-understanding of America would drive many people out of politics. By making second-class citizens of those who had previously participated in politics because of and through their religious and moral commitments, the polity would deprive itself of the insights and interests of a good portion of its citizens.[27] Second, this self-understanding would authorize less democratically responsive institutions and the political and intellectual elites who dominate them—especially the courts, bureaucracies, and national law schools—to declare which forms of political discourse and the beliefs that inform this discourse are compatible with "the essentials of public reason and a democratic society." To empower a particular subculture with this kind of universalizing power, as if their shared doctrines make them immune to the temptations of interest and power, defeats the claim to neutrality and fairness among comprehensive moral doctrines and would, paradoxically, undermine popular loyalty to the very institutions that this theory holds central to maintaining liberal equality.

More broadly speaking, these alternatives question whether one can even treat "comprehensive moral doctrines" as static "things"—as if each person at some stage in his life were given a wardrobe selection of religious and metaphysical doctrines from which to clothe his identity.[28] This abstracted self is posited as disembodied and unencumbered and yet is assumed to be free to choose and to have the intellectual and moral resources to do so—provided perhaps by the addition of an appropriate and compulsory "democratic education."[29] Lastly, this understanding of America and of liberal democracy is charged with being itself a comprehensive and particular moral doctrine of man and society even as it claims to stand above the battle as the political "universal" authorized to judge the benighted "particulars" burdened with narrow interests, prejudice, ignorance, and false consciousness.[30] Viewed historically, this pretension is only another instance of the well-known hegemonic strategies of all ruling establishments (and colonial powers) attempting to turn their particular values and interests into universal truths and common sense. Against this, democratic politics insists that the contemporary culture wars are battles between epistemological equals, both in the larger society, where the challenge is from the right, and in academia, where the challenge is from the left.[31]

Without addressing all of the forms in which these arguments are embedded, I want to highlight three of these forms and suggest how they bring religion, or at least a religious sensibility, back into politics.

Phenomenology and the Human Sciences

The first form is the most firmly grounded in the language of philosophy and its history, namely, a critique of the liberal-enlightenment project in philosophy from the standpoint of phenomenology, tracing its roots back to Hegel. [32] This critique holds that the "human sciences," which include political philosophy, are inescapably both "interpretivist-experiential" and historical: understanding must come from within attempts to discover meaning in the world we experience. In political philosophy, the touchstone is Charles Taylor's *Sources of the Self* (1989) and his writings on Hegel and on language and human agency. [33] This critique of Rawlsian liberalism holds that the very capacity to act as a citizen in a democratic society requires moral sources that are not "chosen" but constitutive and that these moral sources (also termed the "social imaginary") of meaning are the starting point, not the end point, of philosophical reflection. To view both personal and collective identity as constituted from these moral sources integrates ideas and values from religion, philosophy, literature, and history as well as politics and political ideologies. [34]

Civic Republicanism

The second form of criticism is in the form of an alternative understanding of the foundations of contemporary America and liberal-democratic societies generally: the discovery/invention of "civic republicanism" as an alternative model to a rights-based liberalism. [35] Civic republicanism as a general theory subordinates individual rights, both philosophically and in its social theory, to the participatory political community. The bonds of this political community are both deep and constitutive of the individuals within it. These bonds authorize this "community of equals" to engage in extensive moral and civic education and democratically decide on the distributions of rights compatible with communally generated purposes. Conversely, the community seeks to protect this communal liberty by instilling suspicion of any elites, be they judicial, intellectual, economic, or cultural, who claim authority from sources outside the political community. These ideas and values powered the revolutions creating liberal democratic nation-states, and it is these same ideas and values that are undermined by Rawlsian liberalism.

Like the original Antifederalists and many later forms of populism, it is an open question whether civic republican critiques are from the right (to protect traditional and often morally backward ways of life) or from the left (to unmask and discredit great inequalities of wealth and power). The civic republican alternative began as an attempt to reread the origins of liberal-democratic political thought in early modern England, continued as a way of reinterpreting the American revolutionary founding, and only later found its most secure institutional home among "critical legal theorists" in the national law schools. As a counter-theory of contemporary politics it is at once "conservative" (protecting the ligaments of community and loyalty; rediscovering the moral and religious bonds necessary for concerted political action) and "radical" (extending the powers of the democratic community against elites; creating newly empowered political movements). But from either direction, civic republicanism is highly skeptical of "rights talk" abstracted from political democracy, whether this talk is used to shore up established interests and powers or to legitimate self-appointed judicial and bureaucratic elites in creating clienteles dependent upon their sponsorship and goodwill. One powerful element of civic republicanism is a deep critique of the rights talk underwriting contemporary church-state jurisprudence, particularly noteworthy in view of the fact that critical legal theorists think of themselves as critics of liberalism from the democratic left. [36]

Antifoundationalism

The relationship of both of these alternative understandings to religion is both complex and indirect. Insofar as each is a critique of Rawlsian theory and "rights talk" grounded in claims of moral and religious neutrality, each of these alternatives is, at a minimum, less hostile to claims of the spirit, to religiously based identities, and to forms of political obligation grounded in contingency and history. Beyond this minimal conclusion is an openness to discussions of nationalism and patriotism that situates discussion of equality, rights, and freedom inside of traditions, discourses, and feelings that frame all politically salient thinking. The radical historicism that pervades some of these writings and the "antifoundationalism" that feeds their critiques often replicate and restate deeper theological perspectives on politics. Just as Nietzsche lies at the foreground of antifoundationalism, so Augustine is in the background. [37]

MULTIPLE SECULARISMS AND SECULAR-SACRED BOUNDARY PROBLEMS

It is important to adumbrate one issue in the critique of Rawlsian theory that was raised at the start of this chapter. The issue is the charge that the claims of secular liberal political theory are not (and cannot be) universal, based on "a view from nowhere" or from behind some veil of ignorance that screens out self-serving interests and values, but are made by particular historic subcultures with particular traditions and roles and with particular interests and values. This critique takes many forms. One flows simply from the naive question of who authorizes this set of political and legal theorists to speak for America and its core identity and political values. [38] Put differently, what

historical background or legacy is assumed by this particular theory community such that they can claim an a priori right to speak and to be heard
regarding who we are and what we should be about?

Earlier, I had suggested that a progressive-liberal establishment prevailed
in American politics and intellectual culture from the Progressive Era
through the 1970s. Even the electoral victory of Franklin Roosevelt and the
rebirth and dominance of the Democratic Party did not significantly blunt
this dominance.[39] And despite the many and grievous religious, racial, and
gender exclusions by Progressivism and the New Deal, both the liberalism
outlined at the start of this chapter in portrait A and the democracy outlined
in portrait B flourished in tandem: this is the very definition of a successful
establishment. This simultaneous flourishing, however, was increasingly articulated in liberal-universalistic terms, while its religious, assimilationist,
nationalist, moralistic, and patriotic elements were subordinated.

The liberal establishment came under siege by the left beginning in the
late 1960s and was joined by forces from the right soon thereafter. The left
charged this establishment with betraying its own proclaimed ideals of universal rights, while the right charged it with betraying Americanist ideals of
individual and family responsibility, national patriotism, and limited government. The result was perplexing. The left won most of the intellectual, cultural, and elite institutional battles, largely by converting the prevailing establishments from the inside and gradually occupying their seats of authority.
The result is a secular liberalism combined with a principled multiculturalism
that still wins important victories in nondemocratic electoral settings. The
ideological right, however, increasingly consolidated its democratic electoral
victories that it began in the 1980s.

What the twentieth-century Progressive and New Deal liberal establishment successfully joined, the left and right combined to tear asunder.[40] In the
process, however, each side has found it necessary to use arguments from the
opposing camp in order to extend its range of victory. We are familiar with
this set of strategies: the right uses First Amendment and diversity arguments
to enhance the voice of religion and morality in schools and in national
institutions (even in the name of multicultural inclusion). The secular-liberal
left, on the other hand, is seeking to rediscover national narratives that will
lend popular meaning and power to its truths.[41] The important point, however, is that this strategy of mutual encroachment tends to confound the boundaries between sacred and secular and to question the autonomous standing
of both religion and politics. Put somewhat cryptically: the religious right has
had to become less pietistic/moralistic, while the liberal left has had to become less arrogantly enlightened and more skeptical. This strategy of mutual
encroachment has not gone unnoticed by those who would seek to theorize it.
The result is a theory of "multiple secularisms" that, in turn, suggests more
unifying ideas of the sacred.

Many Secularisms

Historians of voluntary religious establishments in America have little trouble in tracing the genealogy of today's liberal intellectual and cultural establishment to liberal evangelical Protestant sources that have been alluded to earlier. Indeed, much of the confidence, reforming zeal, and even alleged intellectual arrogance of liberalism might be traced to this background. These intellectual ancestors came to dominate the professions, finance, education, the foundations, and later the federal bureaucracy and judiciary. They were overtly nationalistic and overtly Protestant, and envisioned America as incarnating both enlightened reason and a world-redemptive spirit. Their confidence was buttressed at the start by the dominant churches and churchmen who shared the secularizing hopes that an ethical, noncreedal, ecumenical, and liberal evangelical Protestantism spirit would triumph in every sector of American life from the family to the business corporation to foreign policy.[42] These earlier religious and academic elites often spoke in a secular, philosophical, and social-scientific language, but the meaning and power of this language was deeply embedded in sacred narrative and nationalist rhetoric. The undoing of Progressivism, and perhaps the undoing of contemporary liberalism, came from their increasing confidence that they could disavow and suppress "contingent" sacred narrative and even national-patriotic rhetoric if it stood in the way of their projects and power.

This argument can be restated in broader terms, taken from arguments increasingly found in postcolonial studies, in intellectual history and the history of philosophy, and in religious studies. The reigning liberal-enlightenment understanding of the distinction between secular and sacred is that rational-secular understandings are one and sacred understandings are many. The social sciences, history, and philosophy that shape and articulate this secular understanding are united in a shared and "public" epistemology derived from Kant that stands against the almost infinite varieties of "private" worldviews that are produced by the historical and contingent nature of bodies, hopes, fears, and events. The sacred understandings that result, they conclude, cannot be the products of reason, any more than its symbols and expressions can be understood from the standpoint of reason: imaginative literature, "imagined communities" (nation-states), the "social imaginary," art, ethnicity, and religion are all contingent facts that await their ratification and ranking by a unitary secular reason.

The Kantian or Enlightenment understanding is rapidly collapsing. In contemporary scholarship the Enlightenment is being deconstructed into "rival enlightenments"[43] or into distinct national enlightenments[44] and secularism itself is increasingly discussed as discrete and often rival secularisms, each with its own origins, experiences, and narratives.[45] The truths produced by secular knowledge are subject to this genealogical critique and reinterpreted as part of the particular narratives of meaning in which they are located. Somewhat parallel to Kuhn's argument concerning paradigms that successively transform and structure scientific truth, the argument concerning truths in the human sciences posits separate and simultaneous ethnocultural and religious paradigms that inform, differentiate, and empower a variety of secularisms. Needless to add, postcolonial studies is practically premised on this assumption.[46] Once one begins to look more closely at the critiques of Rawlsian liberalism from this perspective, it becomes apparent that something like a multiple secularisms argument is implicit in many of these critiques.[47] Whether in the name of political democracy to level the political playing field or to cast doubt on the claims of philosophical and political imperium, the antifoundationalist assumption carries with it the claim that secular reason is neither self-creating nor self-authorizing.

Read this way, and in view of the relative weakness of the church base of contemporary liberal Protestantism, this victory becomes an increasingly hollow one if, as has happened, new religious energies and new religious spirits and new personal identities rise to the fore. The forms of secularization these new spiritual energies might produce are now open because they have not, apart from some national electoral victories, penetrated into much of the larger elite national culture. In some respects, however, from the left and at the most sophisticated level of the American intellect, we already have some provisional indications.[48] What relationship these secularizations from the academic left might come to have to the secularizations of the religious right is, needless to add, a very open question.

CONCLUSION: SACRED DISCOURSE AND POLITICAL TIME

What is not in question is the continuing salience of religion in American political identity. Most obviously, the response to the attack and destruction of the World Trade Center in September 2001, discussed earlier,[49] is proof enough. Many Americans were frightened by this outburst of patriotic-religious rhetoric and symbolism. They saw this release of feeling and emotion as a pretext for breaking faith with our legal and constitutional principles, propelling us into the darkness of political extremism. While this response is understandable, some reflection will remind us that the legal and constitutional principles now being defended were themselves the result of earlier transformative moments, beginning with the election of FDR and the institution of the New Deal, followed by World War II, the Cold War, and, finally, the civil rights movement. Indeed, those transformations were predicated earlier on the nationalization of the federal government occasioned by the Civil War and the long period of Republican Party ascendancy begun with the realigning election of McKinley in 1896.[50] As dramatic as this most recent explosion of sacred rhetoric was, it followed familiar patterns, most obviously in the rhetoric of antislavery and the Civil War.[51] Woodrow Wilson's rhetoric following our entry in World War I was repeated in World War II (Eisenhower's history was called *Crusade in Europe*) and sustained American internationalism in the Cold War era and the later civil rights movement. While not all transformative moments in our politics are marked by the sudden insertion of sacred rhetoric (there are powerful secular narratives and rhetorics as well),[52] all of these moments require a discourse to discredit and overthrow the previous political ideology within which priorities are decided and policies are made. These transformative releases from ordinary time and ordinary priorities set the stage for a new configuration of policies constructed from the new repertoire of possibilities contained in sacred time.

Religious belief and sacred rhetoric are not only powerful cultural and intellectual resources that make these moments conceivable, they legitimate the changes and help us bear the sacrifice and loss (material, psychological, and intellectual) in ways that legal-constitutional principles, standing alone, cannot begin to do. And these same limitations apply to philosophical articulations of American political self-understanding and to histories of liberal political theory read as a seamless and secular "just so" story. Like philosophy, diachronic time fixes the past, orders the present, and severely limits the future.

Perhaps the various articulations of America's emerging self-understanding can best be summarized by reflecting on the tensions implicit in the question of whether America is to be understood as "young" or as "new."[53] By "young" I mean that we see ourselves on a preordained path toward maturity within a fixed set of principles and ideals. By "new" I mean that we see ourselves as capable of democratic renewal/rebirth in ways that we cannot know in advance. Perhaps the best example of the former is that of John Dickinson, one of America's most powerful spokesmen for colonial rights against the British in his *Letters from a Farmer.* An enlightened gentleman, thoroughly conversant with Whig political thought and British constitutional principles, he was entirely unprepared for the revolutionary call for independence. His plaintive question, "Where shall we find another England to supply our loss?" illustrates the vision of America as young and destined to mature within the prevailing European political framework. Dickinson's God was a providential keeper of rational order in diachronic time. Tom Paine, Dickinson's Philadelphia tormentor in this period of decision, illustrates the vision of America as new. In his appendix to *Common Sense*, Paine sees independence as an apocalyptic moment in time that redeems past struggles and failures even as it promises to create a new future for the world: "We have it in our power to begin the world over again . . . The birth-day of a new world is at hand."[54] Needless to add, Paine's God is the prophetic judge of righteousness, breaking through ordinary time and altering its meaning and direction.

American political identity exists in the tension between these two poles, poles that implicate politics and religion, the secular and the sacred, providence and prophecy. The metaphor of "young" with its ideal of maturity has the advantage of rational discourse and common sense because the framework and the future is known and assumed settled. This metaphor sustains the "order of preservation" even as it entails a necessary incapacity to imagine possibilities outside its authorized purview and hides from itself its own origins in war, military or electoral conquest, or new political and religious spirits and movements. The metaphor of "new" sustains our transcendent hopes—the "order of salvation"—and calls us to undertake transformative projects. But these transformative moments in politics entail levels of risk and possibilities for tragedy that threaten the goods and purposes provided by stable political and social institutions.

Religious belief and language can accommodate and serve to ratify either metaphorical self-understanding. I would suggest, however, that religion in the service of a "young" America on a path to maturity will always be a rather tepid civil religion, often in moral and ethical thrall to present powers and interests and, therefore, never quite true to itself. Religion in the service of a "new" America is not only more true to itself, it provides a much more realistic understanding of our political condition, anchored as it is in the necessities of contingency and risk and of coercion and death.

NOTES

1. Kelly, 1984, 7.
2. Kloppenberg, 2003; Greenstone, 1993.
3. Zunz, 1998, chapter 7; Eisenach 1994, chapters 2 and 5.
4. From Lind, 1995.
5. Rogers Smith, 2003, 73–76 and 136–37.
6. Mead, 1975.
7. Rogers Smith, 2003, 74–77.
8. Bercovitch, 1976 and 1975; Heimert, 1966; Phillips, 1999; Clark, 1994.
9. Kelley, 1979, parts 2 and 3; Kleppner, 1970; Gienapp, 1987.
10. Two good examples are Block, 2002; Morone, 2003.
11. Moore, 1986; Hutchison, 2003; Hollinger, 1993.
12. Eisenach, 2000, chapter 2; Ferguson, 1997, 177.
13. Eisenach, 2000, 134–36; Watson, 1997.
14. Stout and Hart, 1997.
15. Brauer, 1968; Richard W. Fox, 1993.
16. Hutchison, 1987; Eisenach, 1994, 67–71 and 112–13; and see chapter 5, below.
17. Marty, 1986, 1996; Hutchison, 1992; Howard Murphy, 1955; Bloom, 1992, 28, 32, 45.
18. Stout and Hart, 1997; Dean, 2002; Eisenach, 2000; Richard W. Fox, 1993; Hamburger, 2002; Moore, 1994; Schmidt, 1997; Stevenson, 1986; Curtis, 1991; Thomas, 1989.

19. Isenberg, 1998; Kern, 2001; Fitzpatrick, 1990; Parker, 1997; Douglas, 1977; McCarthy, 2001, 2003.
20. Gerring, 1998; McGerr, 1986; Jaenicke, 1986.
21. Burnham, 1970; Skowronek, 1993; Gerring, 1998; Gienapp, 1987; Howe, 1979, 1997; Kohl, 1989; Eisenach, 1990, 1994; Richard W. Fox, 1993.
22. Skowronek, 1993.
23. Block, 2002; Morone, 2003.
24. Kuklick, 1985 and see Zakai, 2003.
25. White, 2002.
26. Rawls, 1997, in Owen, 2001, 108–9, 112.
27. See Tomasi, 2001, chapter 2.
28. Sandel, 1996; Taylor, 1989, 1985.
29. Gutmann, 1999.
30. Judith Butler, 1996.
31. See Fish, 1999, 191.
32. Hinchman, 1984; Charles Taylor, 1975, 2001.
33. Charles Taylor, 1975, 1985.
34. Skinner, 1985.
35. Kloppenberg, 1998, 3–70.
36. Tushnet, 1985; Steven D. Smith, 1995; Fish, 1999; and see Hamburger, 2002, and Eisenach, 2000, 29–49, on the nineteenth century.
37. Connolly, 1999, 1991, 1987.
38. Neal, 1997, 125–28 and 158.
39. Plotke, 1996, 113 and 187–88; Morone, 2003.
40. For a trenchant analysis, see Hodgson, 1976.
41. Rorty, 1998; Rogers Smith, 2003; and see Isaac, 2003.
42. See chapter 2 above and chapter 5 below and Hutchison, 2003; Handy, 1991; Richard W. Fox, 1993; Silk, 1988; Reuben, 1996; Eisenach, 1994; Stevenson, 1986; Curtis, 1991; Feffer, 1993.
43. Hunter, 2001, and see Hochstrasser, 2000; Haakonssen, 1996; Waldron, 2002; Harrison, 1996; Charles Taylor, 2001.
44. Ferguson, 1997.
45. Taylor, 1998, and see Jakobsen, 2000; Redhead, 2003.
46. Wendy Brown, 2008, chapter 7.
47. One of the best examples is Rawls himself. See Thomas Nagel's introductory essay to the recently discovered and published writings on religion that Rawls wrote as an undergraduate. Rawls, 2009.
48. Rorty, 1998; Connolly, 1999; Charles Taylor, 1998, 2001.
49. See chapter 1, above.
50. Ackerman, 1993, 2000.
51. Walters, 1977; Tuveson, 1968; White, 2002.
52. Lind, 1995; Rorty, 1998; Rogers Smith, 2003; more generally, Zerubavel, 2003.
53. Kelly, 1984, 63–90.
54. Dickinson, 1895, 326; Paine, 1976, 120.

Part Two: National Identity and American Progressivism

Introduction to Part Two

.

WHY THE PROGRESSIVES SUCCEEDED

Current interest in the Progressive movement—one whose intellectual origins began more than a century ago—lies in the hope that exploring the grounds of their success might help revive contemporary liberalism as a living political force. The two concluding chapters explore some of the philosophical, cultural, and ideological contours of Progressivism and, therefore, suggest some reasons both for its appeal and for the energies and commitments of tens of millions of activist citizens over two generations. This analysis further suggests that this appeal was both intellectually and ideologically coherent: to subscribe to one set of appealing ideas and visions was usually to subscribe to others. Because much of this analysis is implicit and is focused on individual contributors to Progressive ideas, it would be helpful here to step back and outline more generally those sets of ideas that were particularly effective in their capacity to attract, mobilize, and direct such a powerfully transformative force in American political life. Four such sets are prominent.

NATIONALISM

Whatever the state of national patriotism before the Civil War, it was clear to all that a deep sense of national identity was one of the victor's strongest legacies. The harbinger of this transformation was the sudden creation of the Republican Party as a party above parties, pledged to national unity. The force of this creation was sufficient to destroy the Whig Party, split the

Democratic Party, and lead the North to military victory. This memory and model were powerful forces in the appeal of Progressivism. On the model of the soldier and his auxiliary supports, the ideal of citizenship was to serve country first—not party, not church, not region, not interest. This national service could be performed in every site of American life: family; church or school; town, city, or state government; profession, workplace, or union. Through a nationalist ideal, one's daily life would be connected to all of one's fellow citizens, and thereby gain a sense of significance and importance. National pride and personal pride were interdependent—and so were public and private shame.

POLITICS ABOVE PARTY

To organize the citizenry on these values and sentiments was perforce to be opposed to political parties that divided people by riches, region, or religion. A truly national party was necessarily above party and therefore staunchly opposed to politics as an electoral "game" in which victors (however they won) could claim the public purse to be distributed by party leaders to further entrench their power. At the extreme, the Progressives would simply claim that a good party member was necessarily a bad citizen. A large part of Progressive reform effort beginning in the 1890s was addressed to the weakening of party power so that higher forms of citizenship could be practiced. Nonpartisan city government and school board elections; initiative, recall, and referenda; Australian (state-printed) ballots; mandatory primary nominating elections; and funding restrictions and reporting are some of the more obvious measures to attack party power. To engage in these reform efforts was not only to rid the polity of manifest forms of corruption, it was also to create a civic environment that was free from many ordinary temptations to put party or private good above the common good.

POPULAR SOVEREIGNTY

A politics above party and the reforms that this value confirmed sought to restore government by the people, unmediated by party bosses in corrupt alliance with private interests and patronage. If given a chance, so this reasoning went, the people would rise to the demands of a higher citizenship. This populist element, the assumption that the average citizen was virtuous because he was not corrupted by temptations of power, has a strong Jeffersonian resonance and is especially evident in the appeal of such measures as the legislative initiative and referenda, and recall of elected officials. While this appeal often encouraged attitudes of moral arrogance and self-righteousness, it also confirmed the most powerful source of political legitimacy in America: that all power must be answerable to the people; the people are sovereign. This appeal draws on long-standing traditions of civic republicanism in American thought, but now freed from their location in states and homogeneous localities.

SOCIAL JUSTICE

Popular sovereignty must be expressed through laws and the laws must encode equal treatment and embody justice. Drawing on Hebraic ideals of American exceptionalism and Christian ideals of compassion, the appeal for social justice was especially appealing to members of the main Protestant churches. Their universities, colleges, and theological schools and their ecumenical publications and philanthropic associations were imbued with ideals of social justice informed by the moral and intellectual prestige of new social sciences and evolutionary theories of history. Hope for personal salvation, instilled by earlier waves of "awakenings" and revivals, fed into demands for social salvation, giving Progressive reform a religious fervor and evangelical energy that echoed the earlier antislavery crusades. Conversely, appeals to individual rights that did not serve the ends of social justice were condemned as politically and morally retrograde.

***

These four sets of ideas were not only linked at the level of individual and social psychology, they constituted a shared public narrative, part of a national story that combined past, present, and future into a powerful civic religion. It was this narrative that grounded both personal and collective identity. To attack and oppose any given set of ideals was to question both the integrity of the narrative and of the self. Rather than subscribing to a series of abstract *principles*, participants in this narrative were committed to substantive *projects* and to ways of living that were parts of those projects; thus the myriad of institutions, associations and organizations, and publications they both created and co-opted; thus the ways in which personal meaning and public purpose were expressed in voluntary political and social action.

Many of the ideals and styles of earlier Progressivism are alive and well today, but in a more politically disparate and culturally confused way. Nationalist and patriotic appeals are distrusted by much of the intellectual left, even as Democratic Party candidates often go out of their way to wrap themselves in the flag. Leaders of both parties freely use the patriotic rhetoric of "war," whether against poverty, drugs, or terrorism, to mobilize popular will for public ends. Populist appeals to a politics above parties are a recurring a feature of both "left" and "right" political movements and ideologies, as are the periodic creation of third parties to sponsor independent candidates (e.g., Nader, Anderson, and Perot). Appeals for social justice and equality are so entangled with identity and racial politics that it is difficult to see their relationship either to each other or to the larger national community. The downward path from the glory of the civil rights movement (America's last great "Progressive" moment) to the war on poverty and the Great Society so discredited liberal reform that even the term "liberalism" itself was taken as a reproach (indeed, it now appears that the term "progressive" has taken its place).

Many other areas of American life remain infused with earlier Progressive ideals but are, at this point, not part of a coherent political ideology capable of organizing a dominant political will. The first is the rapid and unprecedented rise of volunteer and community service activities in high schools and colleges. This volunteerism is mirrored in American responses to domestic and international catastrophes of every kind, whether man-made or natural. A student of American religion once suggested, only half seriously, that jogging was a Protestant sport (alone, painful, but good for you). In this same spirit, I suggest that certain features of environmentalism have become the post-Protestant American religion. The power of the environmentalist appeal affects conduct that ranges from the "micropolitics" of everyday sustainability rituals and consumption patterns to calls for a world authority to regulate carbon emissions. These values and commitments have had real effects on both political parties and on public policy, but they have not become part of a larger political ideology and national narrative. Whether these and earlier Progressive ideals will attain electoral salience will be explored in the postscript to this study.

Chapter Four

Progressivism as a National Narrative

It is important to get Progressivism right. The authors of its leading ideas founded the modern American university and created its disciplines and the journals that codified their thoughts. They completed the transformation of sectarian American Protestantism, begun before the Civil War, into an embracive, liberal, and evangelical civil religion. They created the ligaments of the national administrative and regulatory state and founded and supplied a mass national journalism independent of political party and church. They witnessed and helped legitimate the creation of a national financial and industrial corporate economy that soon became the engine driving the international economy, transforming America into the dominant world power. In the process, they sought to transform an older American liberalism anchored in natural rights and constitutional jurisprudence into a new socialized liberalism anchored in visions of evolutionary progress and the socialization of the self. If Americans cannot understand Progressivism on these terms, they have little hope of understanding themselves and the place of contemporary America in the world.

Lyman Abbott, Albion Small, and Simon Patten are exemplary figures in the intellectual and political success of Progressive political ideas. Each helped shape Progressive political and social thought in national universities, through national journalism and national professional and reform organizations, and by creating powerful reform networks that permeated American society and mobilized its talents and energies to transform the nation. These figures helped to institutionalize a new liberalism that came to dominate major sectors of American political culture and eventually its national politics.

Lyman Abbott (1835–1922) was chiefly known as the editor of *Outlook* (1881–1922), a weekly that began as *Christian Union*. The son of a New England Congregational minister, Lyman studied at New York University and began his career as a lawyer. Under the influence of the renowned preacher Henry Ward Beecher, however, Abbott left law practice to study theology, first serving churches in the Midwest during the Civil War and then directing the Freedmen's Union Commission that provided aid to white war refugees and black freedmen. Under Abbott's editorship, *Outlook* achieved a circulation of one hundred thousand, becoming the preeminent nonsectarian Protestant publication of its day. Following his presidency, Theodore Roosevelt became an associate editor. Booker T. Washington, Jacob Riis, and Edward Everett Hale,[1] along with Roosevelt, published their autobiographies in *Outlook* before releasing them as books. Albion Small and Richard T. Ely[2] were also contributors. Abbott's major book, *The Evolution of Christianity*, popularized the melding of social progress and liberal Christianity. It was continually published from 1892 through 1926 in seven editions. In addition to a popular biography of Henry Ward Beecher, whose pulpit Abbott himself occupied from 1888 to 1899, another major book was *The Rights of Man*, a series of lectures that advanced a theory of government integrating the writings of Hegel and prominent British and American political and social theorists. His thesis was that "self-government is not an assumption on which we are to start in framing a government; it is the goal which we are to reach by means of government." Democracy is not a form of government, but a way of being, "pervaded by the spirit, not merely of good will toward man, and of large hope for man, but also of faith in man."[3] He is credited with having coined and popularized the term "industrial democracy." Given his standing and connections with so many organizations and institutions, especially in the world of ecumenical Protestantism, his voice and his ideas were amplified to a mass audience.

Albion Small (1854–1926) was professor of sociology at the University of Chicago from its founding in 1892 until his death. He was a founding member and later president of the American Sociological Society and editor of *The American Journal of Sociology* (1895–1926). Small's father was a Congregational minister in Maine; his mother, Thankful Lincoln Small, was a descendent of Samuel Lincoln, Abraham Lincoln's earliest American ancestor. After degrees from Colby College and Newton Theological Institute, Albion studied in Germany and then returned to receive his PhD from Johns Hopkins University, whose social science faculty also trained in Germany. Albion Small was more influential as founding editor of *The American Journal of Sociology* than as a major sociological thinker. For more than thirty years Small used his journal as a sort of clearinghouse for Progressive ideas, welcoming Jane Addams, Florence Kelley, and Charlotte Perkins Gilman[4] to its pages, none of whom was a trained sociologist. The integration of women into sociology and reform was equally true professionally. The sociology department at Chicago welcomed its first female doctoral students in America in 1894 and, by the early 1900s, was producing one-third of all female social science PhDs in America.[5] Small wrote extensively on "social economy"—the relationship of the new industrial economy to family, social, and political life—and on the role of religion in social reform. He was a powerful link between academic sociology, the emerging profession of social work, and the rise of popular weekly and monthly magazines addressed to energetic and reform-minded women.

Simon Patten (1852–1922) was born in Illinois, the descendent of eighteenth-century Scotch-Irish settlers in New York. Educated at Northwestern and at Halle, where he received his PhD, Patten was one of the many German-trained founders and early presidents of the American Economic Association. Along with Albion Small and six of Patten's doctoral students, he was also one of the founders of the American Sociological Society, serving as its president as well. Patten followed Edmund J. James, another son of Illinois and a Halle PhD (and later president of the University of Illinois), to the University of Pennsylvania, where they were professors in the Wharton School, the newly founded professional business school that combined the study of economics, public finance, and business management. Together, Patten and James founded and lead the American Academy of Social and Political Science and edited its publication, the *Annals*. This journal became a high-level meeting place not only for German-trained academics in America, but also for leaders in business, finance, and government. Patton's analysis of wages, profits, and rents provided the basis for Charles Beard's analysis of the sources of political conflicts in America, starting with the Antifederalists and Federalists' conflict over the adoption of the constitution and continuing through party conflicts to the present day. Patten's basic argument that underlay Beard's political party analysis was simple: the major battle is not between workingmen and capitalists, but between the productivity and profits of the industrial economy and the somewhat parasitic benefits from rents, that is, unearned income from rising land values and local market monopolies that typified small-producer capitalism. The lesson is the one preached by William McKinley against William Jennings Bryan in the presidential election of 1896—the interests of workingmen lie in a thriving industrial capitalism producing economic surplus and not in a class alliance with marginal farmers, main street shop owners, and southern rentier interests against capitalists. Herbert Croly, whose book *Promise of American Life* (1909) became the definitive statement of national Progressivism, used this same argument in his discussion of the emergence of a permanent class of industrial wage earners. Patten's many graduate students (called Patten Men) included Walter Weyl of *The New Republic*, Edward Devine, general secretary of the New York Charity Organization Society, and two who later made major contributions to the New Deal: Rexford Tugwell and Frances Perkins. Patten is credited with inventing and popularizing the term "social work." Through the professionalization of social work and charity, articulated through its journal *Survey*, Patten's ideas concerning the social and political requirements of industrial democracy placed both family life and social welfare at the center of his analysis.

Three features animate the thought of Abbott, Small, Patten, and other major Progressive intellectuals. The first is the primacy of a narrative. This narrative was historicist in its outline of American's national history and destiny. This historicism, in turn, was grounded in Protestant evangelical theology and Hegelian philosophy, seeing the structural changes in American social and economic life as signs of an emerging morality and spirit that would lead to the reconstruction of American society and its leading role in world history. It was this shared narrative vision, I suggest, that fused together Progressivism and Protestantism, providing the moral, intellectual, and institutional basis for political mobilization. Placed in this larger narrative framework, their social political ideas reached a large and receptive mass audience. A second feature of Progressive thought flows directly from the primacy of narrative, namely, its hostility to "principled" or abstract-philosophical forms of political and social thought because these were thought to be major barriers to democratic reform. This hostility took many forms, but its chief targets were classical economic theory and prevailing forms of constitutional jurisprudence, both of which treated rights as preexisting, fixed, and freestanding entities that stand outside of social, economic, and political life. The third feature of Progressive thought is its confidence that historical modes of social and political inquiry would produce "laws" of progress that should guide practice and provide a set of values that would integrate self and society on a democratic foundation.

Five topics central to Progressivism contain these animating features. The first is their intense national patriotism. The Progressives believed that the American nation, if it prepared itself, was destined to become a world-historical actor, shaping the history of the modern world. The second is the new industrial economy and its centrality in the new social sciences. Progressives believed that organized social knowledge would make manifest the relationship between material and moral progress. The third topic is the Progressive call for new ethical and civic values required of this new economic and social order. These values were thought to be immanent in the new industrial economy and in the path that social knowledge was taking. The fourth topic is the religious dimension of this same evolutionary argument, expressed by the term the "social gospel." The last topic is the Progressive attack on "principles," with particular attention paid to the role of constitutional jurisprudence and law in American political institutions and practices. I conclude with some reflections on the achievements and ironies of Progressive political thought both in terms of the path of academic political theory after the Progressive Era and in terms of the rise of conservative political thought in the last quarter of the twentieth century.

AMERICA AS A DEMOCRATIC NATION

Progressive intellectuals were children of staunch Republican Party parents who saw Lincoln as the defining figure in American life. Herbert Croly identifies Lincoln as the one American political leader who had the intelligence and courage to see that the issue of slavery in the territories was not resolvable inside the bounds of the constitution and laws as currently understood. And because he forged a new understanding of the constitution, slavery was destroyed and America was refounded on a more national and democratic basis.[6] The challenge in confronting the new industrial economy is a direct parallel to that of slavery. In her textbook on social ideals in English letters, Vida Dutton Scudder, a professor of literature at Wellesley, made the Civil War "the third great episode in the national struggle for freedom," which now calls us to a fourth task, that of realizing "a spiritual democracy for the victims and outcasts of the Old World" now on American shores.[7] To Lyman Abbott, who as a young man heard Lincoln's Cooper Union address in 1860,[8] Lincoln gave us the principles we now need to address the labor problem in America.[9]

Lincoln and the Civil War symbolized for the Progressives a new commitment—they would say "covenant"—of the American people to create a democratic nation. The period following the Civil War was largely a betrayal of that commitment, as American political life retreated back into a party-dominated politics of electoral corruption, patronage, and the dominance of powerful economic interests.[10] Rededication to building a national democracy would require painful adjustments in ways of thinking about American citizenship, about economic life, and even about religion and the family.

In an article, "The Bonds of Nationality," Albion Small nicely summarizes what is required to create a real nation. National bonds primarily consist of four elements, (1) a common language, (2) race solidarity, (3) a coherent family type, and (4) a convincing religion.[11] The achievement and strengthening of all four bonds of nationality require substantial political, economic, and social reforms. The goal of the new science of sociology is to depict, organize, and make meaningful the democratic social forces that serve these bonds of nationality.[12] "The American democracy can trust its interest to the national interest," said Herbert Croly, "because national cohesion is dependent, not only upon certain forms of historical association, but upon fidelity to a democratic principle." The rise of national industrial, financial, legal, political, and labor leaders who operate outside of democratic controls "are driving new wedges into American national cohesion." At the turn of the twentieth century, "the American people are not prepared for a higher form of democracy, because they are not prepared for a more coherent and intense national life." The nationalization of the American people, so brilliantly evidenced by the North in the Civil War, should not mean, however, "merely to centralize their government." Indeed, now, "among those branches of the American national organization which are greatly in need of nationalizing is the central government" itself.[13]

Academics like Small and Patten, and "public intellectuals" like Abbott, placed extraordinary faith in the capacity of national institutions like the universities, public education, churches, professional associations, national magazines, and national reform organizations to become effective schools for national democratic citizenship. From this base, they thought, it might even be possible to transform political parties into nationally oriented institutions instead of temporary and expedient coalitions of local and special interests to capture the national government and reap the spoils of victory. To break through the institutional and legal barriers to reform first requires the emancipation from "traditional illusions," chief among them, according to Croly, the "tendency to regard the existing constitution with superstitious awe, and to shrink with horror from modifying it even in the smallest detail." If this emancipation is not achieved, "the American ideal will have to be fitted to the rigid and narrow lines of a few legal formulas; and the ruler of the American spirit, like the ruler of the Jewish spirit of old, will become the lawyer." To affirm a new covenant between nationality and democracy— what Croly termed a fusion between Hamilton and Jefferson—would be "in truth equivalent to a new Declaration of Independence" because it would affirm of right of the American people "to organize their political, economic, and social life in the service of a comprehensive, a lofty, and far-reaching democratic purpose."[14] Largely through Theodore Roosevelt's "new nationalism" and the formation of the Progressive Party as a party "above parties," Croly's ideas helped translate a generation of academic discourse to a popular audience.

THE NEW POLITICAL ECONOMY

Nowhere were democratic values more lacking than in the organization of the industrial economy. As talented as they were, both business and labor "bosses" wielded undemocratic power to serve narrow and self-interested ends. The existence of a permanent and rapidly expanding class of wage-laborers was the central theme in all braches of the social sciences in the new research universities. Whether the issue be the specific ones of public education, city government, assimilation of the new immigrants, and public health or the broader issues of political democracy and social justice, the new industrial economy was central in their analysis. Two formative books giving shape to this perspective were *Studies in the Evolution of Industrial Society* and *Outlines of Economics*, both by Richard T. Ely. Interestingly, these books were first published as part of a "home reading series" of the Chautauqua movement, a Methodist-inspired summer camp and later a national lectureship series, dedicated to melding together nondoctrinal Christianity, family life, ethical values, and responsible citizenship. *Outlines* became the standard text in college economics courses, published continuously, in many revisions, between 1893 and 1939. A central thesis of both books is this: "The multiplying relations of men with one another give us a new economic world. These relations require regulation, in order to preserve freedom. The regulation by the power of the state of these industrial and other social relations existing among men is an essential condition of freedom."[15] Behind that simple thesis lies a much more complex understanding of what constitutes social knowledge and how that knowledge is to be obtained. Ely and Simon Patten largely drafted the statement of principles adopted at the formation of the American Economic Association in 1895. They might well have been speaking of the Progressive ideals of the social sciences generally:

1. We regard the state as an agency whose positive assistance is one of the indispensable conditions of human progress.
2. We believe that political economy as a science is still in an early stage of its development. While we appreciate the work of former economists, we look, not so much to speculation as to the historical and statistical study of actual conditions of economic life for the satisfactory accomplishment of that development.
3. We hold that the conflict of labor and capital has brought into prominence a vast number of social problems, whose solution requires the united efforts, each in its own sphere, of the church, of the state, and of science.
4. In the study of the industrial and commercial policy of governments we take no partisan attitude. We believe in a progressive development of economic conditions, which must be met by a corresponding development of legislative policy.[16]

Albion Small seconded the primacy of the new industrial economy to the study of sociology.

A large part of the confusion in the present stage of transition is due to our acquiescence in conceptions of capital as an exclusively economic phenomenon, and in corollaries from those conceptions which act as automatic adjusters of conduct to those unmoral conceptions. Conflicts centering around capital press for convincing analysis of capital as a social phenomenon . . .

The clue to a primary analysis of capital from the social standpoint may be found in the question: To what extent is the effectiveness of capital in the economic process due to unaided acts of the owner; and to what extent is its effectiveness conferred by acts of others than the owner?

When the answer to this question is partially made out, it shows that there are three distinct types of capital, considered as a social phenomenon, viz., first, capital which is used solely by the owner; second, capital which is used by the owner in some sort of dependence upon the acts of others; third, capital which is employed, as such, wholly by others than the owner, and under conditions which he does not and could not maintain by his individual power. [17]

The most original and far-ranging of the new German-trained political and social economists was Simon Patten. He took as given the superiority of large-scale, integrated economic organizations and was little troubled by either European cartels or American trusts. What did concern Patten were the social and political implications of these new entities, most especially the implications flowing from their ability to produce ever-cheaper and more abundant goods and services. "In modern nations," he maintains, "the productive power is more than sufficient to produce the minimum of existence. There is a social surplus above the costs of production in which every worker has a right to share." [18] While these rights are different from earlier conceptions of political and civil rights, they share the same ends.

The rights upon which political freedom depends have already been worked out. They were obtained by picturing a primitive society where men were so isolated that their relations were simple and plain. The problem of economic freedom is to find a modern equivalent for the rights that in earlier times went with land. The workman of to-day should have all that the landowner of the past enjoyed. Freedom consists not merely of political rights, but is dependent upon the possession of economic rights, freely recognized and universally granted to each man by his fellow citizens. [19]

The kinds of rights Patten had in mind were all tied, directly or indirectly, to protecting the production of abundance and to the wise use of the social surplus. The first set of rights he lists are "Public or Market Rights," including rights to an open market, to publicity (transparency), to security, and to association. Among "Social Rights" are rights to a home, to personal development, to wholesome moral standards, to homogeneity of population, and to decisions by public opinion. Among "Rights to Leisure" are provisions for recreation, clean air and water, and a pleasing visual environment. Among "Exceptional Rights" Patten calls for family provision in the event of unemployment or industrial accidents and for rights to an income for both single women and for women whose husbands have been injured or killed in the line of work. [20]

Behind these programmatic proposals lay Patten's larger theory of human progress, best summarized in his book on the changing requirements of charity and social work, *The New Basis of Civilization*.

> There can be no permanent progress until poverty has been eliminated, for then only will the normally evolving man, dominant through numbers and keen mental powers, force adjustments, generation by generation, which will raise the general level of intellect and character. And when poverty is gone, the last formidable obstacle to the upward movement of the race will have disappeared.[21]

For Patten, ideals are not outside of material life and history, but are immanent in the phenomenal world. Through *Survey* these ideas and ideals soon permeated religious, charitable, and philanthropic communities and became built into the professional training of social workers—in turn constituting a powerful and ideologically coherent constituency in the Progressive Party.[22]

THE NEW DEMOCRATIC ETHIC

Behind Patten's theory of material progress and the means of its achievement is an evolutionary ethical theory that informed theological speculation as well. The transition that marks the coming age is from a pain and scarcity economy to a pleasure and abundance economy. According to Patten, a Hobbesian world of law backed by fear of punishment required a Judeo-Christian God as ruler and punisher. These beliefs and doctrines are now barriers to God's continuing revelation. The new Christ "comes not as the ruler of men, but as their servant." In a society of plenty, the greatest dangers are not external persecution and exploitation, but internal temptation: we need "a model for imitation, one who remains pure even though subject to the passions and temptations of men." In the coming era, "intelligence and self-control will be the great virtues," spread through imitation and inspiration. This process is already evident in America, the most economically advanced nation on earth.[23]

Many other Progressives voiced this call for a new democratic ethic. In one of his earliest essays, John Dewey sought to identify the specifically ethical dimensions of democracy. Any ethical conception, in his view, must reject from the start an abstract and mathematical conception of democracy, reducing men "into merely numerical individuals, into ballot-projecting units," and this concept's handmaidens, the traditional political parties.[24] Ethical democracy rests on the fact that "Society and the individual are really organic to each other . . . He is not merely its image or mirror. He is the localized manifestation of its life."[25] In a socialized and ethical democracy, social progress and personal development are interdependent because both require "a unified and articulate will."[26] Without this will, every association for the achievement of common ends would remain temporary and artificial. In his coauthored and widely used textbook, *Ethics*, he stated it this way: "A common end which is not made such by common, free voluntary coöperation in process of achievement is common in name only. It has no support and guarantee in the activities which it is supposed to benefit, because it is not the fruit of those activities. Hence, it does not stay put. It has to be continually buttressed by appeal to external, not voluntary, considerations; bribes of pleasure, threats of harm, use of force. It has to be undone and done over."[27]

The effective embodiment of a common moral will requires a coherent and consensual "public opinion." The many Progressive social scientists who wrote on public opinion shared this view of its crucial role in democratic theory. In the words of the social psychologist Charles Horton Cooley, "public opinion is no mere aggregate of separate individual judgments, but an organization, a cooperative product of communication and reciprocal influence." To the sociologist Franklin Giddings, "society is democratic only when all people without distinction of rank or class participate in the making of public opinion and of moral authority."[28]

The increased role of public opinion not only marks the progress of democratic government, it signals a higher moral consciousness. Cooley's social psychology textbook put it this way: "The present epoch . . . brings with it a larger and, potentially at least, a higher and freer consciousness . . . The general or public phase of larger consciousness is what we call Democracy. I mean by this primarily the organized sway of public opinion. It works out also in a tendency to humanize the collective life, to make institutions express the higher impulses of human nature, instead of brutal or mechanical conditions."[29]

Jane Addams was the most eloquent spokesman for a new democratic ethic. Famous for the establishment of Hull House in Chicago, the female residents of which were soon to lead a host of Progressive reform organizations and causes, Addams was also a prolific and influential writer. In an early essay, "The Subjective Necessity of Social Settlements," her starting point is educated young people who "are seeking an outlet for that sentiment of universal brotherhood which the best spirit of our times is forcing from an emotion into a motive." Educated young people especially feel a great gap between their impulses and their actions.

> They feel a fatal want of harmony between their theory and their lives, a lack of co-ordination between thought and action . . . These young men and women, longing to socialize their democracy, are animated by certain hopes . . . These hopes may be loosely formulated thus: that if in a democratic country nothing can be permanently achieved save through the masses of the people, it

will be impossible to establish a higher political life than the people themselves crave; that it is difficult to see how the notion of a higher civic life can be fostered save through common intercourse; that the blessings which we associate with a life of refinement and cultivation can be made universal and must be made universal if they are to be permanent; that the good we secure for ourselves is precarious and uncertain, is floating in mid-air, until it is secured for all of us and incorporated into our common life.[30]

The new democratic ethic was a call to a higher form of democratic citizenship, one that was premised on a citizenry emancipated through education and ethically centered religious beliefs from narrow partisan, regional, and economic interests. It was no wonder, then, that the Progressive Party was premised on just this set of values.

.

THE NEW SOCIAL GOSPEL

Progressives not only acknowledged the importance of moral and religious vanguards, they made identification with this vanguard a large part of their appeal. This, I think, is most evident in those who explicitly combined Protestant evangelicalism and Progressive social reform. In the antebellum period, "evangelizing" America meant planting churches and colleges in the west and forming ecumenical reform associations. Post–Civil War "social Christianity" was unique, first in its alliance with the new social sciences and then in its equanimity at the prospect of having much of the church's social and charitable mission taken over by governmental or other secular institutions.

These two features were not begrudged concessions to something called "modernity" or "secularization," but were welcomed and, indeed, more or less implicit in liberal-evangelical theology and in its evolutionary theory of history. Lyman Abbott wrote three books on the evolution of Christianity. The first traces the history of Christianity as a spiritual force, the second as a social development, and the third as an evolving ethical system.[31] When the three books are set alongside two other books of Abbott's, on the history and evolution of human freedom and on the making of America,[32] the result is a comprehensive narrative underpinning for the Progressive reform project.[33]

Abbott's evolutionary historicism—the theory that higher and more democratic ideals were immanent in the development of new forms of social, economic, and religious life—fed into and reinforced the new national narrative of American exceptionalism. All of his books substantiated what was called a "New Theology" in American Protestantism that sought to integrate the fruits of higher learning and historical scholarship into Christianity. Many of these fruits grew in German universities; in that sense, Abbott was restating at second hand the scholarly conclusions of American churchmen and professors who studied in Germany beginning in the 1830s and extending well into the early twentieth century.[34]

Because it had its origin in the colleges and seminaries of New England Protestantism,[35] the New Theology was also called the New Puritanism.[36] Abbott's formulation was a common one:

> New Theology is neither new nor a theology . . . [but] new only in contrast with the Puritan theology out of which is has sprung, and from which it is a reaction. It is not truly a theology, since its chief inspiration is a deep desire to get away from the questions of the purely speculative intellect, the answers to which constitute theology, to the practical questions of the Hebrew seers, the answers to which constitute religion . . . The church, then, is coming more and more to conceive of God, not as some one outside of his creation ruling *over* it, but as some one inside his creation ruling *within* it.[37]

Most striking in Abbott's religious historicism is his contrast of pagan Rome and holy Israel. While this contrast is central to his analysis of the history of the church after Constantine and up to the Reformation,[38] its larger meaning is theological and political. History is the unfolding of the age-old struggle between Roman "imperialism" and Hebraic "democracy." Fulfillment in history, both spiritual and material, is the victory of democracy. The Reformation, especially as it developed in England and the American colonies, was where the battle between "ecclesiastical imperialism" and liberty was most aggressively joined.[39]

Interwoven in Abbott's political-ecclesiastical history is a history of ideas, a *Geistesgeschichte*. Luther, Calvin, and Cromwell are joined by Copernicus and Bacon, who are soon joined by Rousseau, Voltaire, and Hegel. Abbott's lectures, published as *The Rights of Man*, are accompanied by a list of books that inform each chapter. Hegel is the first listed, joined by John Stuart Mill and his major followers, John Morley and Frederic Harrison, the liberal statesman William Gladstone, and social reformers Sidney and Beatrice Webb. The American churchman Josiah Strong is listed alongside of prominent Progressive intellectuals Franklin Giddings, Richard Ely, and H. D. Lloyd, who are, in turn, joined by political leaders Theodore Roosevelt and Booker T. Washington. To enlist under the banner of the New Theology was to become part of the social gospel narrative of achieving social justice and to march with the most enlightened and morally advanced intellectuals and leaders of the modern era.

The New Theology is a social and not a theological gospel because religion is seen to migrate from out of the constraints of creed and church in order to permeate the larger society with its higher ethic and advancing social knowledge. America, as the highest embodiment of democracy, is also the highest embodiment of Christianity, for the two are one.[40] In the words of an astute historian of the impulses of liberal Protestantism: "A key paradox of [American] liberal Protestantism—one that must be a cornerstone of any history of liberal Protestantism—is that its goal has always been, in part, to sanctify the secular, to bring forth out of the natural and human worlds the divine potential contained within them. Secularization can be seen, in some of its forms, as a sign of success for liberal Protestantism, not a marker of defeat."[41]

The millennial and utopian strains in Progressive political thought came largely from an alliance of social gospel writers with the emerging science of sociology. Indeed, sociology was seen as the special voice of God's progressive revelation.[42] A meeting of Wisconsin Congregationalists in 1895 proclaimed "the right of sociology to demand that theology be ethicized" and that "the best book for social guidance is the New Testament; the best commentaries are the works of scientific sociology."[43] This alliance declared war on "individualism" and its intellectual allies. Echoing the critique of individualism by political economists, but with a more moralistic edge, Samuel Zane Batten declared in *The Christian State*, "just so far as democracy means the enthronement of self-interest and the apotheosis of individual desire . . . so far it becomes an iniquitous and dangerous thing." George Herron, in *The Christian Society*, declared that "the law of self-interest is the eternal falsehood that mothers all social and private woes; for sin is pure individualism." Simon Patten, who often wrote for social gospel publications, lists as one of the ten principles of social Christianity, "the doctrine of social responsibility in contrast to individual rights."[44]

The calls for a new political economy, a new social ethic, and a revitalized social Christianity combined to constitute a deep indictment of America's commitment in the Gilded Age to constitutionalism and a rights-based discourse. Whether the issue be states rights, the claims of private property, the sanctity of contract, or, more generally, the power of courts to intervene in industrial disputes and overturn legislative will, Progressives now had an armory of weapons to challenge prevailing legal values. More broadly, their project was to transform and reconstitute the older liberalism on a new ethical and social basis.

THE PROGRESSIVES' PROBLEM WITH PRINCIPLES

With the exception of Oliver Wendell Holmes (1841–1935), whom Theodore Roosevelt appointed to the Supreme Court in 1902, Progressives displayed a thinly disguised contempt for the American legal mind and its institutional expressions in the upper bar and the courts.[45] Herbert Croly, in his call for reform in *Promise of American Life*, simply dismissed the legal profession as unqualified to make any positive contribution to this effort.[46] In *Progressive Democracy*, Croly extends this criticism to the constitution itself when viewed as standing above and outside of democratic political life:

> Public opinion can no longer be hypnotized and scared into accepting the traditional constitutionalism, as the final word in politics . . .
>
> The Law in the shape of the Federal Constitution really came to be a monarchy of the Word . . . Thus the aspirations and the conviction of the early democrats that popular political authority should be righteously expressed hardened into a system, which consecrated one particular machinery of possibly righteous expression . . .
>
> The Constitution was really king. Once the kingdom of the Word had been ordained, it was almost as seditious to question the Word as it was to plot against the kingdom. A monarch exists to be obeyed. In the United States, as in other monarchies, unquestioning obedience was erected into the highest of political virtues.[47]

Croly admits that, like European monarchy, American constitutionalism initially served educative political purposes.

> The monarchy of the Constitution satisfied the current needs and the contemporary conscience of the American nation. Its government was at once authoritative, national and educational. It instructed the American people during their collective childhood. It trained them during their collective youth. With its assistance the American people have become a nation. They have been habituated to mutual association and joint action.[48]

This age has now passed. Democracy and the monarchy of the constitution are now in conflict, and monarchy must give way.

> The ideal of individual justice is being supplemented by the ideal of social justice. . . . Now the tendency is to conceive the social welfare, not as an end which cannot be left to the happy harmonizing of individual interests, but as an end which must be consciously willed by society and efficiently realized. Society, that is, has become a moral ideal, not independent of the individual but supplementary to him, an ideal which must be pursued less by regulating individual excesses than by the active conscious encouragement of socializing tendencies and purposes.[49]

Behind this critique of the constitution and law lay a social science that posited the growing power of "public opinion" and internal moral controls as the evolutionary mark of democracy. As the sociologist Edward Ross explained,

Public opinion has the advantage of a *wide gamut* of influences. By thus supplementing the coarse and rough sanctions of the law, society avoids putting itself into such undisguised opposition to a man's wishes, and is not so likely to raise the spirit of rebellion. Its blame does not exclude moral suasion, and its ban does not renounce all appeal to the feelings.

Public opinion is *less mechanical* in operation than law. The public can weigh provocation better, and can take into account condoning or aggravating circumstances of time, place, motive, or office. The blade of the law playing up and down in its groove with iron precision is hardly so good a regulative instrument as the flexible lash of public censure. [50]

Given this array of arguments, we should not be surprised at the openness of the Progressive Party to proposals to reign in the courts to make them more responsive to popular will. [51]

In a 1924 essay, "Logical Method and the Law," Dewey drew out the larger implications of this argument. At the forefront of his analysis were the writings of Justice Holmes; in the background lay an evolutionary theory of history and human development. Logical systemization in legal decisions, Dewey begins, is a necessary part of any instrumental reasoning and, "while it may be an end in itself for a particular student, is clearly in last resort subservient to the economical and effective reaching of decisions in particular cases." Legal logic, then, "is ultimately an empirical and concrete discipline," but, by a process of natural selection "of the methods which afford the better type of conclusion," those selected become clarified by logical analysis and hardened into scientific formulas. [52]

Despite this underlying experiential practice, courts must justify their decisions through exposition. The logic of exposition is, however, quite different from the experimental logic of search and discovery.

It is at this point that the chief stimulus and temptation to mechanical logic and abstract use of formal concepts come in. Just because the personal element cannot be wholly excluded, while at the same time the decision must assume as nearly as possible an impersonal, objective, rational form, the temptation is to surrender the vital logic which has actually yielded the conclusion and to substitute for it forms of speech which are rigorous in appearance and which give an illusion of certitude. [53]

Dewey concludes his argument on a historicist note. Most contemporary principles of law, especially those regarding property and contract, were shaped in and through the experience of the eighteenth century, when "the great social need was emancipation of industry and trade from a multitude of restrictions which held over from the feudal estate of Europe." Now, however, one sees "in the present reaction against the individualistic formulae of an older liberalism" an "intermittent tendency in the direction of legislation, and to a less [sic] extent of judicial decision, towards what is vaguely known as 'social justice,' toward formulae of a collectivistic character." Those who continue "the sanctification of ready-made antecedent universal principles as methods of thinking" are "the chief obstacle to the kind of thinking which is the indispensable prerequisite of steady, secure and intelligent social reforms in general and social advance by means of law in particular."[54]

The "kind of thinking" that Dewey had in mind already lay at hand in the new social sciences. In the 1890s, the political economist Henry Carter Adams wrote two definitive articles in which he charged that contemporary legal thinking was so far removed from the realities of contemporary economic relationships that resort to force by both capital and labor became inevitable.[55] In the first volume of *American Journal of Sociology*, also in the 1890s, Albion Small launched a critique of prevailing ideas of property and contract in the face of the rise of large business corporations.[56] Roscoe Pound, who began his twenty-year tenure as dean of Harvard Law School in 1916, wrote three very influential articles in the previous decade that made his reputation and became programmatic statements for legal reformers.[57] He concludes one of them with a call to integrate the new social sciences into jurisprudence.

> Let us look to economics and sociology and philosophy, and cease to assume that jurisprudence is self-sufficient. It is the work of lawyers to make the law in action conform to the law in the books, not by futile thunderings against popular lawlessness, nor eloquent exhortations to obedience of the written law, but by making the law in the books such that the law in action can conform to it, and providing a speedy, cheap and efficient legal mode of applying it. On no other terms can the two be reconciled.[58]

The energy and tenacity of the Progressive attack on prevailing juridical and constitutional thinking eventually had its intended effects. By the 1920s— well after the electoral energies of Progressivism had been spent—the key assumptions and values of Progressivism were institutionalized in the curricula of elite law schools, in the federal regulatory bureaucracy, and eventually in the judiciary. By the time of the great realigning election of 1932, the New Deal not only found a well-developed administrative branch to serve its ends, it found a court system that increasingly deferred to the will of legislative majorities and expert administrators.

ACHIEVEMENTS AND IRONIES

Thanks to the antislavery movement, the victory of the Union armies in the Civil War, and the hegemonic electoral victory of the Republican Party in 1896, the intellectual, moral, and political leadership of the Progressives at the turn of the last century led to a substantial fulfillment of earlier Whig visions of American nationality. Adding to the Whig call to nationalize existing institutions, however, the Progressives created many new and more embracive ones. While many of these institutions were top-down in organization and leadership, an equal number were bottom-up federations, joining local and regional organizations to national ones.

This nationalization—including the nationalization of governmental institutions—had a curious two-edged effect. On the one hand, it "politicized" private and local activities to the extent that they voiced ends that were explicitly tied to larger national purposes. In the earlier world of the Whigs, this transformation was largely within Protestant churches and the ecumenical reform organizations they created. The Progressives went much further in creating a nonsectarian, nationally oriented, and richly complex "civil society" with these same politicized features. And second, like the Whigs, they "moralized" many political organizations and activities by infusing them with quasi-religious purposes. No better example of this process can be found than in the sudden formation of the Progressive Party and its ability to field candidates for state and national office in almost every region of the country.

The election of 1912 represented the highpoint of Progressive ideas in popular political culture. All three parties, but especially the Progressive Party, a newly formed breakaway from the Republicans, touted various aspects of a Progressive agenda. While all three candidates won a substantial share of the vote, the Democratic candidate, Woodrow Wilson, prevailed, with more than 6.6 million votes. However, Theodore Roosevelt, the Progressive candidate, received 4.13 million votes, more than half a million more votes than the Republican Party regular, William Howard Taft. The Progressive Party nominating convention, held in Chicago in August, exhibited a distinctly evangelical Protestant style. Every delegate was given five minutes for political testimony. Theodore Roosevelt's address was titled "Confession of Faith." Periodically, the delegates would break out singing "Battle Hymn of the Republic." Following the keynote address by former senator Albert Beveridge, the audience sang "Onward, Christian Soldiers" as they paraded through the hall—led by the head of the New York delegation, Oscar S. Straus, a prominent Jewish political leader. Their platform documented the success of more than three decades of Progressive political and social thought, especially its planks on social and industrial justice. [59]

In addition to shaping and institutionalizing a national language of democratic reform, a second major Progressive achievement was to link the systematic pursuit of social knowledge to political reform and thereby to tie higher education and the learned professions to the cause of national democracy. Given the undeveloped administrative capacity of the national government, this tie did not yield European "statism," but it did set up durable patterns of cooperation between the universities, the national government, large business corporations, and, later, national charitable foundations, labor unions, and the military.[60] One important result was the development of "welfare capitalism"—what Simon Patten termed "voluntary socialism"—as large corporations took on many functions that in Europe were provided by governments.[61] Another important side effect of these ties was the turning of many academic social scientists into well-known "public intellectuals" (or, better, "public moralists") writing for popular magazines, speaking to large nonacademic gatherings, and cultivating strong personal ties with nonacademic reform leaders from many walks of life.[62] As reform leaders became national institutional elites, so did many academics.

Lastly, the combined effects of Progressive ideas, organizations, and energies helped to complete a new national self-consciousness and national identity. In a recent book on regime periods in American history, Michael Lind, a prominent liberal journalist and public intellectual, distinguishes between "government framers" and "people founders" in shaping new political regimes.[63] Surely, the Progressives can be said to have completed much of Abraham Lincoln's task of refounding America, not so much in terms of formal governmental institutions, but in how we see these institutions in relation to shared national purposes and to the entire complex of other national institutions that shared these purposes. No matter how deeply "rights talk" came later to penetrate American reformist political discourse, an enduring legacy of the Progressives was to ask that all rights claims be tied to durable national ends.[64]

Recent books by political theorists and public intellectuals on the left have reasserted the relevance of the Progressivism tradition for our own times.[65] These commentators see the era beginning in the 1980s—economic restructurings and dislocations, growing inequalities of wealth and income, and the explosive growth of immigration—as a new Gilded Age, calling for an intellectual and political response modeled on that of the Progressive generation one hundred years earlier. Insofar as Progressivism is seen as the progenitor of the New Deal liberalism—itself a contentious view—there is a certain irony in this contemporary hope by the American left for a rebirth of Progressivism. With the exception of a long train of electoral losses (partially stemmed by the election of 2008), liberalism continues to enjoy a hegemonic position in the American university and its law schools, in public education, in most professional associations, in the national media, and in the upper reaches of the mainline Protestant churches and much of the Catholic Church. When to these redoubts are added much of corporate America and almost all of the major charitable foundations, and much of the federal judiciary and bureaucracy, calls by liberals for a rebirth of Progressivism seem excessive.

There is, however, a deeper reason for this call, and it involves narrative. The rise of "value-neutral" readings of liberal democracy begun in the mid-twentieth century[66] and the turn to Rawlsian and Kantian versions of democratic liberalism—especially in constitutional understandings—have entailed the virtual abandonment of national narrative by American liberalism. Contemporary liberalism not only lacks a compelling narrative, it seems actively hostile in principle to the very idea of a national narrative—let alone a *sacred* one—that honors "ascriptive" or "ethnocentric" values.[67] There have been some notable exceptions.

The opening line of Richard Rorty's 1997 Massey Lectures at Harvard reads: "National pride is to countries what self-respect is to individuals: a necessary condition of self-improvement." Lamenting "a widespread sense that national pride is no longer appropriate" among leftist intellectuals, Rorty draws a sharp contrast between contemporary and early twentieth-century leftist thought as between "spectators" and "agents." The agency of these earlier reformers (he cites Herbert Croly) was anchored in the earlier national patriotism of Abraham Lincoln and Walt Whitman.[68] Lacking a patriotic and sacred national story, today's left "has no projects to propose to America, no vision of a country to be achieved by building a consensus on the need for specific reforms." A "thoroughgoing secularism" leaves reformers without either a national narrative or a reform-oriented civil religion of the kind prefigured in John Dewey. Rorty concludes that, while America clearly has a cultural left, it does not have a political one; therefore, "the Left is unable to engage in national politics." To reengage the cultural left in politics requires that it can no longer "take the point of view of a detached cosmopolitan spectator."[69]

A more complex attempt to create a liberal national narrative is made by the political theorist Rogers Smith in *Stories of Peoplehood*.[70] This study is important for three reasons. The first is that it so consciously explores the various forms that national narratives take and the range of purposes they serve. Second, while the study clearly distinguishes stories of peoplehood from universalistic liberal-democratic principles, it recognizes their necessary interdependence. Thirdly, this study comes on the heels of his earlier book *Civic Ideals*, a story of America's seemingly endless betrayal of our universalistic civic ideals.[71] And because it was a wholly principled antinarrative, *Civic Ideals* resonated perfectly with the academic and intellectual left that Rorty charged with being "unable to engage in national politics." Proof of this inability is that *Civic Ideals* quickly became adorned with national academic awards.[72]

Civic Ideals was a mea culpa, cataloging the constitutional and legal ways by which African Americans, Native Americans, and women were denied full membership in the political community. Smith posits that these exclusions flow logically from defining the political community in "ascriptive" terms, that is, terms not based on the universal principle of equal individual consent. The persistent worry in *Civic Ideals* is why Americans seem so willing and able to heed the siren calls of ascriptive national identity in the face of their foundational liberal and civic republican principles. Smith's answer is simple but troubling. In a political democracy "aspirants to power require a population to lead that imagines itself to be a 'people,'" driving "political leaders to offer civic ideologies, or myths of civic identity" in order to achieve power.[73] Smith's somewhat tepid proposal is that holders of universal liberal principles—for him the authentic ground of American identity—must condescend to form a "party" with an ideology and myth of civic identity in order to compete against illiberal narratives.[74]

In *Stories of Peoplehood*, Smith revisits the issues raised in *Civic Ideals*, but with a decided shift in emphasis. All political regimes, even liberal-democratic ones, are now said to *require* "ethically constitutive stories."

> The problem is not only that, politically, we probably cannot hope to shape communities that can long endure unless people see them as expressing more than their procedural agreements and senses of abstract justice . . . On these accounts, so long as one preaches democracy, particular memberships then can be expected to emerge rather organically out of fundamentally extra-political factors. But since those "extra-political" forms of intersection and mutual effect need to be articulated in politics as bases of collaboration . . . the pressures and dangers that impel reliance on ethically constitutive accounts of whole particular political societies cannot be escaped . . . Citizens are at a minimum morally entitled to understand the commitments of those to whom they are entrusting their political destinies.[75]

Even though "the politics of people-making . . . involves continual . . . often invidious, and always exclusionary processes centered on stories and force . . . these processes also do much to make us who we are and to make it possible for us to flourish on this earth." The philosophical requirements of political life seem now to include a national narrative at its very center. "I therefore doubt," Smith concludes, "that any kind of politics of peoplehood . . . is likely to get far in transforming the world for the better if it simply takes the form of an assault on or dismissal of American national identity." These assertions are in direct response to those who would constrain democratic discourse to that which meets philosophically fixed standards of "public reason." These constrainers "appear to deny, either hypocritically or foolishly, that their own views also express controversial ethically constitutive accounts of human beings that are far from self-evident truths."[76]

Whatever the implications the arguments by Rorty and Smith have for the philosophical foundations of contemporary liberal-democratic political theory, there is no question that their calls for national narrative are in response to the rise of a coherently conservative Republican Party over the past three decades. This rise suggests an irony in contemporary American political thought, namely, that the rise of contemporary conservatism bears some close resemblances to the rise of Progressivism. Like Progressivism, contemporary conservatism began as an intellectual counterculture against a prevailing set of frozen possibilities and static visions. It was now liberalism that seemed frozen, first in its static models of "interest-group pluralism" and then in its legalistic formulas of identity-group pluralism. [77] Neither formulation embodied a coherent notion of the public good or a shared ideal of national purpose. Given the demise of Cold War patriotism during the Vietnam War period, the only remaining symbol of national unity for liberalism was an abstract and philosophically grounded rights discourse through which to read the constitution. Unfortunately, this discourse has been used primarily to buttress the traditional favorites in the old system of interest groups or to sponsor new favorites in the emerging system of racial, gender, and identity-group politics.

What this conclusion suggests is that contemporary conservatism in America might owe the Progressives more than it acknowledges, both in shaping public policy consistently oriented to national purposes and in enlisting the political, moral, and spiritual energies of those who wish to participate as public-regarding citizens of their country. The Progressives drew their core values from Lincoln's conception of the American people as a nation with shared substantive purposes. How and through what means these purposes were to be achieved was not preordained and fixed for all time because the nation was a living and evolving organism. In the fight against slavery, for example, Lincoln depended less upon prevailing constitutional truths and more on the moral energies and historical visions of his compatriots. [78] So, too, the best forms of contemporary conservative thought must maintain a national orientation, both in their commitment to a substantive public good and in their understanding of the place and distribution of rights.

APPENDIX 1: THE WHIG ORIGINS OF THE TERM "PROGRESSIVE"

While confirming the revisionary work on the Whigs begun by Daniel Walker Howe and continued by Lawrence Kohl, [79] the story below also foreshadows both the biography and the culture of the generation of academics and intellectuals who provided the philosophical and institutional basis of the Progressive critique of America. The pamphlet discussed here as anticipatory of Progressive ideas half a century later also looks backward. And because it appeals to the continuing power of the Puritan myth of America, it provides additional grounding, direction, and motive for the early Progressive intellectuals. In this reading, the election of Lincoln and the victory over slavery was, for the Progressives, a typological event in biblical-American history.

***

To my knowledge "Progressive Democracy, A Discourse on the History, Philosophy and Tendency of American Politics"[80] contains the first use of the term "Progressive" in American political discourse. This twenty-two-page pamphlet is an address by David Francis Bacon "before a large mass-meeting of Whigs and young men" in New York City's National Hall in 1844. Further research suggested that it was obviously no accident that this man should have been the American inventor of the term. Everything we know about David Francis Bacon (1813–1866) seems to foreshadow the horizons of Progressivism as a coherent body of ideas. First, he was from New Haven, home of Yale College, which was the center of liberal evangelical Christian apologetics, the primary source of presidents of the new American universities (Cornell, Johns Hopkins, Chicago), and a major pathway, via its theologians and philologists, to German universities and scholarship. Bacon's own evangelical piety is evidenced by his major publication, *The Lives of the Apostles of Jesus Christ* (1835), "drawn from the writings of the early Christian Fathers, and embracing the New Testament history." He was also a municipal reformer, writing a pamphlet, "The Mystery of Iniquity, a Passage of the Secret History of American Politics, Illustrated by a View of Metropolitan Society" (1845), an exposé of wrongdoing in New York City elections. Whig, evangelical, and municipal reformer: can antislavery be far behind? In 1843 Bacon wrote a collection of almost two hundred pages for a three-part antislavery report entitled, "Wanderings on the Seas and Shores of Africa."

In addition to antislavery views, no portrait of a proto-Progressive would be complete without a tribute to the importance of women to America's destiny. Here, too, Bacon does not fail us. In 1833 he collected and edited *Memoirs of Eminently Pious Women of Britain and America*. A year earlier, in his first published writing, he combined piety and reform, family and feminism in a two-volume collection, *Missionary Museum*, "an account of missionary enterprises in conversations between a mother and her children."

But back to "Progressive Democracy." The first half is a somewhat tedious and tendentious reading of recent American political history. Its intent is to show that Jackson and Jacksonian "democracy" are a perversion of the Republican-Democratic principles of Jefferson-Madison-Monroe-Adams-Clay—an appropriate lineage for a pamphlet underwritten by the Central

Clay Committee. Bacon wants to rescue the term "democracy" from the Locofocos and other Jacksonian parties by demonstrating the *conservative* character of Jacksonian democracy. As proof, he points to two forms of opposition to "governmental measures necessary to the useful exercise of the people's power, to the development of their capacities of happiness, and to their improvement and elevation in the scale of being." First are those simply satisfied with things as they are—privileged conservatives "who wish the present to be the future, who are satisfied with the good now in possession, who feel no need of the influences which cherish the infancy of enterprise . . . and which raise the mass, or the active portions of the mass, to the large possessions of the blessings of life, to the acquisition of knowledge, respect-ability, property, and all the means of happiness and power." The second type of opposition to Progressive democracy is not only conservative but destructive:

> Those who, despairing of their own improvement and benefit by the action of a beneficent system of government—incapable, by ignorance, indolence or vice, of appreciating and enjoying the advantages which such a system offers to intelligent and and [sic] honest enterprise—and envious of success of those who profit thus by gifts free to all as the air which they breathe—devote the energies which they should have employed for their own good, to the injury of others. They envy and oppose—not so much those who are already prosper-ous—as they do those who, by the wise use of such beneficent agencies of government, rise, or labor to rise, from among them, their equals in all natural advantages, and their inferiors only in the active wisdom and practical sense by which these public benefits are converted into individual happiness.[81]

In a republic, "the true democratic party . . . is the party of progress." The opponents of progress are, on the one hand, conservatives or "The Party of Repose . . . who would be an aristocracy in exclusive enjoyment of honor, wealth, knowledge and political power" and, on the other, "The Party of Retrogression, the ignorant and obstinate and the vicious, who can enjoy their power of numbers only by exercising it to the injury of those that seek to improve and reform themselves and their community."[82]

   Much of the remainder of Bacon's address is a Whig-partisan pastiche of mild nativism, strident national chauvinism, and biblical millennialism com-bined with moralistic condemnation of the patronage, corruption, and oppor-tunism of Locofocoism, "that hideous combination of Toryism and destruc-tive Radicalism." He ends with a prophetic warning to New York City's rich merchants who are tempted to trade present personal and local advantage offered by the Democrats for future national good (the growth of domestic credit, industry, and manufactures) promised by the Whigs. While never expecting the rich as a class to repay as debt to the community what their fortunes would really require, Bacon at least hopes that many of them will be

sensible to one overwhelming fact: in America, "the strength that here se-
cures Possession is not its own. The host of the defenders of peace and order
are not the children of enjoyment; nor are they yet the children of desperate
misery. They are THE CHILDREN OF HOPE!"[83] Their banner is Progressive democracy.

APPENDIX 2: SIMON PATTEN AND SCOTT NEARING

The story below illustrates the power of professional norms of Progressive
academics. Scott Nearing (1883–1983) later became the living link between
a radical social gospel in Progressive political culture, the ecological consciousness in 1960s communes, organic farming, and the Vietnam antiwar
movement.

***

When Simon Patten arrived in Philadelphia to teach economics, the Wharton
School was less than ten years old. Along with his close friend from Illinois
and Germany, Edmund James, and three other faculty members, Patten and
America's first collegiate school of business thrived: by 1908, Wharton had a
faculty of forty and a student body of almost six hundred.[84] Patten was
especially noted for producing graduate students who then went on to lead
the emerging professions in the social sciences. One of his students to
achieve fame—and later, some notoriety—was Scott Nearing. Nearing was
one of Patten's more promising graduate students when he began his studies
at Wharton in 1903, the same year his first book was published, *Social
Religion: An Interpretation of Christianity in Terms of Modern Life*. Following work on the Pennsylvania Child Labor Commission, Nearing was appointed as an instructor on the Wharton faculty and promoted to assistant
professor in 1914. Always a passionate and outspoken social critic, he finally
exceeded the bounds acceptable to the university trustees. The occasion was
a Billy Sunday revival in Philadelphia in early 1915. In a public letter,
Nearing asked Sunday to take notice of the unemployment and poverty
among the city's multitudes. Describing Sunday's sponsors as the "chief
priests, scribes, and Pharisees of Philadelphia" he called on this noted saver
of souls to use his "oratorical brilliancy . . . against low wages, overwork,
unemployment, monopoly, and special privilege."[85] That same year, despite
a unanimous Wharton faculty vote for Nearing's reappointment, the trustees
refused to reappoint him. The Nearing case received wide publicity in this
country and abroad. Patten took the lead in organizing the counterattack, first

by coordinating a muckraking campaign against the special interests represented by the trustees and then by appealing to the newly created American Association of University Professors. Both campaigns failed and Nearing was out of a job (but he was immediately made an associate editor of *Annals of the American Academy of Political and Social Science*, which James and Patten had founded twenty-five years earlier). Given Nearing's opposition to American entry into World War I, that position proved short-lived. Patten, who supported the war, but a bit late and a bit oddly, was not permitted by the trustees to stay at the university past his official retirement date, even though other less distinguished faculty members were. There is one more item to this story: in February of 1915, Professor Patten sat on the stage of the Billy Sunday revival as one of his honored sponsors. Indeed, that same year Patten's *Advent Hymns* was published.[86]

NOTES

1. Washington (1856–1915), born into slavery, became president of Tuskegee Institute in Alabama, an industrial and agricultural training center for freed slaves. He accepted the necessity for legal and social segregation in the south, maintaining that the best path was economic and educational advancement as a prerequisite for claiming civic and political equality. He was a strong supporter of Theodore Roosevelt. Riis (1849–1914) was a Danish-born American journalist. His book *How the Other Half Lives* (1890), illustrated with his own photographs, documented life in the slums of New York City. The book brought him to the attention of Theodore Roosevelt, who was then serving as the city's police commissioner. Hale (1822–1909) was a clergyman and popular writer, most notably of *The Man without a Country* (1863). Married into the Beecher family of prominent abolitionists, he later became a prominent advocate of modernist theology and the social gospel movement.

2. Ely (1854–1943), a German-educated professor of political economy at the University of Wisconsin, was a founder and early president of the American Economic Association and of the American Association for Labor Legislation and author of many books on the relationship between the new industrial economy and political and social reform.

3. Abbott, 1901, 100 and 165.

4. Addams (1860–1935) was the founder of Hull House in Chicago, a famous neighborhood settlement house and social laboratory serving the needs of new immigrants. Its volunteer residents, mostly college-educated young women, led many reform movements for factory legislation, municipal reform, the abolition of child labor, and scientific social work. With Florence Kelley, she drafted the social and industrial justice planks of the 1912 Progressive Party platform. Kelley (1859–1932), an early resident volunteer at Hull House in Chicago, was a founder and longtime president of the National Consumers League and associate editor of *Charities*, a journal advocating scientific social work. She was active in organizing women's trade unions, in factory safety legislation, and in the abolition of sweatshops and child labor. Gilman (1860–1935), a descent of the Beecher family, supported herself and her children as an editor, lecturer, and writer. Her most notable writings are *Women and Economics* (1898) and a short story, "The Yellow Wallpaper" (1899).

5. In 1894, the University of Chicago had twenty-five women and eighty-five men enrolled in graduate study in the departments of political economy, political science, and sociology. Fitzpatrick, 1990, 13, 29–30.

6. Croly, 1909, chapter 4.

7. Scudder, 1898, 205 and 210. The first two episodes were the colonization of New England by the Puritans and the American Revolution.

8. It was this address against the extension of slavery that galvanized Lincoln's campaign for the Republican Party nomination for president later that year.

9. "What is the choice of the American people? Do they prefer Communism or Industrial Democracy? The life and teaching of Abraham Lincoln make perfectly clear his answer to that question" (Abbott, 1922, 309).

10. This era has been termed a regime of courts and parties. See Skowronek, 1982, and Keller, 1977.

11. By race, Small was referring to cultural and moral agreement, or consensus, not biological or genetic identity. By religion, Small does not mean membership in a common church organization or subscription to a particular theological creed, but rather a nationally shared sense of transcendent purposes and projects. For a similar formulation, see Abbott, 1911, chapter 5. For similar understandings by contemporary scholars, see Bloom, 1992 and Mead, 1975.

12. Small, 1915.

13. Croly, 1909, 267, 269, 271, 273.

14. Croly, 1909, 278–79.

15. Ely, 1903, 98–99, and see Ely, 1893.

16. Ely, 1938, 140–41.

17. Small, 1914, 722, 725, 726.

18. Patten, 1902, 224.

19. Patten, 1902, 215.

20. Patten, 1902, passim. And see Florence Kelley, 1905, and Low and Ely, 1890. Abbott, 1901, has two chapters summarizing these same rights of labor.

21. Patten, 1907, 197.

22. Milkis, 2009, 67–68 and 125–27.

23. Patten, 1896, 85, 90, and 107.

24. Dewey, 1888, 8.

25. Dewey, 1888, 14.

26. Dewey, 1888, 16 and 22.

27. Dewey and Tufts, 1908, 304.

28. Cooley, 1909, 121; Giddings, 1898, 315. And see Edward A. Ross, 1901, 93–105.

29. Cooley, 1909. Cooley's social psychology textbook was the founding book in this new field, and was in continuous publication through 1929.

30. Addams, 1893, 2.

31. Abbott, 1892, 1896, 1897.

32. Abbott, 1901 and 1911.

33. His contemporary and president of the University of Wisconsin, John Bascom (1827–1911), wrote four books that almost exactly parallel those by Abbott. For more on Abbott and Bascom, see chapter 2, above.

34. Or received his German scholarship through Coleridge, in the manner of Horace Bushnell, one of Abbott's early heroes. On the influence of German scholarship in this period, see Herbst, 1965; Stevenson, 1986; and see chapter 2, above.

35. For the crucial role of Yale College and its German-trained faculty, see Stevenson, 1986. Yale College went on to produce the founding presidents of Johns Hopkins, Cornell, and the University of Chicago.

36. Abbott, Bradford, et al., 1898.

37. Abbott, 1892, 109–10.

38. Abbott, 1892, 154: "The history of the church down to the period of the Reformation is the history of the way in which Christian principles and the Christian spirit pervaded and transformed pagan institutions, and in which Christian institutions were moulded and pervaded by pagan principles . . . an empire partially christianized, and a church partially paganized."

39. When Abbott wrote in support of the American entry into World War I he repeated this argument: what was at stake for mankind was the victory either of "Rome" or "Israel." Germany and its kaiser represented a soulless, external, and authoritarian Rome. America, represented

by Lincoln and Wilson, stands for the union of reason, matter, and spirit—what Abbott termed Hegel and Christianity. "He who believes that history is anything more than merely a series of accidental happenings, who believes that there is any continuity and coherence in history, who believes in any ordered social evolution, should find it difficult to believe that this march of the century toward liberty will be halted" (Abbott, 1918, 99).

40. The last chapter in Abbott, *Rights of Man*, is subtitled, "To what extent and in what sense democracy and political Christianity are synonymous." The Hegelian element becomes clear when paired with the subtitle of the previous chapter: "The grounds for believing that democracy in some form is the ultimate and permanent form of government." Dewey, 1894, posited this same conflation in an early essay, "Christianity and Democracy."

41. Fox, 1977, 400, and see Curtis, 1991, 131: "A revitalized politics promise new life to religion as social gospelers conceived it. A political system responsible for social service and public morality extended the influence of churches into the secular arena and restored the relevance of religion to everyday life. Most important, progressive politics demanded social gospel Protestantism."

42. Small, 1915, 675–76, stated that "The crucial problem at the present stage of religious development is not whether this, that, or the other doctrinal formula or system is correct; but the incalculably more radical problem is whether religion is a hand-out from an external authority or a deposit of the evolving output of men's objective experience and subjective interpretations and valuations." He concluded that it fell to sociology "to represent among scholars the conviction that the world's knowledge, in the degree in which it approaches objectivity, must be capable of demonstrating its objectivity in part by its composability into an organization of knowledge, each portion of which shall corroborate and vitalize every other portion. Nothing less than this is conceivably adequate intellectual support for a religion that should convince all men." For some parallels with John Dewey, see chapter 2, above.

43. Quoted in Thelen, 1972, 108–9. George Herron, one of the more influential social gospel ministers, added: "Sociology cannot be dissociated from theology. Sociology and theology will ultimately be one science. Society depends upon theology. Men will be what they think God is. We need a Christian theology that we may have a Christian society" (Herron, 1894, 32).

44. Batten, 1909, 215; Herron, 1894, 110; Patten quoted in White and Hopkins, 1976, 133. Batten and Herron were among the most popular social gospel writers and lecturers in America. The centrality of national consensus to achieve "the brotherhood of man" also impelled an attack on existing party-electoral politics. Batten declared that the system of parties and electoral spoils "stands between the people and the government and makes a fully democratic government impossible . . . A good partisan cannot be a good citizen" (Batten, 1909, 239–40).

45. Richard Ely dedicated *Studies in the Evolution of Industrial Society* (1903) to Oliver Wendell Holmes, with the inscription, "In appreciation of the enlightened philosophy so conspicuous in his opinions, which is laying a firm foundation for a superstructure of industrial liberty."

46. Croly, 1909, 135–37. In alliance with corporate business, they manipulated popular constitution worship for their own selfish ends.

47. Croly, 1914, 25, 44–45, 131.

48. Croly, 1914, 145–46.

49. Croly, 1914, 148–49. Charles Beard's textbook that dominated collegiate instruction in American politics from its inception in 1910 through the 1930s made this same historical argument: "No longer do statesmen spend weary days over finely spun theories about strict and liberal interpretations of the Constitution, about the sovereignty and reserved rights of states . . . It is true that there are still debates on such themes as federal encroachments on local liberties, and that admonitory volumes on 'federal' usurpation come from the press. It is true also that conservative judges, dismayed at the radical policies reflected in new statutes, federal and state, sometimes set them aside in the name of strict interpretation. But one has only to compare the social and economic legislation of the last decade with that of the closing years of the nineteenth century, for instance, to understand how deep is the change in the minds of those who have occasion to examine and interpret the Constitution bequeathed to them by the Fathers. Imagine Jefferson . . . reading Roosevelt's autobiography affirming the doctrine that the Presi-

dent of the United States can do anything for the welfare of the people which is not forbidden by the Constitution! Imagine Chief Justice Taney . . . called upon to uphold a state law fixing the hours of all factory labor . . . Imagine James Monroe . . . called upon to sign bills appropriating federal money for roads, education, public health . . . and other social purposes! . . . Why multiply examples?" (Beard, 1928a, 100–1).

50. Ross, 1901, 93–94. Ross adds that public opinion is a progressive force not only with the growth of popular intelligence and character, but when the public defer to "the ascendency of the wise" (102).

51. Milkis, 2009, 57–61 and 68, on proposals at both the state and national levels.

52. Dewey, 1924, 19.

53. Dewey, 1924, 24.

54. Dewey, 1924, 27.

55. Adams, 1954. "Economics and Jurisprudence." The other article, "The Relation of the State to Industrial Action," was equally influential. The latter essay was his presidential address to the American Economic Association.

56. Small, 1895a and 1895b.

57. Pound, 1908, 1909, 1910.

58. Pound, 1910, 36.

59. Four books reflect this optimism and success: Benjamin Parke De Witt, 1915; Walter Lippmann, 1914; Rauschenbusch, 1914; and Walter Weyl, 1912. There were two notable exceptions to this triumph, both involving Negroes in the south. The first was the failure to condemn in the party platform violence against Negroes, their increasing loss of civil and political rights, and their increasing social segregation. The second involved the refusal to accept and seat a racially mixed delegation from a southern state. On the two exceptions to this triumph, the Negro question and the seating of Negro delegates from the south, see Crunden, 1984, chapter 7.

60. See Zunz, 1998, and Balogh, 2009.

61. Brandes, 1976.

62. Crunden, 1984.

63. Lind, 1995.

64. Dorothy Ross, 2009.

65. Dawley, 1991, 2003; McGerr, 2003; Hansen, 2003; Rorty, 1998; Dionne, 1996; Lind, 1995; Tomasky, 1996. Isaac, 2003, critiques much of this literature. Johnston, 2002, 68–91, is the most complete overview of contemporary writings on the Progressive period.

66. Two of the most notable are Truman, 1951, and Dahl, 1956. For an analysis of the rise of a value-neutral conception of the liberal democratic state in America, see Ciepley, 2007.

67. On the philosophical origins of his hostility, see Eisenach, 2006a.

68. Rorty, 1998, 3, 10.

69. Rorty, 1998, 19, 91, 106.

70. Rogers Smith, 2003.

71. Rogers Smith, 1997.

72. Two organized sections of the American Political Science Association (Politics and History and Foundations of Political Theory) each gave the book its annual award. The Social Science History Association made it a cowinner of its annual book award, as did the Organization of American Historians in the category of American intellectual history. Outside of academic organizations, the Association of American Publishers gave the book its highest award in government and political science. Given the number and breadth of the accolades bestowed on the book, to his credit its author was seemingly less satisfied with its conclusions than many of his readers.

73. Rogers Smith, 1997, 6.

74. A party with a built-in arrogance as well: we brave/fearless few risk hard and principled choices in a society of intellectually and morally lazy citizens all too willing to support illiberal values and policies. See Rogers Smith, 1997, 502.

75. Rogers Smith, 2003, 152. There are two other forms of constitutive stories, economic ones that celebrate the material flourishing of a people (60–62, 79–80, 82–83), and political power stories, celebrating the power of citizens in the government, the popular achievement of

independence or revolution, etc. (62–64, 93–95). These two kinds of stories, however, are much less binding and long-lived than ethically constitutive stories, which "are more likely to be religious or quasi-religious, kinship-like, and gendered than economic or political power stories" (69). Smith does not allow that these other stories can be combined into a larger national narrative, a sacred narrative that I argue the Progressives succeeded in creating.

76.   Rogers Smith, 2003, 56, 177, 183. Here Smith comes closer to the pragmatic position in Fish, 1999, chapters 9–11.

77.   Lowi, 1969, is the definitive critique of interest-group pluralism; Lind, 1995, is an effective critique of multiculturalism as a national purpose.

78.   Lincoln responded to the charge that his decree emancipating slaves in areas under Union military occupation violated the constitution by asking, "Was it possible to lose the nation, and yet preserve the Constitution?" Letter to A. G. Hodges, April 4, 1864, quoted in White, Jr., 2002, appendix 2, 207.

79.   Howe, 1979 and 1990; Kohl, 1989.

80.   Bacon, 1844.

81.   Bacon, 1844, 11.

82.   Bacon, 1844, 11–12.

83.   Bacon, 1844, 13 and 19–20.

84.   Daniel Fox, 1967, 41.

85.   Daniel Fox, 1967, 125.

86.   Daniel Fox, 1967, 125. For Nearing's praise of Patten, see Nearing, 1925. Recent studies of these founders of professional social science in American higher education tend either to ignore or to relegate to "formative influences" this persistent evangelical side. See, for example, Daniel Fox, 1967 (Patten); Coats, 1968 (Henry Carter Adams); Ross, 1977 and 1990, on most of the leading social scientists in this period; and Haskell, 1977, and Bledstein, 1976, on the professionalization of knowledge. Although there are many compelling reasons of identity for sustaining this lacuna in today's academic subculture—akin to the saving myth in the larger culture that the Prohibition movement began around World War I as the revenge of the yokels—this representation was not at all the case in the many detailed studies written in the 1930s and 1940s. Studies of these same people and many others by Dombrowski, 1936; Dorfman, 1949; Everett, 1946; Fine, 1956; Gabriel, 1956; and Schneider 1946 are quite straightforward in discussing this side of their lives and writings.

Chapter Five

Progressivism Internationalism

Herbert Croly asserted a century ago that one could not be a serious reformer of American life unless one were also a stalwart advocate of American power abroad. This coupling was another way of saying that a consensual national interest implicit in foreign policy ought to inform domestic policy as well. Politics in the sense of private and regional interest coalitions for mere partisan advantage should not only stop at the water's edge, it should be subordinated to the domestic common good as well. There were in America large constituencies prepared for this message. Liberal evangelical churches had, throughout the nineteenth century, sustained large home and foreign missionary projects to redeem America and the world. Political economists in the new research universities made the link between the new industrial society, foreign trade, and domestic prosperity a central feature of their analysis. Social and settlement-house workers, YMCA leaders, and academic social scientists all drew upon international sources of knowledge and international examples of effective reform. Progressive internationalism, therefore, is an integral part of Progressive nationalism.

This view of Progressive internationalism is more clearly seen when one steps back from partisan-electoral politics and looks instead to the deeper intellectual and cultural currents that increasingly held sway in American public life from the 1890s onward. From here we can see two features that, on the surface at least, seem in some tension. The first is a resurgence of the ideal of America as the covenant nation with a world-redemptive calling. This resurgence was most clearly and convincingly expressed, however, not by Protestant "churchmen," but by philosophers, sociologists, and political economists in the new universities and their counterparts and followers in the national journalistic and organizational complex that came into being at the same time. It is this second feature that warrants our attention because it at

115

once redescribes a long-standing component of American identity and trans-forms that identity into a set of highly sophisticated ideas and explanations that integrate local, national, and international events, issues, and politics.

A good illustration of this conflation is the publication of *The New Encyclopedia of Social Reform*, edited by William D. P. Bliss and published in 1908. Successor to a less ambitious version published eleven years earlier, this new edition of more than 1,300 closely printed pages promised in its subtitle to be a compendium of "all social-reform movements and activities, and the economic, industrial, and sociological facts and statistics of all countries and all social subjects." The articles, statistical tables, reform organization listings, and, especially, the biographies portray social reform as the common enterprise of the civilized world, flowing inexorably from the lives and thoughts of its most intellectually and morally advanced citizens. Every major heading views the status and progress of reform in a comparative perspective. While prominence is given to America and Americans, Great Britain and Germany are always featured and statistical data from every region of the world are presented in superabundance.

Article contributors to the *New Encyclopedia* are overwhelmingly American Progressives, with a sprinkling of British Fabians and Liberal MPs and a few German Social Democrats and academics. American contributors include social workers Edward Devine and Florence Kelley, economists John R. Commons and Arthur Twining Hadley, sociologists Franklin Giddings and Charles Ellwood, labor leaders Samuel Gompers and Morris Hilquit, clergymen reformers Graham Taylor and J. Cardinal Gibbons, and celebrity reformers and war horses such as Booker T. Washington and William Lloyd Garrison. Billed also as "contributing," but only because their writings are extensively quoted, are Jane Addams, Richard Ely, Josiah Strong, Sidney Webb, and President Theodore Roosevelt.

Bliss (1856–1926), like so many of the founding generation of Progressives, had a New England and clergyman background.[1] Indeed, his parents were serving as Congregational missionaries in Turkey when he was born. After a degree at Amherst College, Bliss himself studied divinity at Hartford Seminary. While Bliss devoted his life to reform organizations and journalism and developed close ties to American academics through his encyclopedia ventures, his religious background permeated his reform activities and constituted an important source of his internationalism.[2] The *New Encyclopedia* reflects this combination: its headings "Christ and Social Reform," "Christian Socialism," "Christianity and Social Reform," and "Church and Social Reform" rival in extent and scope such seemingly more central topics as "Child Labor" and "Factory Legislation." The *New Encyclopedia*, one of the most sophisticated and cosmopolitan compilations of social data and legislation in its day, can be read as a handbook for a social gospel Internationale. Encoded in this handbook is a sort of church invisible, headquartered in America but with powerful centers throughout the English-speaking world and in the advanced states in Europe, especially Germany. Its leading lights are academic social scientists and reform leaders whose ideas and spirit radiate throughout many hundreds of reform organizations, many thousands of periodicals, books, and pamphlets, and many millions of enthusiastic followers. America is the leading national actor, Bliss's *New Encyclopedia* seems to say, and its stage is the whole world.

Progressive internationalist ideas were shaped and expressed in two ways, through an evolutionary theory of world history in which America comes to play the leading role and through the emerging discipline of political economy and its recommended public policies. American entry into the war in Europe was seen as an apotheosis of Progressivism. And despite the postwar fragmentation of domestic Progressive reform, its international dimension was institutionalized and persisted through the 1920s and early 1930s. Looking even farther ahead, one sees these same values resurgent during World War II and the Cold War.[3] Despite the intervening New Deal, many policies of which were inward looking, this resurgence had the effect of turning domestic reform away from these directions and into earlier nationalist Progressive (and Republican) pathways, especially in industrial/defense policy and race relations. Because liberalism today is in a state of both intellectual disarray and (at least until 2008) political demoralization, the historiography of Progressivism is the subject of renewed interest. Looking at the international dimension of Progressivism might not only clarify its successes, it might suggest paths for the future restoration of reform liberalism in America.

THE INTELLECTUAL/INSTITUTIONAL FRAMEWORK

We wish, fully and entirely, TO NATIONALIZE THE INSTITUTIONS OF OUR LAND AND TO IDENTIFY OURSELVES WITH OUR COUNTRY; to become a single great people, separate and distinct in national character, political interest, social and civil affinities from any and all other nations, kindred and people on the earth.
—*American Republican*, November 7, 1844

This vision of American nationality was introduced in chapter 1, above. It bears repeating because it foreshadows the "Progressive" call to arms. My point is a simple one. The intellectual founders of Progressive internationalism were Whig-Republican, enthusiastically Protestant, and of New England ancestry and shared a biblical-historicist and social-evolutionary view of America. In their view, the American nation was from the start a "world-historical" people whose political and institutional history was only the overt expression of the unfolding of a covenantal and prefigured destiny. Rooted in the Calvinist and Puritan hermeneutic of Israel and its promised rebirth and victory, it was the rebirth of the American nation under Abraham Lincoln that was, for the Progressives, the defining moment in American/biblical history and prophecy. Perhaps the greatest literary expressions of this idea are Lincoln's second inaugural address and Julia Ward Howe's "Battle Hymn of the Republic."

This "nationalist" intellectual background to Progressive internationalism has an institutional counterpart. Prior to the Civil War there were very few "national" institutions in America. The federal government as defined by constitutional law encoded separate sovereignties, limited national power, and individual and states' rights. The mass-based and electorally oriented political parties were local in the extreme, both in their organization and in their coalitional function. While there were national "movement" parties (e.g., Anti-Masonic League, Liberty Party) prior to the Republican Party, the dominant electoral parties reinforced federalism and provided the patronage conduit for the mobilization of local interests and loyalties. There was, however, one set of antebellum institutional structures that were national in intent, organization, and reach, and that was religion, especially its reform and philanthropic offshoots. This complex of ecumenical reform and missionary organizations existing before the Civil War has been aptly termed "the benevolent empire" or "the evangelical united front."[4] When one includes the individual churches and their local societies, as well as the colleges and seminaries that supplied trained personnel and intellectual leadership, this complex was indeed a potential competitor to political parties for the dominance of our politics and public opinion at the national level. But until the slavery issue emerged in the 1850s, this national complex was more a "voluntarist" alternative than a direct challenge to electoral and party politics. Because of their British connections, the prominence of women and clergymen, and the stress on moral and religious regeneration, these institutions, including the academic ones, symbolized deep estrangement from the increasingly tough, masculine, violent, and interest-dominated universe of party-electoral politics in the Jacksonian era.[5] The Civil War and Lincoln changed all that—at least for one shining moment. When this set of national counterinstitutions did mobilize politically and electorally in the 1850s, the Whig Party disintegrated, the Democratic Party fractured, and the Republican Party was born.[6] It was this memory and model and this institutional setting that formed the organizational and ancestoral-cultural nidus from which Progressive national-internationalism was born. Indeed, the parents of almost the entire first generation of Progressive intellectuals were active abolitionists and Republican leaders.[7]

It was American churchmen, moreover, who taught the early Progressive philosophers, sociologists, and political economists to think in historical-national ways. In the decades prior to the Civil War, American churchmen went to German universities to study the ways in which German scholars had translated narrowly theological and evangelical ideas into a more philosophical and sociological language. It was this romanticized and historicized translation that also transformed theology and moral philosophy into the more political and reformist ideas of national development and the world-historical role of advanced nations. While the Unitarians of Harvard could be said to have played an important role—five of the six divinity school faculty under its dean Charles Everett (1878–1900) had studied in Germany—it was Yale and liberal evangelical theology that carried the day after the Civil War, and it was this transposed liberal evangelical image of America that served as the template of Progressive nationalism and internationalism. Not surprisingly, from this Yale milieu emerged the founding presidents of the three new leading graduate universities: Daniel Coit Gilman at Johns Hopkins, Andrew Dickson White at Cornell, and William Rainey Harper at Chicago. Presidents of two other leading graduate centers, Henry P. Tappan at Michigan and John Bascom at Wisconsin, began their careers as churchmen. Along with Harvard, Columbia, and Yale, these new institutions quickly became powerful intellectual centers for the Progressive critique of American political life and its prevailing moral-political culture. [8]

The academic journals and professional associations established by faculty in these new universities are all listed in Bliss's *New Encyclopedia* as part of the world movement for social reform and properly so, for their associations and journals, along with the universities that housed them, were profoundly at odds with the dominant public philosophies and party-ruled politics of their day. Their shared historical-evolutionary perspective, their analysis of political, economic, and social institutions and practices as parts of larger organic relationships, and their stress on interdependence, cooperation, and the socially formed self were far removed from the hyperindividualism built into Gilded Age constitutional, legal, and party-political culture. In their view, America could only be understood as a national culture, a national economy, and, increasingly, a powerful national state with major interests to project and to protect in a world of powerful nation-states. Taking their cue from the sudden political and economic emergence of Germany, where most of them had studied, they saw our localized party and patronage system, the protection of local monopolies and small-producer capitalism, and prevailing constitutional doctrine as deep-seated barriers to American development and to the achievement of social justice. [9] Paradoxically—and this cannot be stressed too much—one of the greatest barriers to the achievement of national responsibility, national purpose, and national citizenship was the federal government itself. Ruled by an interest-dominated Congress, bereft of a talented and energetic civil service, and profligate and wasteful to a degree that put the powerful European nation-states to shame, the national government was less reliable as a vehicle for nation building than were many state governments, advanced municipalities, and, of course, the emerging national universities, professional associations, and reform societies.[10] These latter "parastates" were—like the institutions of the "benevolent empire" and "evangelical united front" that preceded them—emerging as a powerful intellectual, moral, and political counterculture to the dominant one and became increasingly linked through the new mass circulation magazines of the day.[11]

The books, articles, and lectures by philosophers like John Dewey and James Tufts, sociologists like Charles Horton Cooley and Albion Small, and political economists like Simon Patten and Richard Ely at once articulated this new social and historical philosophy and mobilized a new nationally oriented citizenship dedicated to consciously formulated ideals of social justice. Because this philosophy flowed so seamlessly from a common evangelical and biblical-historical background, these writers found a ready-made and rapidly growing audience and used familiar styles and models for reaching that audience. This complex of Progressive institutions, connected by the new journalism and animated by a shared spirit, was not only a powerful rebirth of the older ecumenical united front, it now directly and successfully challenged the political parties as the primary engine driving the political agenda and the national mobilization of public opinion.[12] The political reforms it inspired defunded, demoralized, and demobilized the political parties, placing the (now considerably diminished) electorate increasingly in the hands of the "nonpartisan" reform press and the intellectuals and activists of the Progressive movement.[13]

This connection may now be restated directly in terms of internationalism. Protestant theology in America was always "internationalist" in the way in which the American church cum American nation was seen as the critical actor in the fulfillment of a universal sacred history and prophecy.[14] By the start of the twentieth century, this national theology had been relocated in the universities and into the new historical-evolutionary social sciences and philosophy—sciences and philosophies with international sources and audiences.[15] This relocation and redirection tended to deepen its intellectual power, broaden its reach, and tie it more directly to the state—not least because its leading ideas had already become severed from an ever-smaller and narrower northern Protestant church base. It was this transformed and relocated vision of America that provided the animating political spirit opposed to that dominating the party-electoral and court system.

The internationalist side of this organizational complex was most manifest in the foreign missionary societies and in the cross-national movements against child labor and drunkenness and for compulsory schooling, women's rights, workmen's compensation, and factory legislation. On college and university campuses at the turn of the century, organizations like the Student Volunteer Movement to recruit candidates for foreign missions complemented the huge international programming and presence of the YMCA and the World Student Christian Fellowship.[16] The organizers of women's clubs, settlement houses, and the emerging profession of social work also saw their institutions as part of an international crusade for justice and developed many international ties and alliances. In marked contrast to national political parties, Progressive national reform institutions were often international and cosmopolitan. This internationalism was strongly reflected in and encouraged by the new higher journalism, especially in successful periodicals like Albert Shaw's *Review of Reviews* and Walter Hines Page's *World's Work*, journals that in turn influenced more popular mass circulation magazines.

Symbolically, the meeting point between the older evangelical theology and the new social science was the same as that between the older institutional churches and the new university: it was the "social gospel." Always the province of lay leaders and ecumenical reform organizations, social Christianity became increasingly "post-Protestant" as it became institutionalized in graduate departments, the settlement movement, the new journalism, and the institutions comprising the women's movement. To these "ministers of reform," the terms "to democratize," "to Christianize," "to Americanize," "to nationalize," and "to internationalize" were largely interchangeable: they all meant to be animated by the moral ideals of personal responsibility, social justice, and a democratic community.[17] If "Christianize" necessarily pointed both to the nation-people and beyond it to the larger world, so too did "nationalize" and even "Americanize." This "people" must have a self-conscious identity and shared purpose, constituting, in the words of the Whig editorialist in 1844, a "race" distinct from "all other nations, kindred, and people on the earth" whose spirit and purposes are destined to rule the world.

THE POLITICAL/ECONOMIC FRAMEWORK

The civilized nations of the old world will yet do homage to the wisdom and learning, the science and arts of our people, and the combined powers of all Europe shall bow before the majesty of our power.
—*American Republican*, November 7, 1844

Given this intellectual and institutional background, it is not surprising that the earliest and most sophisticated American political economists were quick to shape their writings within these larger contours. The social evolutionary perspective posited both increasing integration of economic units and their increasing interdependence, all pointing to a coming era where individualist competition is increasingly supplanted by cooperation and mutual responsibility. When these phenomena are accompanied by vast improvements in productivity, lower costs, and high wages, a higher morality and a higher standard of living necessarily follow. In the words of Columbia professor Edwin Seligman, "with every improvement in the material conditions of the great mass of the population there will be an opportunity for the unfolding of a higher moral life."[18]

For the Progressive professoriate, the development of capital-intensive industry, the mechanization of agriculture, and the integration of national and international markets were marks of moral and spiritual progress. Some, like Wharton professor Simon Patten, saw this as a displacement of a "pain" economy premised on scarcity by a "pleasure" economy resting on abundance. With abundance, competitive motives necessary to ensure survival in the older economy of scarcity come increasingly into conflict with the social bonds created by increasingly interdependent economic networks. Thus, even individual utilities depend on the development of stronger social bonds as expressed in higher conceptions of morality and religion. The virtues demanded in this new age of abundance are "intelligence and self-control."[19] As both an ethical and a social science, political economy should describe this new reality and reveal its inner ethical and moral meanings. For Patten, as for Arthur Hadley at Yale, Henry Carter Adams at Michigan, John Bates Clark at Columbia, Richard Ely at Wisconsin, and Albion Small at Chicago, the new industrial economy constitutes a kind of "voluntary socialism," in that wealth production becomes separated from individual ownership of property. As early as 1887, economists like Adams recognized that because "the source of the increment of product is the new [social] relations that men enter into," we can no longer function as "a society whose moral code is expressed in the language of rights" but must instead see ourselves as "a society whose moral code is expressed in the language of duty."[20]

The hostility of these economists to "laissez-faire" was not hostility to markets as such but rather to certain forms of small-producer capitalism that were barriers to economic and moral progress—and were also the mainsprings powering the current party-electoral system. Not only did this earlier form of capitalism necessarily rest on individual ownership and rights claims opposed to the obligations to the larger national community, but many of its benefits to individuals flowed from undeserved monopoly "rents" and not earned "profits." This rent increment is necessarily entailed in land ownership, but it is also an element wherever local or "main street" advantage prevails. Unlike temporary advantages of successful large-scale corporations, the rents of small-producer capitalism are permanently built into local economies and small markets. The coming of national and international markets and the emergence of large-scale business not only dislodges many of these local monopoly rents, it releases these resources into the community in the form of lower prices—even while earning temporary "super profits" for the entrepreneurs in the process. Local monopoly rent, small-producer capitalism, and an ethic of individualism are as inseparably connected as were the new technology, the new industrial economy, and an emerging social ethic. For the founding generation of Progressive political economists—early presidents of the American Economics Association and authors of the first textbooks—"the present struggle is not between the rich and the poor but between centralized and localized wealth."[21] The entire material and moral future of America rested on preventing the forces of the latter from plundering and disabling the former.

The material and moral promise of the new industrial economy was the Progressive answer to the moral and material limits of the older small-producer or "yeoman" economy. That older economy was trapped in individualism and isolated ownership and the often ruthless struggles necessitated by scarcity. The new industrial economy promised a future in which stewardship, mutual responsibility, and ever-increasing abundance and leisure would prevail. With every increase in the scale and scope of these enterprises and their connecting links, there would be corresponding opportunities and motivations for individual development of skills and talents.

When Richard Ely declared that "mutual dependence is not slavery," but an invitation to a larger freedom, he was writing an academic epitaph to the American yeoman and small-producer ideal of independence as freedom. The American economy, along with those of England and Germany, was the leading engine in "the evolution of industrial society" and thus a major factor in world civilization. Indeed, the very rise of modern industrial society mandated that political economy be a historical and an ethical science because man's spirit and progress were increasingly being revealed in and through these new material forces and institutions. The static science of economics must yield to the dynamic science of political economy because the nation-state, not the individual firm, was now the primary economic unit and mechanism of coordination. This also meant that it increasingly fell to the state to underwrite the conditions of man's future moral progress. In the words of Ely's proposal for founding the American Economics Association: "We regard the state as an educational and ethical agency whose positive aid is an indispensable condition of human progress."[22] This was necessarily true in the case for establishing new standards for industrial relations and in regulating competition among oligopolistic firms. But there were many other reasons as well, reasons that directly tied national economies to international ones. During this period, international capital markets played an increasing role, first in funding American railroads and industry and later in American overseas investments. The mechanization of American agriculture, the development of mass food processing and marketing, and the creation of commodities markets and standards first nationalized and then internationalized agriculture. Indeed, as agriculture in much of the south was becoming increasingly decapitalized and even feudalized, that in the Midwest was literally swamping world markets with its products, making Chicago first the national and then the world center of agricultural commodities. [23]

THE EMERGENCE OF AMERICA AS A WORLD POWER

While many of these changes were taking place as early as the 1870s and 1880s, it was the election of 1896 that marked a decisive shift in policy and practice across many fronts. As a realigning election, the Republican victory condemned both the Democratic Party and competitive partisanship itself to the margins of national political life. [24] Over the next twelve years, waves of antiparty legislation and values swept the country, especially its more advanced regions, effectively displacing localized and patronage-based parties from their primacy in setting agendas, articulating policy choices, and leading public opinion. [25] This displacement had the effect of suddenly empowering those nationally oriented "parastates" and social forces most determined to "Americanize" (democratize, Christianize) both the country and the world.

Given this freedom from prior electoral (and therefore constitutional) constraints, the major policy changes that followed had the effect of committing the national government to an activist international role on a permanent basis. Without recounting this history, its first element was the guarantee of the gold standard, releasing large capital inflows into the American industrial economy and triggering a wave of industrial consolidations and rationalizations. [26] This had the side effect of committing America to a permanent regime of trade and tariff diplomacy premised on reciprocity and international cooperation rather than on a confluence of local domestic interests. A second element was the rapprochement with Great Britain, initially occasioned by the need to abrogate the 1850 Clayton-Bulwer Treaty that prevented the United States from constructing the Panama Canal. This new era of cooperation with Britain was strengthened by our sudden naval and colonial expansion into a universe dominated by the British Empire. Finally, the remarkable success of our trade expansion abroad and industrial profits at home quickly transformed America from a debtor to a creditor nation. The new need to invest large amounts of capital abroad in order to maintain profits, employment, and financial stability at home only intensified the earlier shifts toward internationalization of our political, economic, and institutional culture. [27]

These shifts in policy and direction may also be stated in spatial terms. From 1896 until the New Deal, domestic and foreign policy reflected the national distribution of economic, cultural, and intellectual energies and powers more than it did constitutional separations and distributions of power.

This de facto "core" dominance over the periphery—a dominance precluded de jure by our constitutional arrangements—could only prevail if power shifted from locally based political parties to nationally constituted parastates and from Congress and the courts to the executive and its allies in the larger society.[28] So long as reform journalism, the new universities and professions, and the myriad reform organizations supported by social gospel values and the organizational network of the ecumenical Protestant establishment kept the "antiparty" (i.e., national elements in the Republican Party) dominant, this "core" dominance along the Chicago–New York economic and cultural axis was ensured.[29]

Progressive academics, journalists, and reformers were fully aware of these changes in all of their economic, political, and cultural dimensions. Their writings not only helped to bring these changes about, they integrated these political and economic changes into a cultural-religious narrative of the place of America and Americans in world history. From antiparty reforms, through the increasing divorce of management from owners in corporations, to the rapid expansion of American products, power, and money abroad, these Progressives and their ever-growing and increasingly self-confident audience saw signs of the spirit revealed. But appropriately, perhaps, it was an Englishman—the liberal reformer, evangelical, and journalist William Stead—who combined the intellectual-institutional and the political-economic sides of Progressive internationalism and who most clearly captured this moment of America on the verge of triumph.

William Thomas Stead, a Gladstonian social reformer and editor of the *Pall Mall Gazette*, is noteworthy in three respects: as founder of both the British and the American *Review of Reviews* (1890), as author of a best-selling book, *If Christ Came to Chicago: A Plea for the Union of All Who Love in Service of All Who Suffer* (1894), and as director of a journalistic project tracing America's rise as the world's most dynamic industrial power, compiled and published as *The Americanization of the World* (1902). The purpose of the two *Reviews* is made clear in the first British issue:

> There exists at this moment no institution which even aspires to be to the English-speaking world what the Catholic Church in its prime was to the intelligence of Christendom. To call attention to the need for such an institution, to enlist the co-operation of all those who will work towards the creation of some such common centre . . . are the ultimate objects for which this review has been established . . . Already [the English-speaking man] begins to dominate the world. The [British] Empire and the [American] Republic comprise within their limits almost all the territory that remains empty for the overflow of the world. Their citizens, with all their faults, are leading the van of civilization.[30]

While the British *Review* was moderately successful, the American one, taken over by Albert Shaw in 1892, quickly established itself as the leading organ of Progressive internationalism in America.

The series of reports on American economic expansion first appeared in the British *Review of Reviews* in 1901. These reports stressed how American economic growth was coming to dominate world markets, citing as examples the facts that, in 1900, the United States was supplying the United Kingdom with over half of its salt pork, more than 70 percent of its live cattle and fresh beef, and almost 90 percent of its bacon and ham.[31] The Steel Trust in America brought in ore by rail to its furnaces at one-fifth the British cost per ton mile; railroad shipping costs for heavy goods were one-half of Germany's and one-fourth of Britain's. This material success, Stead writes, only reflects a deeper cultural and political success: America is forging all the nationalities within her borders "into one dominant American type . . . [creating] one uniform texture of American civilization." Conceding American dominance and Britain's secondary role, the book concludes with a quotation from Gladstone: "Will it make us, the children of the senior race, living together under [the American's] action, better or worse? Not the manner of producer, but what manner of man is the American of the future to be? How is the majestic figure, who is to become the largest and most powerful on the stage of the world's history, to make use of his power?"[32]

In a sense, Stead had already answered Gladstone's question. *If Christ Came to Chicago* was an impressive piece of investigative journalism into the economic, social, and moral conditions of Chicago.[33] Following a long tribute to Jane Addams and Hull House, Stead concludes with a prophecy: having already achieved first rank as an ocean port (anticipating the Saint Lawrence Seaway) and as the nation's transport, commercial, and financial center, Chicago is soon to be made the capital of America and become the imperial city of the world. Every reformer's dream has come true: prosperity, religious unity, housing cooperatives, popular education and culture, free medical care, and municipally owned utilities, stores, banks, gymnasiums, parks—even pawn shops and neighborhood saloons (Stead *was* British)— have made Chicago every Progressive's model city. To crown its achievements, the city holds a great festival. The high point is the arrival of the emperor of Germany, who has come to pay homage to "the ideal city of the world." At the City Hall he is received by the mayor, Mrs. Potter Palmer.

THE GREAT WAR AND PROGRESSIVISM

By 1900, most Progressives shared the view expressed by Lyman Abbott, the editor of one of its most influential weeklies: "We are a world power; we are likely to be a leader among the world-powers. We could not help ourselves if we would; we would not help ourselves if we could."[34] As close followers of European events and longtime participants in international reform, charitable, and disaster relief causes, the first response of Progressive political and cultural leaders to the outbreak of war in Europe was to urge "preparedness." While preparedness included governmental plans for military mobilization, its initial thrust was moral and voluntarist—a call for all Americans to prepare themselves for a momentous test of resolve and will. Without question it was Progressives who led the way.[35] Their very willingness to "prepare" for some as yet unknown collective sacrifice was itself proof that republican virtue was more important than individual material comfort—proof that, in the words of Theodore Roosevelt some years earlier, we are not a nation of "well to do hucksters . . . sunk in a scrambling commercialism."[36] Once the struggle in Europe was framed in terms of the fate of democracy in the world, Progressives did not doubt that America would be called to take the leading role in its defense. Herbert Croly, the founding editor of *The New Republic*, had long believed that no European nation or group of nations could be committed unreservedly to the cause of democracy: "A European nation . . . cannot afford to become too complete a democracy all at once, because it would thereby be uprooting traditions upon which its national cohesion depends." In America, however, "we can trust its interest to the national interest, because American national cohesion is dependent . . . upon fidelity to a democratic principle."[37]

When defense of democracy at home and abroad is also a defense of a certain kind of post-Protestant American identity, the call for preparedness takes on the ideal of national regeneration through atonement—the selfless sacrifice by the "innocent" and "righteous" for the evils of others. As preparedness turned to mobilization, and mobilization to the declaration of war, it was almost as if four decades of cultural and political preparation by the Progressives had at last found a object worthy of its impulses. Indeed, Lyman Abbott's *The Twentieth Century Crusade* (1918) stands as a sort of "proof text" for the flood of books and articles written by Progressive intellectuals in that same year.

American civic virtue, according to Abbott, is best embodied in her mothers and their sons: the mothers by the sacrifice of their sons to the larger cause of justice and democracy, the sons by their physical courage and risk of life to atone for the sins of others.[38] Despite its sentimentality, Abbott's appeal to mothers in the form of nine "letters" is a robust call to arms. The first letter recalls Lincoln and the Civil War, telling the mother that her son "has joined the noble army of patriots." By the fifth letter, he is contrasting the "glory in tribulation" to the sordid ends of personal happiness. In the sixth and seventh letters, the reader is reminded that democracy is not a form of government but a way of life, a faith in human brotherhood that informs the character of all American institutions, religious, industrial, educational, and political. Our democratic republic is the modern Israel, a holy nation opposing Rome in all its forms. Lincoln and Wilson stand for Hegel and Christianity; Germany and the kaiser represent materialism, paganism, and power. The concluding letters are triumphal. Democracy and social justice are marching to victory. They "who have offered their lives, not merely for their country, but for an unknown people, of a different land, a different language and often of a different religious faith" will be crowned with immortality "not as a hope for the future [but] as a present possession, . . . the consciousness that I am more than the body which I inhabit."[39]

This understanding of American civic virtue gave early preparedness campaigns and later war mobilization a decidedly voluntarist cast. While this was most evident in the thousands of Americans who served in expeditionary units prior to the declaration of war, it was also manifest in the way in which small federal governmental units functioned largely through unofficial voluntary organizations and efforts. From George Creel's Committee on Public Information, with its volunteer army of 150,000 intellectuals, writers, and speakers, to Herbert Hoover's Food Administration with a paid staff of 1,400 directing 750,000 volunteer housewives allocating and rationing the nation's food supply, it appeared that "official" action was only the final procedural act, not the substantive animating source, of the war effort. Even the initial funding for allied loans was raised through "Liberty Loans." In June 1917, four million Americans joined in offering the government $3 billion—an amount that increased to more than $25 billion within two years. The crowing achievement of this style of mobilization, however, was military conscription itself. Almost the entire apparatus of the draft functioned outside of the official federal government. Of the 192,000 workers administering the draft, just 429 were salaried federal employees. Only a nation already integrated and mobilized in spirit for many decades could have accomplished what still appears almost miraculous today. Two weeks to the day after Congress passed the Conscription Act, nine and a half million men presented themselves to local draft boards. With only the most rudimentary administrative state, the American nation did what the most powerful and centralized European states could barely imagine.

PROGRESSIVE INTERNATIONALISM IN THE 1920S

The period immediately following the war witnessed this heady sense of shared purpose. Returning from the peace conference in 1919, Woodrow Wilson's rhetoric summarized these preparedness and mobilization themes:

> Our participation in the war established our position among the nations . . . the whole world saw at last . . . a Nation they had deemed material and now found to be compact of the spiritual forces that must free men of every nation of every unworthy bondage . . . The stage is set, the destiny is disclosed. It has come about by no plan of our conceiving, but by the hand of God who led us into this way. We cannot turn back. We can only go forward to follow the vision. It was of this that we dreamed at our birth.[40]

While Progressive political leaders were soon disabused of their hope that the spirit and unity of preparedness and mobilization would continue to animate national governmental policy after the war, Progressive leadership in other sectors of American society remained optimistic. This was especially the case with leaders of "parachurch" ecumenical organizations that enjoyed unprecedented prestige and support during the war. In the words of one prominent religious publication, "War drives for world freedom [were] passing into Christian drives for world redemption . . . Christian churches mobilize when armies demobilize."[41] And mobilize they did. The most ambitious of these plans was to create and fund a gargantuan umbrella organization called the Interchurch World Movement. This organization would not only embrace all churches in America, but would call on the support of leaders in government, labor, and industry to help underwrite a sort of national voluntarist parastate to spearhead the drive for democracy and justice at home and abroad.[42] Motivation for the success of this venture was all the stronger after America's rejection of membership in the League of Nations. With a paid staff of 2,600 in New York City and expenditures exceeding a million dollars a month, Interchurch began its drive to raise more than a third of a billion dollars. The campaign was a colossal failure; less than 10 percent of the goal was met.[43]

While there are many explanations for this sudden shift in religious and political culture, the long and gradual theological movement from liberal evangelicalism to "modernism" and the sudden rise of a strident and angry fundamentalism in the 1920s surely played a major part.[44] The immediate result was that Progressivism as a political culture, especially its internationalist side, was now located in institutions that had fewer and less salient connections to a popular base. Its moral and intellectual redoubts were the liberal ecumenical associations and the national universities with their allied colleges and professional associations. It may be true that many Progressive

intellectual and cultural elites suddenly appeared as secular technocrats in
bureaucratic alliance with the new industrial state, but this was an outcome
more inevitable than chosen. The popular base in churches, journalism, labor,
and enlightened small business was so reduced that only the more abstract
and secular language of an emerging liberal cosmopolitanism could hold the
Progressive remnant together.[45] This remnant, however strong at the national
heights of our organizational culture, could no longer command a popular
electoral following and therefore had very little leverage in the national political parties. In 1912 each of the three leading presidential candidates had
some impressive Progressive credentials; in 1924 the Republicans nominated
Calvin Coolidge and the Democrats John W. Davies, a Wall Street lawyer
from West Virginia who ended his career defending state segregation of
schools before the Supreme Court in *Brown v. Topeka.*

John Dewey wrote a sort of epitaph to popular Progressivism in a 1922
article in *The New Republic*:

> What we call the middle classes are for the most part the church-going classes,
> those who have come under the influence of evangelical Christianity. These
> persons form the backbone of philanthropic social interest, of social reform
> through political action, of pacifism, of popular education. They embody and
> express the spirit of kindly goodwill toward classes which are at an economic
> disadvantage and toward other nations, especially when the latter show any
> disposition toward a republican form of government . . . [This middle class]
> followed Lincoln in the abolition of slavery, and it followed Roosevelt in his
> denunciation of "bad" corporations and aggregation of wealth.

In marked contrast to his prewar writings, Dewey now seems to dismiss this
constituency as a source of future reform. Reflecting the rupture in Protestantism between modernism and fundamentalism, he now declares that this
evangelical middle class "has never had an interest in ideas as ideas, nor in
science and art for what they may do in liberating and elevating the human
spirit."[46]

Despite Dewey's pessimism—understandable in the period of the Scopes
trial and the Red Scare—Progressive values remained the defining ones in
the mainline churches through the Federal Council of Churches, in the thriving academic professional organizations and research universities, in the
higher journalism, in the higher reaches of a now increasingly competent and
self-confident federal civil service, and in the labor, business, and financial
sectors organized earlier through the National Civic Federation and permeated with the ideals of welfare capitalism.[47]

At the same time, Progressive values were becoming increasingly powerful in the nation's premier law schools. Long the object of contempt by
Progressive intellectuals for their legal formalism, a fixation on abstract
rights, and an antidemocratic animus, both law schools and courts were

thought constitutionally incapable of understanding the new industrial order and shaping the law to its imperatives. It was almost an article of faith among early Progressive academics and intellectuals that the constitution and its high priests were a barrier to overcome rather than a source of social and political direction.[48] In the 1920s, however, major law schools more and more reflected the teachings of the Progressive political economists, sociologists, and philosophers, under the banners first of "sociological jurisprudence" and then of "legal realism." Critical of an abstract and mechanical jurisprudence and accepting of both administrative law and the administrative-regulatory state, these new legal cadres were becoming cosmopolitans, equally capable of serving government, international finance, and large business corporations in managing and coordinating the larger economic and legal framework of America.

Hoover's election and the responsible role that the United States played in sustaining the international economy in the 1920s also testify to the enduring power of Progressive political values.[49] But this popular electoral strength was somewhat illusory: the demobilization of the electorate and the dramatic decline in voting in this period ensured that Progressive values most attuned to new industrial values would remain powerful while more popular (and populist) ones would not. Investment bankers, large oligopolistic business and its labor union beneficiaries, scientific proponents of efficiency and rationalization in government, and the foundations, universities, and national publications that propounded these values were especially advantaged. Those Progressive followers and values more heavily influenced by an earlier populism and by ideals of social Christianity were not.

PROGRESSIVE INTERNATIONALISM FROM THE NEW DEAL THROUGH THE COLD WAR

The long fall in agricultural commodity prices, the stock market crash, the collapse of international trade, and the defeat and discrediting of Hoover almost reversed the electoral equation and therefore the fortunes of Progressivism in the 1930s. Its financial and industrial redoubts collapsed from the inside, while its educational, professional, and philanthropic allies were in moral and intellectual disarray. Combined with its earlier fragmentation, this collapse set the stage for a new public philosophy of New Deal liberalism very different in intellectual origins and constituencies from Progressivism. Without reopening the debate about the relationship of Progressivism to the New Deal in its domestic relief, welfare, and regulatory policies, 1932–1939, it is surely the case that the simultaneous rise of the New Deal lawyer and the Washington law firm was both a link to and a major subversion of Progressive values. The New Deal, especially after the election of 1936, was a victory of marginals at the periphery of national life and of a resurgent politics of patronage, party, and elections, necessarily subjecting policy to localism and policy making to elaborate coalitional games. None of this maneuvering, of course, had much to do with sustained economic recovery. Indeed, many of the initial New Deal programs were extensions of what Hoover began. It is clear, however, that Progressive internationalism as a national policy collapsed along with international investment and trade and was implicitly repudiated by the autarkic economic policies by both Hoover and Roosevelt in response to the Depression.

If the Depression undermined Progressive economic internationalism and discredited both international finance and large industrial corporations, the war quickly restored the centrality of both sectors—and revitalized the other centers of 1920s Progressivism as well. Unlike in World War I, mobilization for World War II was much more extensive, "state-centered," legalistic, and bureaucratic. Nevertheless, because of its scale and duration, mobilization drew even more heavily upon the energies and talents of those parastates utilized in the earlier war, especially the universities, professional and trade associations, and the national media.

This presidentially centered relationship between nationally minded political leaders, universities, churches, foundations, corporate law, finance and business, and labor continued and grew stronger in the Cold War. The "national security state" was much more than a system of anti-Soviet military alliances abroad and a military-industrial complex at home. Abroad, the American government managed postwar European and Asian economic and political reconstruction, presided over the decolonization of much of Africa and Asia, and dominated international monetary and trade policies. It was precisely this American identity abroad—its "mission to the world"—that was the engine for sustaining liberal-progressive modes of reform at home. [50]

Given international economic policies, those policies of the New Deal undertaken in the spirit of Wilsonian "New Freedom" and the older small-producer capitalism were consistently subordinated to the demands of large-scale industrial and financial capitalism. The demands of labor were met selectively according to these same criteria. Even the persistent impulses in Democratic Party ideology for acknowledging religious, regional, cultural, ethnic, and racial "difference" were subordinated to the demands of American internationalism. This was also true at the level of political beliefs. The first demands to purge suspected communists and "fellow travelers" came from New Deal liberals—loyalty screening began under Truman—and were widely supported by the liberal establishment in all of its major locations, from national universities and foundations, through mainline churches, to the American Civil Liberties Union, the National Association for the Advancement of Colored People, and Americans for Democratic Action. [51]

But there is also the other side to this demand for national unity for international ends: the imperative to dismantle racial segregation in the south. As anticommunism abroad drove anticommunism at home, so too anticolonialism and leadership of the "third world" abroad impelled desegregation at home, even if it meant repudiating the last vestige of constitutional federalism. These projects were initiated, led, and driven by liberal national elites and institutions—elites and institutions who had the most direct connection to earlier Progressive ones.[52]

Another sign of a postwar Progressive restoration was the emerging norm of "bipartisanship" in foreign policy. By common elite consensus lasting more than a quarter of a century, American foreign policy, that is, internationalism as a dominant value, was removed from the normal tug of domestic interests and party-electoral politics. So long as this consensus prevailed and so long as foreign policy imperatives could prevail over domestic interests, the newly institutionalized presidency, standing above party, became the official repository of American identity and purpose in the world. Through these executive institutions, the spirits of antiparty Republican Progressivism still provided the limiting conditions within which both New Deal liberals and Republican conservatives could function.

Postwar bipartisanship can be restated in two other ways. The first way is by James MacGregor Burns, whose books codified and rationalized our ideological, political, and constitutional situation between the New Deal and the Vietnam War. Burns postulated a "four-party" system in America, wherein each party had a responsible, presidentially oriented nationalist/internationalist wing and an irresponsible, interest-dominated congressional/localist wing.[53] The most important institutional locations of Progressive internationalism were associated with the presidency, as Burns describes, but its power and reach were often hidden. From the antifascist Office of Strategic Services to the anticolonial and anticommunist Central Intelligence Agency, strong but hidden ties were established between the national security apparatus and most of the liberal establishment, ranging from national labor, student and youth organizations through universities, foundations, publishing houses, the national media, and ecumenical church organizations. These connections and forms of informal cooperation were willingly entered into by the leaders of these national institutions, which became known in the 1960s as "the liberal establishment." This establishment shared the same liberal cosmopolitan political and cultural values and the same set of enemies on the left (largely abroad) and on the right (largely at home).[54]

This "internationalist" restoration of Progressivism in midcentury differed in significant ways from its earlier period of glory at the beginning of the century. Because of the continued electoral dominance of the New Deal coalition, domestic policy was largely in the hands of locally oriented congressional leaders and not national elites, and thus there was little "fit," rhetorically or socioculturally, between domestic and foreign policy.[55] The justifications and practices of "interest-group liberalism" at home were simply incommensurate with the justifications and practices (not to speak of the economic needs) of our policies abroad. The former was both "populist" and "constitutional," while the latter was neither but tended to dominate important policy areas—as in extracting domestic resources to support defense and foreign aid spending and trade policies. Liberal internationalism was not constitutional because neither the "intelligence community" nor its clandestine allies and extralegal powers could be contained within any formalist reading of the constitution. They existed outside the constitution because Congress and the courts permitted it. Liberal internationalism lacked a coherent popular electoral base because domestic interests were neither intellectually nor economically integrated into international policies, except insofar as some foreign aid and defense-related spending became pork and thus held hostage to powerful congressional leaders and interest groups.

The only post–New Deal domestic policies that were at once national in purpose, clearly within constitutional understandings, and possessed of a powerful electoral base were the attempts to address persistent and grinding poverty and to achieve some measure of racial integration. What has been termed the "nationalization of rights" associated with the Warren Court could never have come from the New Deal electoral coalition. But given World War II and the Cold War, it bore many of the marks of an earlier Progressive vision translated into a new form of an organic and nationalist constitutional law. This nationalization of rights paralleled in purpose and support the "internationalization of rights" as the foundation for our anticommunist foreign policy.[56] With some exceptions, this nationalization of rights still lacks a truly popular base and appears increasingly removed from any easily recognizable constitutional foundations.

THE HISTORIOGRAPHY OF PROGRESSIVISM

The preceding analysis incorporates a reading of Progressivism that is, to say the least, not without controversy. Because contemporary attempts to reorient and restore American liberalism necessitate a rethinking of Progressivism, the controversy about the identity and history of Progressivism is also controversy about the identity and future of American liberalism.[57] It may be useful to conclude, therefore, by sketching the dimensions and import of my reading, both to clarify its understanding of Progressivism and to contrast it to alternative readings.[58]

My starting point is that Progressivism began as a movement to restore the American *nation*, to inculcate a substantive idea of public good and infuse its purposes into all areas of American life from family government to national government, from academic culture and religion to public education, from small businesses to international investment banks. Readings of Progressivism that slight or subordinate this nationalist orientation will miss the only intellectual and organizational framework that brought together and connected its leading figures, institutions, and practices over many decades. This nationalist orientation forces attention on ideas and social theories; on institutions, civil society, and culture; and, at least initially, away from "interests," their interplay, and events in party-electoral politics. [59]

This cultural/intellectual orientation is a powerful way of understanding and of explanation because it is authentically historical; it assumes that actions and behaviors are deeply embedded in self-understandings and systems of social meaning. Only as and until these are significantly altered is it possible, literally, to conceive of new political and social institutions and practices. Because these new self- and social understandings can only be forged from materials already at hand—another explicitly historical perspective—this reading of Progressivism is able to connect with earlier languages and practices in American culture that were reformulated and relocated into coherent and powerful social and political forces. It necessarily follows that this nationalist reading restores the role of religious ideas and institutions to a central place in our political culture precisely because religious language was the most compelling and powerful language of national identity within an American-centered narrative of universal (world) history. When this narrative is directly infused into social movements and politics, as it was during the American Revolution and the American Civil War, it can become a hegemonic national culture and even a "civil religion." Progressivism in the hands of its most articulate philosophers and social theorists both aspired to that goal and, in most national institutions, achieved it, that is, achieved an intellectual/cultural dominance that was unquestioned from the 1890s until the 1920s and, though contested, remained very powerful until the early 1970s.

In contrast to this approach, most current studies of Progressivism begin with the success of Progressivism as a political ideology in party-organized electoral contests from the early 1900s through 1915, chart its party-electoral collapse following World War I, and then reconstruct its past—and its future. This anachronistic way of proceeding has the corresponding tendency to encourage a flowering of nostalgic speculation about "alternative Americas" that "might have been"—as if each generation of Americans can reinvent itself. Neither time nor topic warrants a close analysis of these readings, but a brief sketch of some prominent ones and their implications provides an instructive contrast to my own.

One influential interpretation is that Progressivism never existed or, if it did, it took so many disparate forms that the term cannot stand for any coherent or unified view.[60] This interpretation makes sense only if the Progressivism one searches for is almost exclusively a party-electoral one in local, state, and national politics. If no substantively coherent Progressive ideas are to be found in the legislative policies in this period, then the "Progressive movement" lacks coherent identity as a public philosophy. While this method might have made sense during the party period of American politics, it is deeply ironic that Progressivism should be judged on this basis, since its chief aim was to break the grip of party-dominated institutions as the final arbiter of political ideas. Indeed, the very success of Progressivism in national institutions and intellectual culture and the increasing power of that culture in our political life discredits this test. Moreover, after 1900, the test is largely irrelevant to an understanding and explanation of US foreign policy and of our emergence as a world power. Precisely because nongovernmental but national institutions and leaders, combined with an increasingly autonomous presidency, shaped foreign policy and foreign-policy thinking, a party-electoral test of both coherence and saliency is misplaced.[61] The moral and material mobilization for World War I is the best example.

A variant of this same insular perspective reaches a complementary conclusion. It also starts by simply denying the coherence of Progressivism but, lacking confidence that the term marking an entire political era will simply disappear in our historical consciousness, takes the demotic route of including marginals and subalterns as constitutive actors in the formation and success of Progressivism. Whether the increasingly ethnic political machines of the north and Midwest or the one-party semifeudal Democratic south, these political forces are made an integral part of Progressive identity and meaning.[62] Richard Hofstadter's earlier incorporation of the Populist movement into "the age of reform" is the model for this mistake.[63] This incorporation of marginals is possible because Progressivism was assumed at the start to lack any philosophical or sociocultural soul—that is, one constitutive of a national identity—but was only a loosely connected series of ad hoc responses by decent Americans to perceived wrongs and social problems. Thus reduced to a wide array of innovative policy proposals or "reforms" to which various interests could and did attach themselves variously and from which they received direct and differential benefits, even the intentionally procedural and soulless soul of the Democratic Party as an institution could be incorporated into this understanding of Progressivism and therefore into the mainstream of American history.[64] Put directly, it is as if both the Civil War and the realigning and hegemonic election of 1896 never happened.[65] Put indirectly, this perspective denies the brute facts of winners and losers and the intractable horizons that winning establishes for future conflicts.

Recent attempts to divide Progressives into "good" ones (i.e., anti-imperialist, pacifist, protosocialist, multicultural) and "bad" ones (i.e., imperialist, technocratic, welfare-capitalist, WASP) represent a further retreat from or evasion of our history.[66] Reading back from the 1920s and taking its cue from the beautiful souls of the "Young Americans," this interpretation sees this confused and hopeless critique as a lost remnant of "good" Progressivism pointing to an alternative that might be reclaimed today. This understanding is not so much bad history as it is history's denial—as if the truly free American can exist outside of history and the larger world and reclaim a lost freedom by mere assertion and will. Needless to say, this "idealism" is not only isolationist, it puts America in opposition to its national history and therefore to the history of the modern world that America has done so much to shape. One might call this reading of Progressivism a yearning for a new Jeffersonian moment when America did see itself as existing alone in endless space and not with others in historical time.[67] In this discussion, Randolph Bourne is the hero, Walter Lippmann the goat, and John Dewey the subject of interpretive struggle.

These misreadings and distortions of Progressivism become most apparent when Progressive internationalism is given prominence. The coherence of Progressivism as a public philosophy stands out most clearly when its vision is placed on a world stage, where the nation as the actor must possess both articulate purposes and a unified will if it is to act effectively. To see Progressivism as its intellectual founders articulated it—as a historically grounded public philosophy designed to create a democratic nation under new social and economic conditions—is also to see Progressivism as part of a worldwide endeavor to create the conditions in which a world of democratic nations can also come into being. As Croly recognized more than a century ago, given the constitutional structures that frame our politics, without the national focus, historical perspective, and discipline that American power in the world requires, domestic policies might easily degenerate into a politics of distribution that sustains extant and narrow interests, encourages dependencies of all sorts, and lowers the standards of citizenship.

As these chapters assert in various registers, the coherence of Progressive thought rests on an embracive ideal of national patriotism. That ideal, in turn, is structured within a narrative understanding—often a sacred one—of both nation and citizenship. This coherence gave agency and power to both citizen and nation. To remove or to, in retrospect, deny the centrality of national patriotism in large projects of political, social, and economic reform is to weaken the power of those reform efforts even while diminishing the meaning and worth of citizenship. In contemporary America academics and intellectuals might reassess this legacy of Progressivism and reevaluate the civic and moral resources that the American nationality has in such abundance.

NOTES

1. Eisenach, 1994, 31–36, 42–44.
2. In the 1890s, Bliss was founder of the Christian Socialist Society of the United States, secretary and national lecturer for the Christian Social Union in America, president of the National Social Reform Union, founding editor of *Dawn*, and editor of the *American Fabian*. After serving two years as an investigator for the US Bureau of Labor, he worked with Josiah Strong's American Institute of Social Service, 1909–1914, and compiled and edited writings from John Stuart Mill and John Ruskin.
3. Inboden, 2008, is especially persuasive on the role of liberal-ecumenical religious bodies in support of Cold War policies both at home and abroad.
4. Charles Foster, 1960, 274–80 for the list of missionary and reform societies in America and Great Britain. See also Howe, 1990.
5. On women and clergymen see Cott, 1977 and Douglas, 1977.
6. Two studies that combine to clarify this relationship are Walters, 1977 and Gienapp, 1987.
7. For biographies of prominent Progressive intellectuals and reform leaders see Eisenach, 1994, 31–36 and Crunden, 1984.
8. This transposition from churchman to philosopher is seen most vividly in scholarly journals and academic publication. See details in chapter 2, above.
9. See Eisenach, 1994, 92–93, and Herbst, 1965, 207–14 and 230.
10. The best general discussion of localism, expenditures, and governmental growth during this period is Keller, 1977.
11. Leaders of the new professional associations regularly wrote for the new national magazines and, in turn, opened the pages of their professional journals to prominent reformers. For examples, especially of women reformers, see Eisenach, 1994, 13–15, 149, and 183.
12. Even in the new journalism, the religious press was the forerunner and provided the first models. Both the *Independent* and *Outlook*, for example, started as denominational publications and evolved into major mass circulation reform periodicals (Mott, 1957, 422–35 and 292–94).
13. McCormick, 1986, 332–48. A good analysis of the institutional ramifications of these reforms is found in Shefter, 1978.
14. The most coherent and convincing case for this view is Bercovitch, 1975.
15. Kloppenberg, 1986. He is especially persuasive in showing that, between 1870 and 1920, "two generations of American and European thinkers created a transatlantic community of discourse in philosophy and political theory" (3).
16. The scale and reach of these internationally oriented organizations are difficult to comprehend today. The Student Volunteer Movement was founded by a Cornell undergraduate in 1888; shortly thereafter, six thousand college students pledged to become foreign missionaries in a one-year period. More than twenty thousand missionaries were eventually recruited by this group, whose founder, John R. Mott, went on to work for the international YMCA and to head the World Student Christian Federation. Immediately after World War II Mott was instrumental in the founding of the World Council of Churches. The "secular" and social service dimension of foreign missions is indicated in the fact that, of every one hundred American missionaries serving abroad, only thirty were clergymen. For more on Mott, see chapter 2, above. See also Marsden, 1994, 343–44, and Handy, 1991, 77–96.
17. Crunden, 1984.
18. Seligman, 1907, 132.
19. Quoted in Eisenach, 1994, 89.
20. Adams, 1954, 159 and 152–53. His immediate purpose was to restructure industrial relations so that workers have more weapons than strikes and managers have more legitimacy than as agents of owners enforcing property rights through force. With union recognition, subsidiary state law, and long-term collective bargaining agreements, wage earners, he argues, will acquire a quasi-property right in their jobs.

21. Patten, 1912, 336. While Patten had formulated these ideas much earlier, this was the article that so deeply influenced Herbert Croly in *Progressive Democracy* (1914) and Charles Beard's distinction between Jeffersonian "realty interests" and Hamiltonian "capitalist interests."

22. Ely, 1938, 136. Charles Beard called this era of small-producer and agricultural capitalism "a type of economic society such as had never before appeared in the history of the world and can never exist again" (Beard, 1928b, 132). See also Zunz, 1990, and Livingston, 1994.

23. See Cronon, 1991, and Zunz, 1990. On the decline in southern agriculture, see Eisenach, 1994, 151, 176, and 179–81.

24. On realigning elections and the "system of '96," see Burnham, 1970.

25. McGerr, 1986, 69–105; McCormick, 1986, 197–227; Silbey, 1990, 224–41; and Eisenach, 1994, 104–22.

26. See Perkins, 1968; Collin, 1985; and Rosenberg, 1982.

27. See Rosenberg, 1982, 24–27, and Sklar, 1992, 78–101. On the navy, see Arnold, 1996, 333–59.

28. The term "parastate" refers to nationally oriented institutions and organizations (e.g., universities, professional and reform organizations, the new national journals, ecumenical church organizations) that came to shape both public and Republican Party opinion in this period. Those within the Republican Party who called for a national orientation and leadership by "educated man" were voicing this same antiparty idea. See Eisenach, 1994, 117–22, 135–36, and 161–63.

29. Bensel, 1984, is an excellent study of "core-periphery" politics in this period.

30. Quoted in Mott, 1957, 657.

31. Estimates are that, while the United States accounted for about 23 percent of world production in the 1870s and 35 percent in the period 1906–1910, British shares fell from 32 percent to 15 percent in this same time period. In roughly this time span, America's per capita income rose from $764 to $1,813 while Britain's grew from $972 to $1,491. See Chandler, 1990, 52.

32. Stead, 1902, 149, 440.

33. Matthew Arnold had earlier hailed Stead as the inventor of a new genre of journalism that combined human interest narrative with the cause of social reform. See introduction by Harvey Wish in Stead, 1964.

34. Abbott, 1901, 266.

35. See McClymer, 1980, chapters 5 and 6, on social workers; Kennedy, 1980, 33–44, on the universities; Wynn, 1986, 36–38 and 43–44, on Progressive journalists, reformers, and women's rights activists; Schaffer, 1991, 90–95, on women reformers, and 127–48 on the universities; and Ernst, 1974, 35–69, on liberal evangelical churches and ecumenical associations.

36. Quoted in Giankos and Karson, 1966, 52–53.

37. Croly, 1909, 266–67.

38. The counterpart of this image is that adult males embody liberal individualism and truncated ideas of citizen as voter. This argument is developed in Kann, 1990.

39. Abbott, 1918, 52–54, 106.

40. Speech to the Senate, July 10, 1919.

41. Quoted in Ernst, 1974, 59. For more on Interchurch and other ecumenical initiatives, see chapter 2, above.

42. A more correct image might be that of a massive, nonsectarian established church that embraced the entire range of democratic institutions constituting American civil society, infusing them with shared purpose and value. This initiative is discussed more fully in chapter 2, above, and see Handy, 1991, 184–88.

43. See Marsden, 1994, 343.

44. See Ernst, 1974, and Marsden, 1980.

45. Indicative of the consciousness of this shift is Ames, 1918.

46. Dewey, 1922, 303.

47.   On the churches, see William McGuire King, 1989 and Inboden, 2008; on the federal bureaucracy, see Skowronek, 1982 and Balogh, 2009; on corporatism, the National Civic Federation, and welfare capitalism, see Weinstein, 1968.

48.   See chapter 4, above; Rabban, 1996.

49.   See Paul Johnson, 1983, 230–50.

50.   Hodgson, 1976.

51.   Plotke, 1996, 293–335.

52.   King, 1989, 122–40, and Dudziak, 2002.

53.   Burns, 1967. Burns also wrote a Progressive-style critique of congressional politics, 1949, and a later (1965) defense of a powerful presidency.

54.   Hodgson, 1976.

55.   The extreme statement of Burns's position is Huntington, 1965, which holds that the two thousand new presidential appointments every four or eight years are a more nationally representative and therefore "democratic" body than a locally elected—and endlessly re-elected—Congress. Executive appointees come from dynamic national institutions and address issues from a national and cosmopolitan perspective; congressmen represent local, provincial, and essentially stagnant interests.

56.   Dudziak, 2002.

57.   A book that nicely captures some of the earlier Progressive nationalist perspective is Lind, 1995. See also Sandel, 1996, which restates Progressive arguments against rights-based individualism but, unfortunately, ignores the teachings of earlier Progressive political economy in favor of a nostalgic economic populism.

58.   Some of these issues are discussed more fully in Eisenach, 1994, 18–31, 205–24, and 259–66.

59.   An excellent example of this kind of historical perspective is Gerring, 1998.

60.   Filene, 1970, 20–34; Rodgers, 1982.

61.   An equivalent misreading is to explain national security policy, leadership, and practices, 1950–1970, from the interest-group or "pluralist" reading of American domestic and electoral politics that dominated this period. Since this reading is false on its face, given the autonomous power of the executive establishment and its nongovernmental allies in foreign policy, those who insist that electoral/constitutional politics are everything must resort to capitalist "power elite" (left) or world government (right) conspiracy theory.

62.   See Buenker, 1978, on the north and Midwest; Sarasohn, 1989, on the south.

63.   Hofstadter, 1955.

64.   On the inconsistencies in these readings, see Eisenach, 1994, 21–25, especially footnotes 19 and 21. On the procedural ideal of the Democratic Party, see Jaenicke, 1986.

65.   It also confuses Woodrow Wilson's sudden and necessary conversion to Progressive nationalist rhetoric with a sudden conversion of the Democratic Party rather than as the only viable rhetoric available in that presidential election campaign.

66.   The best of these attempts are Dawley, 1991, and Hansen, 2003.

67.   Livingston, 1994, is the most sophisticated but complex response to this position. Wilson, 1974, and Greenstone, 1993, chapter 2, discuss the relationship between the development of American national identity and a historicist perspective.

Postscript

The 2008 and 2010 Elections in Recent Political Times

"The average American is nothing if not patriotic." Herbert Croly began *The Promise of American Life* with these words and proceeded to argue that national reform, from whatever governmental or other institutional source, must be explicitly premised on and infused with national patriotism. In some of the chapters above, I concluded with rather gloomy predictions about the political future of the Democratic Party and liberal-progressive reform generally in guiding—let alone transforming—the national polity. Two primary reasons were adduced for this outlook. First, the party remains, as it has always been, a coalition of activists from identity groups and material interests. *As identity groups and as material interests* these elements do not ideologically cohere: blue-collar union members, African Americans, feminists, gay and lesbian rights activists, schoolteachers, public employees, trial lawyers, and, most importantly, a large segment of affluent professionals and "idea workers" of all ages and kinds. While most of these groups share a negative consensus (a long tradition in Democratic Party history), most recently a deep dislike of President George W. Bush and his administration, this dislike, often turning to outright hatred and mockery, takes many different forms. For some Bush was an economic royalist, representing powerful economic interests such as big oil, banks, and drug companies. This same president was, to others, a dangerous right-wing populist, appealing to and politically dependent upon the reactionary values of the religious right and the growing influence of evangelical Protestants and conservative Catholics within American Christianity. For still others, Bush represented a resurgent American imperialism. Well-educated professionals focus on military imperialism through the wars in Iraq and Afghanistan; for them, especially those in academia and the media, the heroic legacy of the Vietnam antiwar movement must be protected. For others, especially blue-collar industrial workers, economic imperialism in the forms of free trade, labor migration, and globalization is the target of their ire and discontent. These contradictory forms of contempt and hatred have now been transferred to the Republican Party. It is obvious that this negative consensus does not necessarily contain the materials capable of shaping a coherent positive set of national policies—let alone a coherent narrative that ranks the relative importance of those policies.

The Republican Party, in contrast, despite an active membership that includes great economic, religious, and regional diversity, somehow manages to produce legislators more disciplined regarding public policies and more ideologically coherent both in the critique of their political opponents and in the direction they want the nation to move.

Barack Obama's stunning victories in 2008—first in Democratic Party primaries and then over the strongest candidate the Republican Party could possibly have mustered—might be read as a refutation of this analysis. Obama's compelling appeal is precisely the belief that he would *transcend* differences within the Democratic Party and even transcend party itself in his appeal to all Americans. His ability to attract the enthusiastic support of such broad swaths of America from all races, regions, and income and occupational groups, and an impressive variety of ethnic and religious groups, surely signals a new political era in America. Even through the devastating congressional election of 2010, his personal popularity remained high, the mainstream media continued to swoon and support, and the major national institutions and organizations in American civil society seemed willing to back his major policy initiatives. The meltdown in finance, housing, and credit during the 2008 election and the rising unemployment and economic contraction that followed initially gave an air of urgency and generated added support for most of the president's ambitious domestic agenda.

To be sure, some jarring were notes sounded, especially in the ears of his most ardent and enthusiastic supporters from the left, represented immediately by Obama's "faith-based secularism" (represented by the selection of Rick Warren as the inaugural prayer giver), then by his decision to deploy large numbers of new troops in Afghanistan and his continuation of Bush's extraordinary powers over the capture, holding, and trials of enemy combatants. For his smaller populist economic base, the administration's response to the financial crisis seems crafted more to underwrite Wall Street than to rescue the beleaguered home owner and create jobs for the unemployed. Evidence for all of these fissures and discontents is most clearly found within the body of House Democrats, both when they constituted a numerical majority and, two years later, when they constituted a minority. The event that has most recently symbolized the internal contradictions and disarray among Democratic officials (and voters) is their widely differential response to the Occupy (Wall Street, Seattle, Los Angeles, Tulsa) movements. These protests are treated at once with the greatest attention and respect—as signally important for our political life—and as quite irrelevant as any possible guide for either election strategy or policy proposals. In the meantime, the Republican "tea party" activists all over the country continue their local rounds of voter education and registration—the last believers in the ethic of the League of Women Voters.

Given the congressional results of the election of 2010, the question of whether Obama's resounding victory of 2008 signaled a new Democratic political era has probably been answered in the negative—even if Obama is reelected in 2012. There is a big difference between the repudiation of President Bush and his administration and a repudiation of the ideas, values, and policies begun in 1980 with the victory of Ronald Reagan and strengthened with the later Republican takeover of both houses of Congress during Clinton's second term. Then, as a "wild-card" victor—a Democratic president in a Republican era—Clinton was unable to carve out a policy agenda that differed appreciably from a moderately conservative Republican one. Earlier, the policies of Nixon, who was Clinton's wild-card double in a Democratic era, were, by all measures, more part of a liberal agenda than the beginnings of a conservative one.[1]

A significant change in political regimes not only requires a new set of policy ideas, it requires legislative majorities willing to submit to the discipline and leadership required to mandate and enforce these policies. While this willingness is often purchased with benefits for individual congressmen, highly disruptive and new policies often require the subordination of such interests. The model of a successful legislative majority was the 1994 "Contract with America" that created a common platform for Republican candidates for the House of Representatives. We political scientists well recall its derisive reception by our colleagues and by public intellectuals who specialized in American politics: this isn't how congressmen are elected; this isn't how the House is run; the "Contract" is a public relations device to be quickly forgotten once the election is over. These judgments were not only wrong, the resulting Republican midterm victory—their first winning House election since 1952—led to a series of decisive legislative victories for the Contract's platform and to a major overhaul of congressional procedures, an overhaul that altered the institution to favor disciplined and policy-innovative partisan majorities. The 2008–2010 Democratic majorities in the House (Democrats were also in the majority during the entire presidencies of Nixon/ Ford, Reagan, and H. W. Bush) and in the Senate (Democrats were also in the majority during the entire presidencies of Nixon/Ford and H. W. Bush) have so far evidenced few of these same characteristics. If a *conservative* agenda could be legislated with Democratic legislative *majorities* in the 1980s (tax cuts, deregulation, privatization), why were these same majorities, now backed by a president from their own party, now unable to enact a liberal one?[2] Unless the Democratic Party can create over the next five years as disciplined a majority (or minority) as the Republicans did during the previous eight years, President Obama will be unable to implement a coherent and transformative political agenda.

The Contract with America was later evidence that the initial political success of contemporary conservatism was underwritten, since the early 1980s, by a clear (if highly contentious) set of governing ideas premised on clearly articulated ideals of national patriotism and common good. These ideas were quickly translated into a mobilizing ideology that created enthusiastic platoons of locally based Republican partisans committed to the success of these ideas. And complementing these platoons were well-funded state and national party organizations that supported and directed them, especially in swing states and congressional districts. The capture of the Republican Party by conservatives in most states was also the *creation* of a disciplined party organization made possible by ideologically charged activists. This mobilization was repeated, with the added impetus of the "tea party" movement, in the election of 2010. Moreover, because of locally based party activists, Republican victories in national elections have been replicated by Republican takeovers of increasing numbers of state governments.

During this same period (1980–2010), the Democrats let their already rusty party machinery atrophy, becoming more and more dependent for funding and (often paid) volunteers on outside organizations (often the creation of individual multimillionaires) and interest groups, each with their own priorities and agendas.[3] And while Democratic *presidential* candidates have been well served by these groups and by the candidates' personal campaign organizations, these resources do not easily translate into a common ideological and political will. After his election victory, propelled by funding that dwarfed that of his opponent, President Obama used his large funding surplus not to build a strong Democratic Party from the ground up but to institutionalize his many millions of Internet-based supporters into Organizing for America, a top-down organization designed to mobilize support for his agenda on energy, health care, and education and his reelection campaign. And while President Obama's volunteer ranks are full to overflowing with intellectuals and highly educated professionals of all types, there is no infrastructure of think tanks, publications, and intellectuals to which the Democratic *Party* defers and from which they take their leading ideas. Thus, despite the sweep of the Democratic Party in the election of 2008, Richard Rorty's 1998 critique of American left intellectuals, especially in the universities, still largely holds.[4]

This somewhat bleak prognosis might be tempered by the historical analogy of FDR's 1932 election victory. As we know, his platform and the Democratic Party generally had no significant alternative policy ideas at all (balance the budget?). It wasn't until a durable New Deal electoral coalition was formed in the elections of 1934 and 1936 that the emergency measures taken during the first two years became augmented and shaped into a relatively cohesive set of policies now identified as the New Deal. With that second victory, the Democratic Party (at least its northern portion) became the primary vehicle to carry modern American liberalism. Why haven't the financial rescue and stimulus policies put in place by the Obama administration, augmented by his domestic policy agenda for energy, health, and education, resulted in a coherent ideological restatement of contemporary liberalism of sufficient power to govern America for the next generation?

Given the distinction I drew in earlier chapters between big government and a strong authoritative "state," the ideological liberalism of the New Deal and the ideological conservatism of the past thirty years were both capable of sustaining high levels of public authority even as their respective regimes implemented major policy changes that called for the subordination and sacrifice of many particular interests. In contrast to the conservative Republican regime, however, the reforming impulses of the New Deal were quickly absorbed by World War II and then the Cold War.[5] This is not to say that vast changes were not introduced by government after entry into war, only that national patriotism and elite consensus, not liberal reform ideology and not the Democratic Party, were the driving forces. Put differently, initiative shifted from party majorities in Congress and the president as party leader to the Executive Office of the President and the White House Office as the coordinating center of what became termed a bipartisan "liberal establishment" in both government and society. These bodies had very tenuous ties to Congress but very strong and permanent associations with major national institutions in American life, both public and private. What came to be known as the military-industrial complex of the Cold War was of much greater extent than that term implies: the national media, foundations, churches, research universities, professional and trade associations, and Wall Street were also integral parts of executive power.

In this new context, liberalism as political theory and governing ideas declined into interest-group politics and a rather complacent political science, which not only lost its ideological and reformist edge, but celebrated the loss as "the end of ideology." Attacked first from the New Left and then from the New Right, this kind of liberalism (and the Democratic Party itself) could mount no articulate defense. It is no wonder then that Democratic Party majorities in Congress after the 1970s were quite helpless against the ideas and the policy initiatives of conservative Republican presidents from the 1980s onward. The issue that now presents itself regarding the Democratic Party recapture of power across the board is the state of its "ideational resources":[6] is there now or is there emerging a political theory and an ideology of reform liberalism that can command the support of the electorate, state and local elected officials, Congress, the bureaucracy, and the major institutions of civil society? Can this capture of power be translated into authority?

If these resources are now lacking—and I think they are—the only resource that can hope to take its place is the personal charisma and power of the president. Absent war or other national emergencies, however, this alternative is both unstable and constitutionally dangerous.[7] Moreover, lacking a coherent and ruling ideology, the use of such power has led to "bigger government" (if only to reward major constituency groups in the Democratic Party) without creating a "stronger state." Reform by nostalgia will not suffice,[8] and neither will reform by regulatory fiat. Although it is probably asking too much, one hopes that the immense intellectual and institutional resources of *cultural* liberalism in our universities and in the professions might turn to the serious task of reconstructing an ideology of *political* liberalism premised on a understanding of and commitment to American national patriotism adequate to the task of contemporary governance. We and President Obama need it.

NOTES

1. These terms and their political logic were first framed in Skowronek, 1993, and updated in 2008.

2. But see the collection in Glenn and Teles, 2009, that shows relative ineffectiveness in implementing a conservative agenda in environmental policy, social security, and, to a lesser extent, education.

3. Galvin, 2009, who traces Republican party building back to the Eisenhower administration in the 1950s, notes this failure by the Democrats, but thinks that party building is primarily a function of presidential initiatives—ones that Democratic presidents failed to take in the past, but might take in the future.

4. Rorty, 1998.

5. Brinkley, 1995; Hodgson, 1976.

6. Pierson, 2007, 290, uses the term "ideational infrastructure" to express this failing.

7. Lowi, 1985, who had already declared the "end of liberalism" (1969), argues that this kind of reliance on the presidency has been a prominent feature of our politics since the New Deal.

8. See the collection by Skocpol and Jacobs, 2011, and the response suggested by Skowronek, 2010, chapter 6.

Master Bibliography

Abbott, Lyman. 1892. *The Evolution of Christianity*. Boston: Houghton Mifflin.
———. 1896. *Christianity and Social Problems*. Boston: Houghton Mifflin.
———. 1897. *The Theology of an Evolutionist*. Boston: Houghton Mifflin.
———. 1901. *The Rights of Man*. New York: Houghton Mifflin.
———. 1911. *America in the Making*. New Haven, CT: Yale University Press.
———. 1918. *The Twentieth Century Crusade*. New York: Macmillan.
———. 1922. *Silhouettes of My Contemporaries*. Garden City, NY: Doubleday, Page & Company.
Abbott, Lyman, Amory H. Bradford, et al. 1898. *The New Puritanism*. New York: Fords, Howard, and Hulbert.
Abrams, M. H. 1973. *Natural Supernaturalism: Tradition and Revolution in Romantic Literature*. New York: Norton.
Ackerman, Bruce. 1993. *We the People: Foundations*. Cambridge, MA: Harvard University Press.
———. 2000. *We the People: Transformations*. Cambridge, MA: Harvard University Press.
Adams, Henry Carter, ed. 1893. *Philanthropy and Social Progress*. New York: Thomas Y. Crowell.
———. 1954. Edited by Joseph Dorfman. *The Relation of the State to Industrial Action and Economics and Jurisprudence*. New York: Columbia University Press.
Addams, Jane. 1893. "The Subjective Necessity of Social Settlements." In *Philanthropy and Social Progress*, edited by Henry Carter Adams. New York: Thomas Y. Crowell, 1893.
Altholz, Josef. 1977. "Periodical Origins and Implications of *Essays and Reviews*." *Victorian Periodicals Newsletter* 10:140–54.
American Republican. 1844. November 7.
Ames, Edward Scribner. 1918. *The New Orthodoxy*. Chicago: University of Chicago Press.
Arnold, Peri E. 1996. "Policy Leadership in the Progressive Presidency: The Case of Theodore Roosevelt's Naval Policy and His Search for Strategic Resources." *Studies in American Political Development* 10, no. 2: 333–59.
Bacon, David Francis. 1844. *Progressive Democracy, A Discourse on the History, Philosophy and Tendency of American Politics*. New York: Central Clay Committee.
Balogh, Brian. 2009. *A Government Out of Sight: The Mystery of National Authority in Nineteenth-Century America*. New York: Cambridge University Press.
Barrow, Clyde. 1990. *Universities and the Capitalist State: Corporate Liberalism and the Reconstruction of American Higher Education*. Madison: University of Wisconsin Press.
Barth, Karl. 1959. *Protestant Thought: From Rousseau to Ritschl*. New York: Harper & Brothers.

Bascom, John. 1891. *A New Theology*. New York: G. P. Putnam's Sons.

―――. 1893. *An Historical Interpretation of Philosophy*. New York: G. P. Putnam's Sons.

―――. 1897. *Evolution and Religion; or Faith as a Part of a Complete Cosmic System*. New York: G. P. Putnam's Sons.

―――. 1899. *Growth of Nationality in the United States*. New York: G. P. Putnam's Sons.

Bateman, Bradley W. 2001. "Make a Righteous Number: Social Surveys, the Men and Religion Forward Movement, and Quantification in American Economics." *History of Political Economy* 33 (annual supplement): 57–85.

Batten, Samuel Zane. 1909. *The Christian State: The State, Democracy and Christianity*. Philadelphia: Griffith and Rowland Press.

Beard, Charles. 1928a. *American Government and Politics*. New York: Macmillan.

―――. 1928b. *The American Party Battle*. New York: Workers Education Bureau Press.

Bensel, Richard. 1984. *Sectionalism and American Political Development, 1880–1980*. Madison: University of Wisconsin Press.

Bercovitch, Sacvan. 1975. *The Puritan Origins of the American Self*. New Haven, CT: Yale University Press.

―――. 1976. "How the Puritans Won the American Revolution." *The Massachusetts Review* (Winter): 597–630.

―――. 1978. *The American Jeremiad*. Madison: University of Wisconsin Press.

Bird, Arthur. 1899. *Looking Forward*. Utica, NY: L. C. Childs & Son.

Bledstein, Burton J. 1976. *The Culture of Professionalism: the Middle Class and the Development of Higher Education in America*. New York: Norton.

Bliss, William Dwight Porter, ed. 1908. *The New Encyclopedia of Social Reform*. New York: Funk and Wagnalls.

Block, James. 2002. *A Nation of Agents: The American Path to a Modern Self and Society*. Cambridge, MA: Harvard University Press.

Bloom, Harold. 1992. *The American Religion: The Emergence of a Post-Christian Nation*. New York: Simon and Schuster.

Bowden, Henry Warner. 1971. *Church History in the Age of Science: Historiographical Patterns in the United States, 1876–1918* Chapel Hill, N.C.: The University of North Carolina Press.

Brandes, Stuart D. 1976. *American Welfare Capitalism, 1880–1940*. Chicago: University of Chicago Press.

Brauer, Jerald C., ed. 1968. *Reinterpretation in American Church History*. Chicago: University of Chicago Press.

Brinkley, Alan. 1995. *The End of Reform: New Deal Liberalism in Recession and War*. New York: Knopf.

Brown, Wendy. 2008. *Regulating Aversion: Toleration in an Age of Identity and Empire*. Princeton, NJ: Princeton University Press.

Brown, William Adams. 1906. *The Essence of Christianity: A Study in the History of Definition*. New York: Charles Scribner's Sons.

―――. 1921. *Christian Theology in Outline*. New York: Charles Scribner's Sons.

Buenker, John D. 1978. *Urban Liberalism and Progressive Reform*. New York: Norton.

Burnham, Walter Dean. 1970. *Critical Elections and the Mainsprings of American Politics*. New York: Norton.

Burns, James MacGregor. 1947. *Congress on Trial: The Legislative Process and the Administrative State*. New York: Harper.

―――. 1965. *Presidential Government: The Crucible of Leadership*. Boston: Houghton Mifflin.

―――. 1967. *Deadlock of Democracy: Four-Party Politics in America*. Englewood Cliffs, NJ: Prentice-Hall.

Butler, Jon, and Harry S. Stout, eds. 1998. *Religion in American History*. New York: Oxford University Press.

Butler, Judith. 1996. "Universality in Culture." In *For Love of Country: Debating the Limits of Patriotism* by Martha Nussbaum, edited by Joshua Cohen. Boston: Beacon Press.

Carwardine, Richard J. 1993. *Evangelicals and Politics in Antebellum America*. New Haven, CT: Yale University Press.

Chandler, Alfred. 1990. *Scale and Scope: The Dynamics of Industrial Capitalism*. Cambridge, MA: Harvard University Press.

Cherry, Conrad. 1995. *Hurrying Toward Zion: Universities, Divinity Schools, and American Protestantism*. Bloomington: Indiana University Press.

Christian Century. 1951. "Pluralism—National Menace." Vol. 68 (June 13): 701–3.

Ciepley, David. 2007. *Liberalism in the Shadow of Totalitarianism*. Cambridge, MA: Harvard University Press.

Clark, J. C. D. 1994. *The Language of Liberty, 1660–1832: Political Discourse and Social Dynamics in the Anglo-American World*. New York: Cambridge University Press.

Coats, A. W. 1968. "Henry Carter Adams: A Case Study in the Emergence of the Social Sciences in the United States, 1850–1900." *Journal of American Studies* 2 (October): 177–97.

Collin, Richard. 1985. *Theodore Roosevelt, Culture, Diplomacy, and Expansion*. Baton Rouge: Louisiana State University Press.

Connolly, William E. 1987. *Politics and Ambiguity*. Madison: University of Wisconsin Press.

———. 1991. *Identity/Difference: Democratic Negotiations of Political Paradox*. Ithaca, NY: Cornell University Press.

———. 1999. *Why I Am Not a Secularist*. Minneapolis: University of Minnesota Press.

Cooley, Charles. 1909. *Social Organization: A Study of the Larger Mind*. New York: Scribner.

Cott, Nancy F. 1977. *The Bonds of Womanhood: "Women's Sphere" in New England, 1780–1835*. New Haven, CT: Yale University Press.

Croly, Herbert. 1909. *The Promise of American Life*. New York: Macmillan.

———. 1914. *Progressive Democracy*. New York: Macmillan.

Cronon, William. 1991. *Nature's Metropolis: Chicago and the Great West*. New York: Norton.

Cross, Whitney. 1950. *The Burned-Over District: The Social and Intellectual History of Enthusiastic Religion in Western New York, 1800–1850*. Ithaca, NY: Cornell University Press.

Crunden, Robert M. 1984. *Ministers of Reform: The Progressives' Achievement in American Civilization 1889–1920*. Urbana: University of Illinois Press.

Cuddihy, John M. 1978. *No Offense: Civil Religion and Protestant Taste*. New York: Seabury Press.

Curtis, Susan. 1991. *A Consuming Faith: The Social Gospel and Modern American Culture*. Baltimore: Johns Hopkins University Press.

Dahl, Robert. 1956. *Preface to Democratic Theory*. Chicago: University of Chicago Press.

———. 1967. *Pluralist Democracy in the United States*. Chicago: Rand McNally.

Dawley, Alan. 1991. *Struggles for Justice: Social Responsibility and the Liberal State*. Cambridge, MA: Harvard University Press.

———. 2003. *Changing the World: American Progressives in War and Revolution*. Princeton, NJ: Princeton University Press.

Dean, William. 2002. *American Spiritual Culture and the Invention of Jazz, Football, and the Movies*. New York and London: Continuum International.

Dewey, John. 1888. "The Ethics of Democracy." *Philosophical Papers*, second series, no. 1. Ann Arbor: University of Michigan.

———. 1893. "The Relation of Philosophy to Theology." In *The Early Works, 1882–1898*, vol. 4. Carbondale: Southern Illinois University Press, 1971.

———. 1894. "Christianity and Democracy." In *The Early Works, 1882–1898*, vol. 4. Carbondale: Southern Illinois University Press, 1971.

———. 1897. "My Pedagogic Creed." *The Early Works, 1882–1898*. Vol. 5, 1895–1898. Carbondale: Southern Illinois University Press, 1972.

———. 1908. "Religion and Our Schools." *The Middle Works, 1899–1909*. Vol. 4, 1907–1909. Carbondale: Southern Illinois University Press, 1977.

———. 1922. "An American Intellectual Frontier." *The New Republic*, May 10, 303–5.

———. 1924. "Logical Method and the Law." *Cornell Law Quarterly* 10:17–27.

———. 1934. *A Common Faith*. New Haven, CT: Yale University Press.

Dewey, John, and James Tufts. 1908. *Ethics*. New York: Henry Holt.

De Witt, Benjamin Parke. 1915. *The Progressive Movement*. New York: Macmillan.

Dickinson, John. 1895. *Writings*. Edited by Paul Leicester Ford. Philadelphia: Historical Society of Pennsylvania.

Dionne, E. J. 1996. *They Only Look Dead: Why Progressives Will Dominate the Next Political Era*. New York: Simon and Schuster.

Dombrowski, James. (1936) 1966. *The Early Days of Christian Socialism in America*. New York: Octagon Books.

Dorfman, Joseph. 1949. *The Economic Mind of American Civilization, Vol. 3, 1865–1880*. New York: Viking Press.

Dorrien, Gary. 2001. *The Making of American Liberal Theology: Imagining Progressive Religion, 1805–1900*. Louisville, KY: Westminster John Knox Press.

———. 2003. *The Making of American Liberal Theology: Idealism, Realism & Modernity, 1900–1950*. Louisville, KY: Westminster John Knox Press.

Douglas, Ann. 1977. *The Feminization of American Culture*. New York: Knopf.

Dudziak, Mary L. 2002. *Cold War Civil Rights: Race and the Image of American Democracy*. Princeton, NJ: Princeton University Press.

Eisenach, Eldon. 1979. "Cultural Politics and Political Thought: The American Revolution Made and Remembered." *American Studies* 20, no. 1 (Spring): 71–97.

———. 1981. *Two Worlds of Liberalism: Religion and Politics in Hobbes, Locke, and Mill*. Chicago: University of Chicago Press.

———. 1990. "Reconstituting the Study of American Political Thought in a Regime Change Perspective." *Studies in American Political Development* 4:169–228.

———. 1994. *The Lost Promise of Progressivism*. Lawrence: University Press of Kansas.

———. 1996. "Bookends: Seven Stories Excised from *The Lost Promise of Progressivism*." *Studies in American Political Development* 10, no. 1: 168–83.

———. 1998. "Mill and Liberal Christianity." In *Mill and the Moral Character of Liberalism*, edited by E. Eisenach. University Park: Penn State Press.

———. 2000. *The Next Religious Establishment: National Identity and Political Theology in Post-Protestant America*. Lanham, MD: Rowman & Littlefield.

———. 2002. *Narrative Power and Liberal Truth: Hobbes, Locke, Bentham, and Mill*. Lanham, MD: Rowman & Littlefield.

———. 2006a. "Can Liberalism Still Tell Powerful Stories?" *European Legacy* 11, no. 1: 47–71.

———, ed. 2006b. *The Social and Political Thought of American Progressivism*. Indianapolis: Hackett.

Ellis, Ieuan. 1980. *Seven against Christ: A Study of "Essays and Reviews."* Leiden: E. J. Brill.

Ely, Richard. 1893. *Outlines of Economics*. Chautauqua, NY: Chautauqua Press.

———. 1903. *Studies in the Evolution of Industrial Society*. Chautauqua, NY: Chautauqua Press.

———. 1938. *Ground under Our Feet*. New York: Macmillan.

Engster, Daniel. 2001. *Divine Sovereignty: The Origins of Modern State Power*. Dekalb: Northern Illinois University Press.

Epstein, Richard A. 2006. *How the Progressives Rewrote the Constitution*. Washington, DC: Cato Institute.

Ernst, Eldon G. 1974. *Moment of Truth of Protestant America: Interchurch Campaigns Following World War I*. Missoula, MT: Scholars' Press.

Essays and Reviews. 1860. London: John W. Parker & Son.

Everett, John R. 1946. *Religion in Economics: A Study of John Bates Clark, Richard T. Ely and Simon N. Patten*. New York: King's Crown Press.

Feffer, Andrew. 1993. *The Chicago Pragmatists and American Progressivism*. Ithaca, NY: Cornell University Press.

Ferguson, Robert. 1997. *The American Enlightenment*. Cambridge, MA: Harvard University Press.

Filene, Peter. 1970. "An Obituary for the 'Progressive Movement.'" *American Quarterly* 22, no. 1 (Spring): 20–34.

Fine, Sidney. 1956. *Laissez-Faire and the General Welfare State*. Ann Arbor: University of Michigan Press.

Fish, Stanley. 1999. *The Trouble with Principle*. Cambridge, MA: Harvard University Press.

Fitzpatrick, Ellen. 1990. *Endless Crusade: Women Social Scientists and Progressive Reform*. New York: Oxford University Press.

Follett, Mary Parker. 1918. *The New American State: Group Organization in the Solution of Popular Government*. New York: Longmans, Green.

Foster, Charles. 1960. *Errand of Mercy: The Evangelical United Front, 1790–1837*. Chapel Hill: University of North Carolina Press.

Foster, Frank Hugh. 1907. *A Genetic History of the New England Theology*. Chicago: University of Chicago Press.

Fox, Daniel. 1967. *The Discovery of Abundance: Simon N. Patten and the Transformation of Social Theory*. Ithaca, NY: Cornell University Press.

Fox, Richard W. 1977. "Experience and Explanation in Twentieth-Century American History." In *New Directions in American Religious History*, edited by Harry S. Stout and P. G. Hart. New York: Oxford University Press, 1997.

———. 1993. "The Culture of Liberal Protestant Progressivism, 1875–1925." *Journal of Interdisciplinary History* 23:639–60.

Fox, Richard W., and Robert B. Westbrook, eds. 1998. *In Face of the Facts: Moral Inquiry in American Scholarship*. Washington, DC: Woodrow Wilson Center Press, and New York: Cambridge University Press.

Freeden, Michael. 1996. *Ideologies and Political Theory: A Conceptual Approach*. New York: Oxford University Press.

———. 2003. *Ideology: A Very Short Introduction*. New York: Oxford University Press.

———. 2004. *Liberal Languages: Ideological Languages and Twentieth-Century Progressive Thought*. Princeton, NJ: Princeton University Press.

Gabriel, Ralph H. (1940) 1956. *The Course of American Democratic Thought*. New York: Roland Press.

Galvin, Daniel. 2009. *Presidential Party Building in the United States*. Princeton, NJ: Princeton University Press.

Gaustad, Edwin S. 1989. "The Pulpit and the Pews." In Hutchison, 1989, 21–47.

Gerring, John. 1998. *Party Ideologies in America, 1828–1996*. New York: Cambridge University Press.

Giankos, Perry E., and Albert Karson, eds. 1966. *American Diplomacy and the Sense of National Destiny*. 2 vols. Belmont, CA: Wadsworth.

Giddings, Franklin. 1898. *Elements of Sociology*. New York: Macmillan.

Gienapp, William E. 1987. *The Origins of the Republican Party, 1852–1856*. New York: Oxford University Press.

Glendon, Mary Ann. 1991. *Rights Talk: The Impoverishment of American Political Discourse*. New York: Free Press.

Glenn, Brian J. 2004. "The Two Schools of American Political Development." *Political Studies Review* 2, no. 2: 153–65.

Glenn, Brian J., and Steven M. Teles, eds. 2009. *Conservatism and American Political Development*. New York: Oxford.

Green, William Scott. 1996. "Religion Within the Limits." In *Bulletin of the American Association of University Professors*, supplement, *Academe* 82, no. 6: 24–28.

Greenstone, David. 1993. *The Lincoln Persuasion: Remaking American Liberalism*. Princeton, NJ: Princeton University Press.

Gutmann, Amy. 1999. *Democratic Education*. Princeton, NJ: Princeton University Press.

———. 2003. *Identity in Democracy*. Princeton, NJ: Princeton University Press.

Haakonssen, Knud, ed. 1996. *Enlightenment and Religion: Rational Dissent in Eighteenth-Century Britain*. New York: Cambridge University Press.

Hamburger, Philip. 2002. *Separation of Church and State*. Cambridge, MA: Harvard University Press.

Handy, Robert. 1967. *The Protestant Quest for a Christian America, 1830–1930*. Philadelphia: Fortress Press.

——. 1971. *A Christian America: Protestant Hopes and Historical Realities*. New York: Oxford University Press.

——. 1991. *Undermined Establishment: Church-State Relations in America, 1880–1920*. Princeton, NJ: Princeton University Press.

Hansen, Jonathan. 2003. *Lost Promise of Patriotism: Debating American Identity, 1890–1920*. Chicago: University of Chicago Press.

Haroutunian, Joseph. 1964. *Piety Versus Moralism: The Passing of the New England Theology*. Hamden, CT: Archon Books.

Harrison, Peter. 1996. *"Religion" and the Religions in the English Enlightenment*. Cambridge: Cambridge University Press.

Haskell, Thomas. 1977. *The Emergence of Professional Social Science: The American Social Science Association and the Nineteenth Century Crisis of Authority*. Urbana: University of Illinois Press.

Hatch, Nathan. 1977. *The Sacred Cause of Liberty: Republican Thought and the Millennium in Revolutionary New England*. New Haven, CT: Yale University Press.

Heimert, Alan. 1966. *Religion and the American Mind: From the Great Awakening to the Revolution*. Cambridge, MA: Harvard University Press.

Herberg, Will. (1955) 1983. *Protestant, Catholic, Jew*. Chicago: University of Chicago Press.

Herron, George. 1894. *The Christian Society*. Chicago: Fleming H. Revell.

Herbst, Jurgen. 1965. *The German Historical School in American Scholarship*. Cambridge, MA: Harvard University Press.

Higonnet, Patrice. 2007. *Attendant Cruelties: Nation and Nationalism in American History*. Other Press.

Hinchman, Lewis P. 1984. *Hegel's Critique of the Enlightenment*. Gainesville: University of Florida Press.

Hinchman, Lewis P., and Sandra K. Hinchman, eds. 1997. *Memory, Identity, Community: The Idea of Narrative in the Human Sciences*. Albany: State University of New York Press.

Hochstrasser, T. J. 2000. *Natural Law Theories in the Early Enlightenment*. Cambridge: Cambridge University Press.

Hodgson, Godfrey. 1976. *America in Our Time*. Garden City, NY: Doubleday.

Hofstadter, Richard. 1955. *The Age of Reform: From Bryan to FDR*. New York: Knopf.

Hollinger, David A. 1993. "How Wide and Circle of the We? American Intellectuals and the Problem of the Ethnos since World War II." *American Historical Review* 98:317–37.

Horwitz, Morton J. 1992. *The Transformation of American Law, 1870–1970: The Crisis of Legal Orthodoxy*. New York: Oxford University Press.

Howe, Daniel Walker, ed. 1976. *Victorian America*. Philadelphia: University of Pennsylvania Press.

——. 1979. *The Political Culture of the American Whigs*. Chicago: University of Chicago Press.

——. 1990. "Religion and Politics in the Antebellum North." In *Religion and American Politics from the Colonial Era to the 1980s*, edited by Mark A. Noll. New York: Oxford University Press.

——. 1997. "Protestantism, Voluntarism, and Personal Identity in Antebellum America." In *New Directions in American Religious History*, edited by Harry S. Stout and P. G. Hart. New York: Oxford University Press.

Hughes, Richard T. 2004. *Myths America Lives By*. Urbana: University of Illinois Press.

Hunter, Ian. 2001. *Rival Enlightenments: Civil and Metaphysical Philosophy in Early Modern Germany*. Cambridge: Cambridge University Press.

Huntington, Samuel. 1965. "Congressional Responses to the Twentieth Century." In *The Congress and America's Future*, edited by David Truman. Englewood Cliffs, NJ: Prentice-Hall.

——. 1980. *American Politics: The Promise of Disharmony*. Cambridge, MA: Harvard University Press.

Hutchison, William R., ed. 1989. *Between the Times: The Travail of the Protestant Establishment in America, 1900-1960*. New York: Cambridge University Press.

Hutchison, William R. 1987. *Errand to the World: American Protestant Thought and Foreign Missions*. Chicago: University of Chicago Press.

———. 1992. *The Modernist Impulse in American Protestantism.* Durham, NC: Duke University Press.

———. 2003. *Religious Pluralism in America: The Contentious History of a Founding Ideal.* New Haven, CT: Yale University Press.

Inboden, William. 2008. *Religion and American Foreign Policy, 1945–1960: The Soul of Containment.* New York: Cambridge University Press.

Isaac, Jeffrey C. 2003. *Poverty of Progressivism; The Future of American Democracy in a Time of Decline.* Lanham, MD: Rowman & Littlefield.

Isenberg, Nancy. 1998. *Sex and Citizenship in Antebellum America.* Chapel Hill: University of North Carolina Press.

Jacobs, Lawrence, and Desmond King, eds. 2009. *The Unsustainable American State.* Princeton, NJ: Princeton University Press.

Jaenicke, Douglas W. 1986. "The Jacksonian Integration of Parties into the Constitutional System." *Political Science Quarterly* 101:85–107.

Jakobsen, Janet R. 2000. "World Secularisms at the Millennium: Introduction." *Social Text* 18 (Fall): 1–27.

Jensen, Richard. 1971. *The Winning of the Mid-West: Social and Political Conflict, 1888–1896.* Chicago: University of Chicago Press.

Johnson, Donald B., and Kirk H. Porter, eds. 1975. *National Party Platforms, 1840–1972.* Urbana: University of Illinois Press.

Johnson, Paul. 1983. *A History of the Modern World, from 1917 to the 1980s.* London: Weidenfeld and Nicholson.

Johnston, Robert D. 2002. "Re-Democratizing the Progressive Era: The Politics of Progressive Era Political Historiography." *Journal of the Gilded Age and Progressive Era* 1, no. 1: 68–92.

Jones, H. S. 2007. *Intellect and Character: Mark Pattison and the Invention of the Don.* Cambridge: Cambridge University Press.

Jumonville, Neil, and Kevin Mattson, eds. 2007. *Liberalism for a New Century.* Berkeley: University of California Press.

Kahn, Paul W. 2005. *Putting Liberalism in its Place.* Princeton, NJ: Princeton University Press.

Kann, Mark E. 1990. "Individualism, Civic Virtue, and Gender in America." *Studies in American Political Development*, 4:46–81.

Keller, Morton. 1977. *Affairs of State: Public Life in Late Nineteenth Century America.* Cambridge, MA: Harvard University Press.

Kelley, Florence. 1905. *Some Ethical Gains through Legislation.* New York: Macmillan.

Kelley, Robert L. 1979. *The Cultural Pattern in American Politics: The First Century.* New York: Alfred A. Knopf.

Kelly, George Armstrong. 1984. *Politics and Religious Consciousness in America.* New Brunswick, NJ: Transaction.

Kennedy, David M. 1980. *Over Here: The First World War and American Society.* New York: Oxford University Press.

Kern, Kathi. 2001. *Mrs. Stanton's Bible.* Ithaca, NY: Cornell University Press.

Kerr, Clark. 1963. *The Uses of the University.* Cambridge, MA: Harvard University Press.

Kestenbaum, Victor. 2002. *The Grace and Severity of the Ideal: John Dewey and the Transcendent.* Chicago: University of Chicago Press.

King, Henry Churchill. 1902. *Theology and the Social Consciousness.* New York: Hodder & Stoughton.

King, William McGuire. 1983. "'History as Revelation' in the Theology of the Social Gospel." *Harvard Theological Review* 76:109–29.

———. 1989. "The Reform Establishment and the Ambiguities of Influence." In Hutchison, 1989.

Kleppner, Paul. 1970. *The Cross of Culture: A Social Analysis of Midwestern Politics 1850–1900.* New York: Free Press.

———. 1987. *Continuity and Change in Electoral Politics, 1893–1928.* Westport, CT: Greenwood Press.

Kloppenberg, James T. 1986. *Uncertain Victory: Social Democracy and Progressivism in European and American Thought.* New York: Oxford University Press.

———. 1998. *The Virtues of Liberalism.* New York: Oxford University Press.

———. 2003. "From Hartz to Tocqueville: Shifting the Focus from Liberalism to Democracy in America." In *The Democratic Experiment,* edited by Meg Jacobs, William Novak, and Julian Zelizer. Princeton, NJ: Princeton University Press.

———. 2011. *Reading Obama: Dreams, Hope, and the American Political Tradition.* Princeton, NJ: Princeton University Press.

Kohl, Lawrence F. 1989. *The Politics of Individualism: Parties and American Character in the Jacksonian Era.* New York: Oxford University Press.

Kuklick, Bruce. 1985. *Churchmen and Philosophers: From Jonathan Edwards to John Dewey.* New Haven, CT: Yale University Press.

Landis, James M. 1938. *The Administrative Process.* New Haven, Conn.: Yale University Press.

Levy, David. 1985. *Herbert Croly of the New Republic.* Princeton, NJ: Princeton University Press.

Levy, Michael. 1982. *Political Thought in America.* Boulder, CO: Waveland.

Lieberman, Robert C. 2002. "Ideas, Institutions, and Political Order: Explaining Political Change." *American Political Science Review* 96:697–712.

Lind, Michael. 1995. *The Next American Nation: The New Nationalism and the Fourth American Revolution.* New York: Free Press.

———. 1996. *Up From Conservatism: Why the Right Is Wrong for America.* New York: Free Press.

Lippmann, Walter. (1914) 1961. *Drift and Mastery: An Attempt to Diagnose our Current Unrest.* Englewood Cliffs, NJ: Prentice-Hall.

Livingston, James. 1994. *Pragmatism and the Political Economy of Cultural Revolution 1850–1940.* Chapel Hill: University of North Carolina Press.

Low, Seth, and Richard T. Ely. 1890. "A Programme for Labor Reform." *Century Magazine* 39, no. 6: 938–51.

Lowi, Theodore. 1969. *The End of Liberalism.* New York: W. W. Norton.

———. 1985. *The Personal President: Power Invested, Promise Unfulfilled.* Ithaca, NY: Cornell University Press.

Lustig, R. Jeffrey. 1982. *Corporate Liberalism: The Origins of Modern American Political Theory.* Berkeley: University of California Press.

MacIntyre, Alasdair. 1984. *After Virtue: A Study of Moral Theory.* South Bend, IN: University of Notre Dame Press.

MacPherson, James M. 1991. *Abraham Lincoln and the Second American Revolution.* New York: Oxford University Press.

Marsden, George. 1980. *Fundamentalism and American Culture.* New York: Oxford University Press.

———. 1994. *The Soul of the American University: From Protestant Establishment to Established Unbelief.* New York: Oxford University Press.

Marsden, George, and Bradley J. Longfield, eds. 1992. *The Secularization of the Academy.* New York: Oxford University Press.

Marty, Martin. 1986. *Modern American Religion.* Vol. 1, *The Irony of It All, 1893–1919.* Chicago: University of Chicago Press.

———. 1996. *Modern American Religion.* Vol. 3, *Under God, Indivisible, 1940–1960.* Chicago: University of Chicago Press.

McCarthy, Kathleen D. 2001. *Women, Philanthropy, and Civil Society.* Bloomington: University of Indiana Press.

———. 2003. *American Creed: Philanthropy and the Rise of Civil Society.* Chicago: University of Chicago Press.

McClymer, John E. 1980. *War and Welfare: Social Engineering in America, 1890–1925.* Westport, CT: Greenwood Press.

McCormick, Richard L. 1986. *The Party Period and Public Policy: American Politics from the Age of Jackson to the Progressive Era.* New York: Oxford University Press.

McGerr, Michael. 1986. *The Decline of Popular Politics: The American North, 1865–1928*. New York: Oxford University Press.

———. 2003. *A Fierce Discontent: The Rise and Fall of the Progressive Movement in America, 1870–1920*. New York: Free Press.

Mead, Sidney E. 1975. *The Nation with the Soul of a Church*. New York: Harper and Row.

Meyer, D. H. 1976. "American Intellectuals and the Victorian Crisis of Faith." In *Victorian America*, edited by Daniel Walker Howe. Philadelphia: University of Pennsylvania Press.

Milkis, Sidney M. 2009. *Theodore Roosevelt, the Progressive Party, and the Transformation of American Politics*. Lawrence: University Press of Kansas.

Monsma, Stephen V. 1996. *When Sacred and Secular Mix: Religious Nonprofit Organizations and Public Money*. Lanham, MD: Rowman & Littlefield.

Moore, R. Laurence. 1986. *Religious Outsiders and the Making of Americans*. New York: Oxford University Press.

———. 1994. *Selling God: American Religion in the Marketplace of Culture*. New York: Oxford University Press.

Morone, James. 2003. *Hellfire Nation: The Politics of Sin in American History*. New Haven, CT: Yale University Press.

Mott, Frank Luther. 1957. *A History of American Magazines, Vol. 3: 1865–1885*. Cambridge, MA: Harvard University Press.

Mulford, Elisha. 1882. *The Republic of God*. New York: Houghton.

Murphy, Andrew R. 2001. *Conscience and Community: Revisiting Toleration and Religious Dissent in Early Modern England and America*. University Park: Penn State Press.

———. 2008. *Prodigal Nation: Moral Decline and Divine Punishment from New England to 9/11*. New York: Oxford University Press.

Murphy, Howard. 1955. "The Ethical Revolt against Christian Orthodoxy in Early Victorian England." *American Historical Review* 60:800–17.

Neal, Patrick. 1997. *Liberalism and Its Discontents*. New York: New York University Press.

Nearing, Scott. 1925. *Educational Frontiers: A Book about Simon N. Patten and Other Teachers*. New York: T. Seltzer.

Neumann, Franz L. 1957. *The Democratic and Authoritarian State: Essays in Political and Legal Theory*. Glencoe, IL: Free Press.

Neustadt, Richard. 1976. *Presidential Power: The Politics of Leadership with Reflections on Johnson and Nixon*. New York: Wiley.

New Yorker. 2008. "The Mail." April 26, 5.

Noll, Mark, ed. 1990. *Religion and American Politics*. New York: Oxford University Press.

Novak, William J. 1996. *The People's Welfare: Law and Regulation and Nineteenth Century America*. Chapel Hill: University of North Carolina Press.

———. 2008. "The Myth of the 'Weak' American State." *American Historical Review* 113:752–72.

Orren, Karen, and Stephen Skowronek. 2004. *The Search for American Political Development*. New York: Cambridge University Press.

Oshatz, Molly. 2008. "The Problem of Moral Progress: The Slavery Debates and the Development of Liberal Protestantism in the United States." *Modern Intellectual History* 5:225–50.

Owen, J. Judd. 2001. *Religion and the Demise of Liberal Rationalism: The Foundational Crisis of the Separation of Church and State*. Chicago: University of Chicago Press.

Paine, Thomas. 1976. *Common Sense*. Edited by Isaac Kramnick. New York: Penguin.

Parker, Alison. 1997. *Purifying America: Women, Cultural Reform, and Pro-Censorship Activism, 1873–1933*. Urbana: University of Illinois Press.

Patten, Simon. 1896. *A Theory of Social Forces*. Philadelphia: American Academy of Political and Social Science.

———. 1902. *The Theory of Prosperity*. New York: Macmillan.

———. 1907. *The New Basis of Civilization*. New York: Macmillan.

———. 1912. "The Reconstruction of Economic Theory." In *Essays in Economic Theory*, edited by Rexford Tugwell. New York: Knopf.

Perkins, Bradford. 1968. *The Great Rapprochement: England and the United States, 1895–1914*. New York: Atheneum.

Phillips, Kevin. 1999. *The Cousins' Wars: Religion, Politics, Civil Warfare, and the Triumph of Anglo-America.* New York: Basic Books.

Pierson, Paul, and Theda Skocpol, eds. 2007. *The Transformation of American Politics: Activist Government and the Rise of Conservatism.* Princeton, NJ: Princeton University Press.

Plotke, David. 1996. *Building a New Democratic Political Order: Reshaping American Liberalism in the 1930s and 1940s.* New York: Cambridge University Press.

Posner, Richard. 1995. *Overcoming Law.* Cambridge, MA: Harvard University Press.

Pound, Roscoe. 1908. "Mechanical Jurisprudence." *Columbia Law Review* 8:605–23.

———. 1909. "Liberty of Contract." *Yale Law Journal* 18:454–87.

———. 1910. "Law in Books and Law in Action." *American Law Review* 44: 12–36.

Rabban, David. 1996. "Free Speech in Progressive Social Thought." *Texas Law Review* 74:951–1038.

Rauschenbusch, Walter. 1914. *Christianity and the Social Crisis.* London: Macmillan.

———. (1917) 1945. *A Theology for the Social Gospel.* Nashville: Abingdon Press.

Rawls, John. 1971. *A Theory of Justice.* Cambridge, MA: Harvard University Press.

———. 1997. "The Idea of Public Reason Revisited." *University of Chicago Law Review* 64:765–807.

———. 2009. *A Brief Inquiry into the Meaning of Sin and Faith: With "On My Religion,"* edited by Thomas Nagel. Cambridge, MA: Harvard University Press.

Redhead, Mark. 2003. "Alternative Secularisms." Unpublished American Political Science Association paper, Philadelphia.

Reidy, David A. 2010. "Rawls's Religion and Justice as Fairness." *History of Political Thought* 31:309–44.

Reuben, Julie. 1996. *The Making of the Modern University; Intellectual Transformation and the Marginalization of Morality.* Chicago: University of Chicago Press.

Rodgers, Daniel T. 1982. "In Search of Progressivism." *Reviews in American History* 10, no. 4: 113–32.

Rogers, Melvin L. 2008. *The Undiscovered Dewey: Religion, Morality, and the Ethos of Democracy.* New York: Columbia University Press.

Rorty, Richard. 1998. *Achieving Our Country: Leftist Thought in Twentieth-Century America.* Cambridge, MA: Harvard University Press.

Rosenberg, Emily. 1982. *Spreading the American Dream: American Economic and Cultural Expansion, 1890–1945.* New York: Hill and Wang.

Ross, Dorothy. 1977. "Socialism and American Liberalism: Academic Social Thought in the 1890s." *Perspectives in American History* 11:5–79.

———. 1990. *Origins of American Social Science.* New York: Cambridge University Press.

———. 2009. "Lincoln and the Ethics of Emancipation: Universalism, Nationalism, Exceptionalism." *Journal of American History* 96:379–99.

Ross, Edward A. 1901. *Social Control: A Survey of the Foundations of Order.* New York: Macmillan.

Ruthven, Malise. 2007. *Fundamentalism: A Very Short Introduction.* New York: Oxford University Press.

Sandel, Michael. 1996. *Democracy's Discontent: America in Search of a Public Philosophy.* Cambridge, MA: Harvard University Press.

Sarasohn, David. 1989. *The Party of Reform: Democrats in the Progressive Era.* Jackson: University Press of Mississippi.

Schaffer, Ronald. 1991. *America in the Great War: The Rise of the War Welfare State.* New York: Oxford University Press.

Schleiermacher, Friedrich. 1969. *On Religion: Addresses in Response to Its Cultured Critics.* Richmond, VA: John Knox Press.

———. 1989. *Introduction to Christian Ethics.* Translated by John C. Shelley. Nashville: Abingdon Press.

Schlesinger, Arthur M., Jr. 1949. *The Vital Center: The Politics of Freedom.* Boston: Houghton Mifflin.

Schmidt, Leigh Eric. 1997. *Consumer Rites.* Princeton, NJ: Princeton University Press.

Schneider, Herbert W. 1946. *A History of American Philosophy*. New York: Columbia University Press.

Scudder, Vida Dutton. 1898. *Social Ideals in English Letters*. New York: Houghton Mifflin.

Seligman, Edwin R. A. 1907. *The Economic Interpretation of History*. 2nd ed., revised. New York: Columbia University Press.

Shefter, Martin. 1978. "Party, Bureaucracy, and Political Change in the United States." In *Political Parties: Development and Decay*, edited by Louis Maisel and Joseph Cooper. Beverly Hills: Sage Publications.

Silbey, Joel. 1990. *The American Political Nation, 1838–1893*. Stanford, CA: Stanford University Press.

Silk, Mark. 1988. *Spiritual Politics: Religion and America since World War II*. New York: Simon and Schuster.

Skinner, Quentin, ed. 1985. *The Return of Grand Theory in the Human Sciences*. New York: Cambridge University Press.

Sklar, Martin J. 1992. *The United States as a Developing Country*. New York: Cambridge University Press.

Skocpol, Theda. 2003. *Diminished Democracy: From Membership on Management in American Civil Life*. Norman: University of Oklahoma Press.

Skocpol, Theda, and Lawrence Jacobs, eds. 2011. *Reaching for a New Deal: Ambitious Governance, Economic Meltdown, and Politics in Obama's First Two Years*. New York: Russell Sage Foundation.

Skowronek, Stephen. 1982. *Building a New American State: The Expansion of National Administrative Capacities, 1877–1920*. New York: Cambridge University Press.

———. 1993. *The Politics Presidents Make*. Cambridge, MA: Harvard University Press.

———. 2006. "The Reassociation of Ideas and Purposes: Racism, Liberalism, and the American Political Tradition." *American Political Science Review* 100, no. 3 (August): 385–401.

———. 2010. *Presidential Leadership in Political Time: Reprise and Reappraisal*. 2nd expanded revised ed. Lawrence: University Press of Kansas.

Small, Albion. 1895a. "The State and Semi-Public Corporations." *American Journal of Sociology* 1, no. 4: 398–441.

———. 1895b. "Private Business Is a Public Trust." *American Journal of Sociology* 1, no. 3: 276–289.

———. 1914. "The Social Gradations of Capital." *American Journal of Sociology* 19, no. 6, 721–752.

———. 1915. "The Bonds of Nationality." *American Journal of Sociology* 20, no. 5, 629–683.

Smith, Elwyn. 1971. "The Voluntary Establishment of Religion." In *The Religion of the Republic*, edited by Elwyn Smith. Philadelphia: Fortress Press.

Smith, Rogers. 1997. *Civic Ideals: Conflicting Visions of US History*. New Haven, CT: Yale University Press.

———. 2003. *Stories of Peoplehood: The Politics and Morals of Political Membership*. New York: Cambridge University Press.

Smith, Steven D. 1995. *Foreordained Failure: The Quest for a Constitutional Principle of Religious Freedom*. New York: Oxford University Press.

Smith, Ted. 2007. *The New Measures; a Theological History of Democratic Practice*. Cambridge, MA: Cambridge University Press.

Spragens, Thomas, Jr. 2009. *Getting the Left Right: The Transformation, Decline, and Reformation of American Liberalism*. Lawrence: University Press of Kansas.

Stead, William T. 1902. *The Americanization of the World*. New York and London: H. Markley.

———. 1964. *If Christ Came to Chicago: A Plea for the Union of All Who Love Service to All Who Suffer*. New York: Living Books.

Stears, Marc. 2004. *Progressives, Pluralists, and the Problems of the State: Ideologies of Reform in the United States and Britain, 1896–1926*. New York: Oxford University Press.

———. 2010. *Demanding Democracy: American Radicals in Search of a New Kind of Democracy*. Princeton, NJ: Princeton University Press.

Steiner, Edward A. 1909. *The Immigrant Tide, Its Ebb and Flow*. New York: Fleming H. Revell

Stettner, Edward A. 1993. *Shaping Modern Liberalism: Herbert Croly and Progressive Thought*. Lawrence: University Press of Kansas.

Stevens, Robert. 1983. *Law School*. Chapel Hill: University of North Carolina Press.

Stevenson, Louise L. 1986. *Scholarly Means to Evangelical Ends: The New Haven Scholars and the Transformation of Higher Learning in America, 1830–1890*. Baltimore: Johns Hopkins University Press.

Stout, Harry S., and P. G. Hart, eds. 1997. *New Directions in American Religious History*. New York: Oxford University Press.

Strong, Josiah. 1900. *Religious Movements for Social Betterment*. New York: The Baker and Taylor Company.

———. 1915. *The New World Religion*. New York: Doubleday, Page, and Co.

Swierenga, Robert P. 1990. "Ethnoreligious Political Behavior in the Mid-Nineteenth Century: Voting, Values, Cultures." In Noll, 1990, 146–71.

Taylor, Charles. 1975. *Hegel*. New York: Cambridge University Press.

———. 1985. "What is Human Agency?" In *Human Agency and Language: Philosophical Papers I*. Cambridge, MA: Cambridge University Press.

———. 1989. *Sources of the Self*. Cambridge, MA: Harvard University Press.

———. 1991. *The Ethics of Authenticity*. Cambridge, MA: Harvard University Press.

———. 1998. "Modes of Secularism." In *Secularism and Its Critics*, edited by Rajeev Bhargava. London and Delhi: Oxford University Press.

———. 2001. "The Immanent Counter-Enlightenment." In *Canadian Political Philosophy: Contemporary Reflection*, edited by Ronald Beiner and Wayne Norman. Oxford: Oxford University Press.

———. 2007. *A Secular Age*. Cambridge, MA: Harvard University Press.

Taylor, Nathaniel. 1859. *Lectures on the Moral Governments of God*. 2 vols. New York: Clark.

Teles, Steven. 2007. "Conservative Mobilization against Entrenched Liberalism." In Pierson and Skocpol, 2007, 160–88.

———. 2008. *The Rise of the Conservative Legal Movement: The Battle for Control of the Law*. Princeton, NJ: Princeton University Press.

———. 2009. "Transformative Bureaucracy: Reagan's Lawyers and the Dynamics of Political Investment." *Studies in American Political Development* 23:61–83.

Thelen, David Paul. 1972. *The New Citizenship: The Origins of Progressivism in Wisconsin, 1885–1890*. Columbia: University of Missouri Press.

Thomas, George M. 1989. *Revivalism and Cultural Change: Christianity, Nation Building, and the Market in the Nineteenth-Century United States*. Chicago: University of Chicago Press.

Tomasi, John. 2001. *Liberalism beyond Justice: Citizens, Society, and the Boundaries of Political Theory*. Princeton, NJ: Princeton University Press.

Tomasky, Michael. 1996. *Left for Dead: The Life, Death, and Possible Resurrection of Progressive Politics in America*. New York: Free Press.

Truman, David. 1951. *The Governmental Process*. New York: Knopf.

Tushnet, Mark. 1985. "The Constitution of Religion." *Connecticut Law Review* 18:701–38.

Tuveson, Ernest. 1968. *Redeemer Nation: The Idea of America's Millennial Role*. Chicago: University of Chicago Press.

Waldron, Jeremy. 2002. *God, Locke, and Equality: Christian Foundations in Locke's Political Thought*. Cambridge: Cambridge University Press.

Walters, Ronald G. 1977. *The Antislavery Appeal: American Abolitionism after 1830*. Baltimore: Johns Hopkins University Press.

Watson, Justin. 1997. *The Christian Coalition: Dreams of Restoration, Demands for Recognition*. New York: St. Martin's Press.

Weinstein, James. 1968. *The Corporate Ideal in the Liberal State: 1900–1918*. Boston: Beacon Press.

Welch, Claude. 1972. *Protestant Thought in the Nineteenth Century, Volume 1, 1789–1870*. New Haven, CT: Yale University Press.

―――. 1985. *Protestant Thought in the Nineteenth Century, Volume 2, 1870–1914*. New Haven, CT: Yale University Press.

Weyl, Walter. 1912. *The New Democracy*. New York, Macmillan.

White, Ronald C., Jr. 2002. *Lincoln's Greatest Speech: The Second Inaugural*. New York: Simon and Schuster.

White, Ronald, and Charles Hopkins, eds. 1976. *The Social Gospel: Religion and Reform in Changing America*. Philadelphia: Temple University Press.

Whitman, Walt. 1955. *Leaves of Grass*. New York: Holt, Rinehart and Winston.

Williams, Daniel Day. 1970. *The Andover Liberals: A Study in American Theology*. New York: Octagon Books.

Wilson, Major. 1974. *Space, Time and Freedom: The Quest for Nationality and the Irrepressible Conflict, 1815–1851*. Westport, CT: Greenwood Press.

Wilson, Woodrow. 1908. *Constitutional Government*. New York: Columbia University Press.

Wolff, Robert Paul. 1969. *The Ideal of the University*. Boston: Beacon Press.

Wynn, Neil A. 1986. *From Progressivism to Prosperity: World War I and American Society*. New York: Holmes & Meier.

Zakai, Avihu. 2003. *Jonathan Edward's Philosophy of History: The Reenchantment of the World in the Age of Enlightenment*. Princeton, NJ: Princeton University Press.

Zerubavel, Eviator. 2003. *Time Maps: Collective Memory and the Social Shape of the Past*. Chicago: University of Chicago Press.

Zunz, Olivier. 1990. *Making America Corporate, 1870–1920*. Chicago: University of Chicago Press.

―――. 1998. *Why the American Century?* Chicago: University of Chicago Press.

Index

Abbott, Lyman, 22, 32, 32, 85–86, 88, 89, 90, 95–96, 127

Adams, Henry Carter, 50, 100, 113n85, 122, 138n20

Addams, Jane, 24, 34, 37, 40, 50, 94, 116. *See also* social settlements

African Americans, 103, 112n58, 132, 141

agriculture, 109n1, 122, 123, 131, 139n22–139n23

American Economics Association, 37, 87, 90, 109n2, 112n54, 122, 123

American exceptionalism, xv, 83, 95. *See also* nationality

Augustine, Saint, xv, 71

authority, x, xii, xvi, xvii, xviiin2–xviiin3, 7, 10, 26, 35, 46, 70, 72, 81, 145, 146; authoritative / governing ideas, x, xi, 144, 145; moral / religious, 27, 30, 31, 35, 66, 94, 98, 111n41

Bacon, David Francis, 106–107

Barth, Karl, 52n22, 53n25

Bascom, John, 22, 29, 54n56, 110n32, 119

Batten, Samuel Zane, 40, 97, 111n43

Beard, Charles, 111n48, 139n22

Beecher, Henry Ward, 22, 29, 31, 86

Bercovitch, Sacvan, 4, 19n9, 76n8, 138n14

Bliss, William Dwight Porter, 34, 116, 119, 138n2

Block, James, 57n130, 67, 76n10, 77n23

Bloom, Harold, 17, 76n17, 110n11

brotherhood, 21, 51, 94, 111n43, 127

Brown v. Board of Education, 41, 129

Burns, James MacGregor, 56n103, 133, 140n53

Bush, George W., 13, 141, 143

Bushnell, Horace, 22, 26, 28, 31, 110n33

Calvin / Calvinism, xv, 96, 119

capitalism, 87, 119, 122, 132, 139n22; industrial, 35, 85, 86–88, 90, 91, 115, 122–123, 124, 125, 129, 130, 132; welfare, 101, 130, 140n47

Channing, William Ellery, 22, 26, 27

character, 93, 99, 110n29; national, 7, 117

Chesterton, G. K., 18, 62

Christ, 4, 21, 27, 28, 38, 50, 51, 53n30, 93, 125, 126

Christianity, 24, 27, 28, 51, 59, 130; and democracy, 21, 31, 54n60, 57n114, 96, 111n39, 127; evolution of, 32, 54n54, 86, 95, 110n38; liberal, 29, 52n13, 52n22, 53n26, 55n81, 86, 90. *See also* social gospel / social Christianity

churches: American Baptist, 36, 43, 64; Catholic, 12, 24, 37, 44, 102, 125, 141; Church of England, 27, 53n31; Congregational, 24–25, 29, 36, 43, 50, 51, 53n31, 64, 86, 97, 116; Disciples of Christ, 36, 43; Jewish, 12, 51, 57n137, 101; Methodist, 36, 43, 55n81, 64, 90; Presbyterian, 24, 36, 43, 53n31, 64;

About the Author

Eldon J. Eisenach is professor emeritus of political science at the University of Tulsa. Raised in Yankton, South Dakota, he received his undergraduate degree from Harvard University and his graduate degrees from the University of California at Berkeley; he has taught previously at Penn State and Cornell University. He is the author of numerous books, including *The Lost Promise of Progressivism* (1994), *The Next Religious Establishment: National Identity and Political Theology in Post-Protestant America* (2000), and *Narrative Power and Liberal Truth: Hobbes, Locke, Bentham, and Mill* (2002). He also edited and contributed to *Mill and the Moral Character of Liberalism* (1999) and *The Social and Political Thought of American Progressivism* (2006). He serves on editorial boards for *History of Political Thought, Studies in American Political Development*, and *Politics and Religion*.